Corporate assessment

Books by the same authors

Furnham, A. and Gunter, B. (1989) *The Anatomy of Adolescence,* London: Routledge.

Furnham, A. (1990) *The Protestant Work Ethic: The Psychology of Work-Related Beliefs and Behaviours,* London: Routledge.

Gunter, B. and Furnham, A. (1992) *Consumer Profiles: An Introduction to Psychographics,* London: Routledge.

Furnham, A. (1992) *Personality at Work: The Role of Individual Differences in the Work Place,* London: Routledge.

Gunter, B., Furnham, A. and Drakeley, R. (1993) *Biodata: Biographical Indicators of Business Performance,* London: Routledge.

Corporate assessment
Auditing a company's personality

Adrian Furnham and Barrie Gunter

London and New York

First published 1993
by Routledge
11 New Fetter Lane

Simultaneously published in the USA and Canada
by Routledge
29 West 35th Street, New York, NY 10001

Typeset in Times by Solidus (Bristol) Limited
Printed and bound in Great Britain by
Mackays of Chatham plc, Chatham, Kent

British Cataloguing in Publication Data
A catalogue reference for this book is available from the British Library.
ISBN 0–415–08118–1

Library of Congress Cataloging in Publication Data
has been applied for.
ISBN 0–415–08118–1

For
Alison and Jill
respectively, respectfully, respectworthingly

Contents

Figures and Tables

FIGURES

TABLES

Preface

A number of factors led us to write this book. They arose from the two quite distinct worlds in which we live: the academic world and the consulting world. As academic occupational psychologists we have been surprised, intrigued and interested by recent developments in management science and organizational behaviour. We have noticed the enthusiasm with which students of organizational behaviour have embraced the concept of corporate culture, and the various attempts to distinguish between it and another concept, namely corporate climate. Our own work with many varied organizations and management consultants has led us as academics, to explore ways in which these two complex concepts can be operationally defined and distinguished, and then in turn, how organizations can obtain maximal benefits through self-assessment in terms of either culture or climate audits, or both.

The academic world is certainly as faddish and fashion-conscious as the business world. In the 1950s a scientific approach to management was regarded as the key to management success; in the 1960s the emphasis shifted to how the organization was structured; the 1970s promised success if corporate strategy was well thought out and researched; throughout the 1980s, the focus moved yet again to the 'softer' feature of corporate culture. Each change of fashion has brought a fresh wave of theory-building and empirical research, and is to be welcomed because of this.

Within the 1980s business world, the fashion for mergers and acquisitions meant for the many participating organizations a difficult process of 'marrying' a very different corporate 'personality' from their own. The transition from the old to the new did not invariably follow a smooth passage. One way to predict, and thus to be in a better position to prevent, certain difficulties arising in these new partnerships, is to understand as fully as possible how each organization in the process works. That involves not only understanding the products or services of the mergees (whatever they may be), but also the process whereby they are provided. Through design, accident, and historical precedent, organizations develop norms of behaviour, belief systems and espouse certain values that may, or may not, be adaptive. For both the researcher and the practitioner to understand how these processes work, so that ways might be found of changing or maintaining such crucial organizational features, it is necessary to describe and understand the process. One way of shedding light on this matter is by conducting corporate audits, and that is the topic of this book. The theory and methodology of corporate audits (or whatever synonym they are called by: e.g. employee surveys) is attracting more attention among academics, consultants and professional managers.

The second reason for our writing this book has been due to our experience as organizational consultants. On a number of occasions we have advised clients on how to do corporate audits, where it seemed to us an audit was necessary. Some managers had started by wanting to carry out extensive personality or skills testing which seemed irrelevant to their stated concerns. Others assumed they already knew all about the culture and climate in different parts of their organization, and wanted advice on how to implement change systems. In each of these instances, it seemed useful to point out the advantages of the corporate audit.

We have also had organizations approach us whose express interest was in doing an audit of one sort or another. Many did not know how to go about it; others were not sure which type of audit to choose. We have helped organizations to develop their own audit instruments and techniques; to choose between published audits, selecting the one that is both psychometrically sound and best suited to their needs; and we have adapted our own instruments to provide an audit for clients. We have also developed a National Organizational Audit (NOA), whereby every year numerous organizations are invited to take part in a climate audit. We have created a robust, sensitive, employee climate survey which measures their attitudes and perceptions on fourteen different facets of organizational climate. Organizations that join NOA and who use this audit with a sample of their work-force, not only get a full feedback report on their organizational climate, but also receive an overview of other organizations taking part. Such comparative data can provide extremely interesting and informative benchmarks, allowing managers to consider the profile of their own organization against a normative profile for organizations in the same sector.

This practical consultancy experience, especially that involved with the NOA, has taught us some important lessons. There is nothing as practical as good theory, and nothing as theoretically useful as putting ideas into practice. This book is an attempt to put some of this experience down on paper.

We have both our clients and colleagues to thank for challenging ideas. David Pendleton of Kaisen Consulting helped us to be more sensitive to current issues in the business world, and Liam Forde of Corporate Assessment proved to be the spur that led us to take our early ideas further. Nigel Oakes at Behavioural Dynamics has challenged us to conceive the potential of corporate audits in the widest sphere of business applications, far beyond the range of corporate problem-solving to which they are normally applied. Lee Drew has, as usual, transformed various scrappy pieces of paper, badly processed floppy discs, and near illegible comments on various drafts into a beautiful processed manuscript with speed, efficiency, charm and biscuits.

Adrian Furnham
Barrie Gunter
Thornhill Square
London

1 Management audits

INTRODUCTION

This book is concerned with the practice and, where it exists, the theory of auditing employees' perceptions of their organization's culture, climate, communications and customers. Most organizations have a plethora of 'statistics' of differing kinds by which they measure operational performance and provide prospective and retrospective data and on the basis of which they hope to make rational business decisions. The quality of organizational planning and decision-making is therefore partly a function of this information.

It has often been said that a company's most valuable asset is its employees. Audits, such as those described in this book represent procedures designed to find out what an organization's employees think, how they behave, and what they value.

Many organizations carry out audits on various aspects of their functioning and performance. Here are some examples:

The total company Getting indices like return on investment, sales revenue by product group, profit as a percentage of production/ marketing/distribution costs, market share, debtor-to-sales ratio, asset utilization, and so on.

Production trends Doing audits of departmental production costs, material conversion rates for major product groups, direct labour costs per department, by skill, and machine utilization.

Sales and marketing trends Doing separate audits on such things as the market share of various product groups, competitive position, and market segmentation.

Administrative audits On monitoring costs, and efficiency in terms of the ratio of administrative staff to production workers.

Research and development audits   On issues like profit gained, direct contribution to profit or rate of product growth or decline in the company of amount of innovation and development.

Relationships between resources and results   Where resources are capital investment, administration, marketing and product costs, and results are profit or production and sales revenue.

The audits just listed tend to comprise hard financial, marketing, or production data. They are used by companies to provide a systematic and objective account of their internal functional efficiency and their external business effectiveness. These, however, are not the kinds of corporate audit we will be discussing in this book. Our primary concern will be with audits which use softer currencies, namely the perceptions, values and self-reported behaviours of employees. Such audits attempt to be just as systematic as their 'harder' counterparts, but are based on what are essentially subjective data. The nature of the issues addressed by this second family of audits – monitoring, measuring, and defining corporate culture and climate and closely associated communications and customer care systems – is often more qualitative than quantitative, although we will describe research techniques which can yield valuable corporate data in a quantifiable form. Indeed they can be treated as 'hard data'.

The corporate audits we will discuss provide a means of gathering perceptual data about organizations. They are 'democratic', in that they 'poll' either the entire work-force, or a respectable and representative sample of it. They can provide information such that management may begin to realize they have a problem before it reaches epidemic or unmanageable proportions. It is important to stress, even this early in our exposition, that auditing corporate culture or climate is not without its potential drawbacks. The mere fact of a survey will not in itself resolve an organization's problems. Indeed, mismanaged, a survey can cause problems all of its own, or serve only to exacerbate those which already exist. Sometimes, organizations may set up barriers to doing an audit for fear of how it may backfire on them. These barriers to adopting audits take many forms, and may not always be clearly and openly articulated. The most frequent objections are:

- 'Audits have insufficient benefit, in that they are time-consuming.'
- 'I know my people; the grapevine keeps me pretty well and accurately informed. Hence audits are unnecessary.'
- 'There are much better and simpler alternatives, like MBWA (management by walking about) and I hear the reactions of the company then.
- 'They are simply too expensive.'
- 'This organization [or department] is too small to warrant a full audit.'

- 'Publishing of the results would probably mean a serious loss of (informational) power on the part of management.'

It is true that the act of surveying can influence attitudes. This is more frequently the case if organizations use them only rarely. Employee audits are often provoked by fashion, but some organizations have been doing them annually for twenty years or so, and use audits to calculate various indices that are very important in their strategic planning. Such audits can provide companies with important benchmarks about how they are doing over time. Some more adventurous companies use audits to measure or benchmark themselves against other close corporate performers. There are, in fact, various groupings of companies who share employee survey data from responses to questions they all agree to carry in their surveys. By doing so they obtain valuable comparative data which is most helpful in interpreting the causes of their specific results.

THE ROLE OF THE PERSONNEL FUNCTION

Pendleton and Furnham (1992) believe that the judicious use of human resource and organizational behaviour audits could substantially enhance the power, prestige and professionalism of personnel directors. They asked, 'Why do very few chief executives come from personnel backgrounds?' For most service companies and many in other sectors, the salary bill is the single largest revenue expense, yet those whose principal function is advising on human resource management rarely make it to the top.

One clue is to be found in their history. The background of the personnel specialist usually derives from one of these main areas: administration, welfare and industrial relations. Each of these functions is changing. Administration is becoming increasingly computerized requiring less specialized knowledge of procedures but more knowledge of systems; 'Welfare' is seen as anachronistic, though its function remains important, even in those companies in which the synonym 'counselling' is also avoided. Industrial relations, in much of the industrial world, is tending to operate in a greater spirit of co-operation. This is especially true in Europe and America, where many managers seem to have understood that entire industries could die unless conflict is replaced by collaboration, in increasingly competitive markets. Thus, many traditional personnel functions are becoming redundant or have changed completely.

Other reasons for personnel's apparent decline are more often self-inflicted:

Personal attributes Many current personnel specialists are gentle, 'caring' characters who are asked to help with damage limitation when tough decisions have had to be taken. They are widely consulted on how to implement redundancy programmes in a sensitive way, but are frequently unsuited to taking the tough decisions themselves.

Reactivity Coming from an administrative background, other personnel specialists have a detailed and reactive approach to work, and find it difficult to make a contribution to the creation of future strategy, even when the creative use of human resources may make the most enormous difference to a company's competitive strength. They are neither used to nor trained in strategic planning, nor frequently in any sort of collection and analysis of data. If the language of business is money, the alphabet must be numbers. Some personnel departments, of course, collect extensive data (which they analyse) on absenteeism, performance appraisal and payrolls, but less on attitudes, behaviours and values.

Information Unlike their colleagues in operations, research and development or finance, they frequently lack important sources of management information which will guide senior managers' decision-making. The operations director brings information about throughput, delivery times and distribution. The finance director will bring management accounts and details of unit costs; the sales director will have data about revenue; the marketing director will be able to detect trends in the market place to which the company needs to respond. Yet the personnel director very often brings little more than an intuitive feel for morale or misleading data drawn from exit interviews about why people leave the company (when what they really need is clues about why they stay). The personnel departments which have carefully thought through the information their senior colleagues need in order to guide their decision-making are disconcertingly few. A properly designed and executed organizational audit (e.g. exploring the climate or communications in a company) could provide just the information required.

Invisibility It is all too frequently difficult or impossible to detect the effect of the personnel department. If the sales department fails, the revenue goes down. Most other departments' effects are readily discernible and their impact is immediate. However, if their administrative duties were to continue, it would be hard to detect much of an impact of the closure of many personnel departments. This does not mean that the company would not be harmed, but that the effect might be attributed to other factors, such as a downturn in the market or an insensitive decision taken by senior management. If a benchmark audit is conducted concerning employees prior to the introduction of a change programme, with a follow-up audit to quantify the effects of that programme, all under the charge of personnel, then a significant organizational role for the personnel department more readily emerges.

Pendleton and Furnham (1992) have argued that, by acting as an internal consultant, personnel managers can perform their function more efficiently. The former has many case studies which demonstrate the efficacy of this position. Thus, corporate audits can be seen as crucial instruments in helping professional human resource people with three problems they frequently face:

1 **Development** As markets change, organizations need to change. Helping to develop the organization and its work-force requires a great deal of skill and insight which it would be legitimate for many line managers to seek in the personnel function. Personnel specialists should be at the forefront of planning, monitoring and implementing much-needed change. Audits (before and after change) help monitor the efficacy of organizational change programmes and can suggest which facets of the organization need most attention, when and how.

2 **Tracking** With most major business decisions there are consequences for employees. But what mechanisms currently exist to keep senior managers in touch with the thoughts and feelings of others in the organization? Those who advocate management by walking about (MBWA) imply that managers will automatically discern that which is important. But this does not take into account the difficulties of tracking the mood of a large and complex organization. Devising sensible tracking systems, i.e. regular audits, to challenge the monopoly of the more numerate disciplines, is an important need.

3 **Strategy** The need to use human resources creatively and to come up with increasingly compelling reward schemes which do not contribute to salary inflation, is ever present. Organizations need performance-related strategies which are logical, coherent, future-orientated and integrated both with other departments' plans and the overall business plan. Strategy, however, has to be information-based, and it is the corporate audit which can supply this information.

Corporate human resources audits are seductive; they often sell themselves. It is not hard to believe in them. There is a persuasive logic in attempting to acquire real, accurate, representative feedback upon which to make decisions. Indeed, the results of audits frequently give impetus to strategic planning (Sayle, 1988). This faith is well-founded if the audits are properly designed and analysed. The argument that they are expensive is relatively easily and justly counteracted by the proposal that ignorance is even more expensive.

There has been a significant growth in corporate human resources audits over the past decade or so (Walley, 1974). This has come about for two reasons:

1 **Demand** Line managers, corporate planners and chief executives have quite rightly demanded to know what the culture, climate, and communications are like in their organization (or part of it) before engaging on some plan of action. There is a growing realization that it is only the naive or foolish who presume to know, or who don't care.

2 **Supply** A growing army of single consultants as well as numerous well-established firms are selling their expertise in survey design and analysis. Some have repackaged old ideas in more fashionable terminology, and others have adapted old measures to fit new purposes. These salesmen have done a good job in convincing organizations of the need for such corporate audits.

THE HEALTH AND ILLNESS OF ORGANIZATIONS

Since the beginning of this century psychologists and psychiatrists have attempted to devise a parsimonious but sensitive and robust system to classify mental illness. Over the years a recognized international nomenclature has arisen and the taxonomy of mental states and their attendant behaviours been refined. Whilst it is untrue to say that there is universal agreement and acceptance of the latest offering (DSM III), it is probably fair to state that each succeeding attempt yields greater consensus as to the applicability of the system.

For some time management scientists and other students of organizational behaviour have wondered if some of the ideas from psychology – the study of the behaviour of individuals – might not be equally usefully applied to organizations – collections of individuals. Although there are inherent problems in 'borrowing' terms and concepts from other disciplines, there is also much to be gained, at least in the initial period of conceptual development. In adopting the terminology of individual psychology, organizations have at various times been described as 'neurotic', 'healthy' or 'unhealthy'.

Kets de Vries and Miller (1984) have argued that there are striking similarities between the neurotic behaviour of individuals and the practices of ailing and failing businesses. In such companies, strategy, structure and organizational climate often reflect the neurotic styles and fantasies of the top echelon of managers. More specifically, the neurotic characteristics of these executives seem to create uniformities of organizational culture, which in turn foster common neurotic organizational styles.

These writers identified five such neurotic styles for organizations, which had formerly been well established in the psychoanalytic and psychiatric literature: dramatic, depressive, paranoid, compulsive and schizoid. Each style has its specific individual characteristics, pre-dominant motivating fantasies and associated dangers, and each was found to have its organizational counterparts in the structure, strategic behaviour and climate of a number of troubled companies. We will examine each of these company personality types in more detail.

The dramatic organization

Dramatic firms are hyperactive, impulsive, dramatically venturesome and dangerously uninhibited. Their decision-makers live in a world of hunches, intuition and impressions rather than facts, as they haphazardly address an array of disparate markets. Their dramatic flair encourages the top people to centralize power, reserving their prerogative to initiate bold ventures. Audacity, risk-taking and diversification are major corporate themes. Instead of reacting to the business environment, top decision-makers attempt to create their own environment. Entering some markets and leaving others, they constantly switch to new products while abandoning other ones, placing a sizeable proportion of the firm's capital at risk.

Unbridled growth is the goal, reflecting the top manager's considerable narcissistic needs and desire for attention and visibility. Naturally these organizations are unlikely to use corporate audits, and may pooh-pooh those which do.

> The structure of the dramatic organization is usually far too primitive for its broad markets. First, too much power is concentrated in the chief executive, who meddles even in routine operating matters because he wants to put his personal stamp on (and take credit for) everyting. A second problem follows from this overcentralization – namely, the absence of an effective information system. The top executive does too litle scanning of the business environment because he has too little time and prefers to act on intuition rather than facts. Finally, the leader's dominance obstructs effective internal communication, which is mostly from the top down.
> (Kets de Vries and Miller, 1984, p. 28)

The depressive organization

Depressive firms tend to be characterized by inactivity, lack of confidence, extreme conservatism and insularity. There is an atmosphere of passivity and purposelessness. What is achieved is what has been programmed and routinized and requires no special initiative. These organizations may institute a corporate audit among their employees – indeed, they may have institutionalized them into an annual ritual – but are unlikely to act on the results.

Most depressive firms are well-established and serve a mature market, one that has had the same technology and competitive patterns for many years. Trade agreements, restrictive trade practices and substantial tariffs are the rule. The low level of change, the absence of serious competition and the homogeneity of the customers make the administrative task fairly simple.

Although formal authority tends to be centralized and based on position rather than expertise the issue of power is not very important. Control is really exercised by formalized programmes and policies rather than by managerial initiatives. Suggestions for change are resisted, and action is inhibited. It is almost as if the top executives share a sense of impotence and incapacity. They just don't feel they can control events or that they have what it takes to revitalize the firm. And they are loath to stir up expectations by having employees fill out a questionnaire. Content with the status quo, these organizations do little to discover the key threats and weaknesses in markets or customer stagnation. Generally little use is made of systematic information-gathering via audit techniques.

The sense of aimlessness and apathy among top managers precludes any attempt to give the firm a clear direction or goals. Strategy is never explicitly considered, even though important, so no meaningful change occurs. Yesterday's products and markets become today's, not because of any policy of conservatism, but because of lethargy. Managers spend most of their time working out routine details while procrastinating on major decisions. Where there should be effort to adapt, to grow and to become more effective, there is only inactivity and passivity. A typical fat, non-profit-orientated bureaucracy fits into this category.

The paranoid organization

In this type of company, managerial suspicions are manifest in an emphasis on organizational intelligence and controls. Managers develop sophisticated information systems to identify threats by the government, competitors and customers, and they develop budgets, cost-centres, profit-centres, cost-accounting procedures and similar methods to control internal business. This reflects their desire for perpetual vigilance and preparedness for emergencies.

This paranoia influences decision-making, such that key executives decide that it may be safer to direct their distrust externally rather than withhold information from one another.

They share information and make concerted efforts to discover organizational problems and to select alternative solutions for dealing with them. Unfortunately, this type of decision-making can become overly consultative, with different people being asked for similar information. Such 'institutionalization of suspicion' ensures that accurate information gets to the top of the firm, but it may also lower morale and trust, as well as waste valuable time and energy. Paranoid firms tend to react rather than anticipate. If competitors lower prices, the firm may study the challenge and, eventually, react to it. If other firms introduce a product successfully, the paranoid firm will probably imitate them. But strategic paranoia carries with it a sizeable element of conservatism. Fear often entails being afraid to innovate, overextend resources or take risks.

This reactive orientation impedes development of a concerted and consistent strategy. The paranoid firm's direction has too much to do with external forces and not enough with consistent goals, plans or unifying themes and traditions. Paranoid firms frequently try product diversification, to reduce the risk of reliance on any one product, but because diversification requires more elaborate control and information-processing mechanisms, it actually reinforces the firm's paranoia.

(Kets de Vries and Miller, 1984 p. 34)

Corporate paranoia may result from a period of traumatic challenge, such as a strong market drying up, a powerful new competitor entering the market, or damaging legislation being passed. The harm done by these events may cause managers to become very distrustful and fearful, and to recognize the need for better intelligence. Indeed, over-auditing may occur, which threatens the quality of the data, as jaded employees become suspicious of having to complete so many audits.

The compulsive organization

The compulsive firm is dedicated to rites and rituals. Every detail of all operations is planned carefully in advance and carried out in routinized fashion. Thoroughness, completeness and conformity to established procedures are emphasized. This can almost reach the point of fetishism. Like the paranoid organization, the compulsive organization emphasizes formal controls and information systems. There is a crucial difference, however, in that in compulsive organizations, controls are *really* designed to monitor internal operations, production efficiency, costs and the scheduling and performance of projects, while the paranoid firm is interested chiefly in external conditions. Thus, the paranoid firm monitors corporate culture and climate and the compulsive organization monitors corporate customers and competitors. Operations are standardized as much as possible, and an elaborate set of formal policies and procedures evolves.

The compulsive organization is often exceedingly hierarchical, a reflection of the leader's strong concern with control. The compulsive organization is always worried about the next move and how it is going to make it. Compulsive executives try to reduce uncertainty and to attain a clearly specified objective in a carefully planned manner. Surprises and the unexpected must be avoided at all costs.

Compulsive firms show the same preoccupation with detail and established procedures in all their business strategies. They create a large number of action plans, budgets and capital expenditure plans because each project is designed with many check-points, exhaustive performance evaluations and detailed schedules.

The compulsive firm can have a particular orientation and distinctive competence, and its plans reflect them. This orientation, rather than what is going on in the world, serves as the major guide for the firm's strategy. For example, some organizations take pride in making the safest product endorsed in the market-place; they try to produce the most safety-checked products, whether or not these are called for by customers. Safety (of the sort defined by the manufacturers) may be inappropriate in the light of new market conditions, but the firm's strong inward focus prevents any realization of this fact.

The schizoid organization

Finally, this kind of company can suffer from a leadership vacuum. Its chief executive, often because of past disappointments, believes most contacts will end painfully and is inclined to daydream, to compensate for lack of fulfilment. In some of these organizations, executives on the second level of authority are able to make up for the leader's deficiencies with their own sociability and extroversion. Too often, however, the executives see in the withdrawn nature of the top person an opportunity to pursue their own goals rather than those of the organization as a whole.

The second tier thus becomes a political battlefield for gamesmen who vie to win favour from an unresponsive leader. The combination of leadership vacuum and political in-fighting produces interesting strategies and structural results because no integrated strategy develops. The leader is usually insecure, withdrawn and non-committal, and vacillates between the proposals of one favoured subordinate and those of another.

Strategy-making resides in a shifting coalition of egotistical second-tier managers who try to influence the indecisive leader and simultaneously advance their pet projects and minor empires. The organization thus frequently muddles through and drifts along, making incremental changes in one area and then reversing them whenever a new group of managers wins favour. The initiatives of one group of managers are often neutralized or severely blunted by those of an opposing group. The divided nature of the organization thwarts effective co-ordination, communication and production. Information from audits is used more as a power resource than as a vehicle for effective adaptation; in fact, managers erect barriers to prevent the free flow of information. Thus, while audits may be done, their results are never released or seriously acted upon. This is not the only shortcoming of the information system. The absence of information on the outside business environment is apparent in companies of this type. The company's focus is internal – on personal ambitions and catering to the top manager's desires. Second-tier managers find it more useful to ignore real-world events (e.g. customers' demands, competitors' strategies) that might reflect poorly on their own behaviour or conflict with the wishes of the detached leader.

Kets de Vries and Miller (1984) conclude:

As organizational researchers, we have wondered why certain decisions are made and particular strategies chosen. Why does an organization end up with a particular kind of structure? Why is a certain individual selected for a particular job? If the observations we have outlined are accurate, the problems of many troubled companies are deeply ingrained, based on the deep-seated neurotic styles and fantasies of top executives.

Since our five common pathologies seem so multifaceted and thematically unified, it is unlikely that they can be adequately addressed by management consultants with a standard bag of tools. New information systems, committees and quality-of-work-life programmes will be of little help as long as executives cling to their dysfunctional fantasies and shared organizational ideologies. The new programmes should be complemented either by more realistic views of the business and its environment, or by more adaptive executives.

We are not suggesting that neurotic executive styles always require changing. They may sometimes be quite compatible with a firm's environment. But too often they foster a kind of rigidity that inhibits adaptation. In the long run, only a healthy mixture of styles can ensure corporate success.

(p. 341)

The fivefold classification system described above is of course not the only one available. In the following exercise, we have taken from clinical psychology a variety of terms, whose genesis resides within the analysis of individual psychology, and ascribed them as descriptors of organization types. Consider the following personality disorders where the word personality/individual has been replaced by organization:

- **The inadequate organization.** These are organizations which show inadaptability, ineptness, poor judgement, lack of physical and emotional stamina, and social incompatibility.
- **The schizotypic organization** These are organizations that are incapable of encouraging close relationships with other employees and which value cold, aloof, and emotionally detached behaviours.
- **The cyclothymic organization** These organizations show sudden, considerable and often unpredictable mood-swings in the direction of elation or depression. They accentuate economic cycles, being manic when things are going well, and severely depressed in the bad times.
- **The paranoid organization** These organizations are dominated by characteristics such as suspiciousness, envy, jealousy and stubbornness. People do not share information within these organizations and may plot against each other consistently.
- **The immature organization** These organizations have little control over their emotional reactions and are characterized by impulsiveness, quick changes in mood, and a generally unsettled emotional life.

- **The emotionally unstable organization** This organizational culture has an emotional life which is erratic and unpredictable, and may be exaggerated in any direction. Organizations may be either passive-dependent, passive aggressive, or aggressive.
- **The compulsive organization** Organizations of this type are rigid, meticulous, and perfectionistic, and tend to be totally preoccupied with the correctness of their behaviour. They tend to like rituals, established ways of doing things, and predictable orderliness.
- **The sociopathic organization** These organizations have a form of moral insanity, and do not profit from experience. They tend to have no real loyalties to any person, group or code and have an extra-ordinary ability to rationalize their behaviour in order to justify it.

This strategy of describing organizational cultures in terms of psycho-pathological types has some promise as well as dangers. One advantage of this approach is that it could 'drive' an audit, in the sense that it sets out deliberately to diagnose neurotic or unhealthy features of the organization. A disadvantage of this approach, however, is to become locked into the nomenclature and taxonomy of other disciplines which are inappropriate, and to become restricted to, even obsessed by, the negative aspects of company functioning. Certainly the above categorization concentrates only on the form of 'ill' or 'sick' organizations, rather than on healthy ones.

WHY DO A HUMAN RESOURCES AUDIT?

There are many sound reasons for an organization to audit its human resources. It is proper to deal with this question at the outset. Audits are performed by people, and people are expensive. Before deciding to embark on any audit an organization needs to know the justification for committing manpower, time and effort to pursuing it.

To separate fact from opinion   A human resources audit provides factual information on how a company is perceived by its employees. Audits yield quantifiable data grounded in the views of the work-force, and thus go far beyond vague 'gut feeling' beliefs of managers who may not always be in touch with staff opinions. The quality of plans and objectives devised for an organization depend on the quality of the information upon which these plans are made.

All managerial decisions and plans require factual input, and this includes systematic feedback from staff. Many companies practise a policy of formulating annual, medium-term and long-term plans. Some manage-ments call their plans 'objectives' and operate what are commonly known as 'management by objectives' exercises. These plans are often only vaguely formulated in terms of the human resource data on which they are based. Professionally conducted audits which survey relevant areas of management and staff opinions about the organization can provide the hard empirical data upon which solid, workable plans are based.

To obtain unbiased management information   Since a human resources audit systematically analyses 'objective' evidence (albeit about subjective perceptions) and presents facts rather than value judgements, it corrects preconceived ideas about the status of a company's management systems and procedures, and false ideas about whether or not the various parts of the company are working in a manner which is consistent with the policies and objectives delegated from the board of directors. It is common for senior and middle management to see their own operation through rose-coloured spectacles, ignoring or misinterpreting the ideas, beliefs, and experiences of those lower down in the organization.

A human resources audit provides a direct flow of opinion from whichever part of the company it originates to the most senior management, thus bypassing any filtering process which may alter its shape or contents on its passage through middle management levels. This can give a more accurate view of how the company is perceived to function and the effectiveness of various departments and managers within the organization.

To know factually if the company is at risk   A human resources audit provides vital feedback to management as to whether the organization is meeting its legal and contractual obligations. This reduces the possibility of customer complaints and expensive legal suits. Moreover, it provides even more vital feedback concerning the organization's ability to compete in the future and hence of the wisdom or otherwise of becoming involved in contracts and product markets which the organization does not currently have the capacity to satisfy. Many companies increase their problems through ignorance of their real capacity in relation to market needs and demands and other external factors. An appropriate human resources audit can also help to determine whether the company is meeting its contractual and legal obligations within the company to its staff.

To identify areas of opportunity   An audit analyses evidence concerning the effectiveness of the organization and its structure: it can identify the circumstances under which resources and time are utilized ineffectively. By specifically concentrating on how people spend their time, utilize space, machinery and technology and so on, waste of various forms can be examined. An audit can challenge decisions and the original basis for them, thus ensuring that the status quo is constantly challenged in the light of changing business and technological circumstances.

To improve communications and motivation   Since the audit report reaches top management, it can promote communication between the lowest and the highest levels within the company. It enables employees at all levels to suggest improved methods of operation. The lower echelons are those most closely involved with the actual product and are normally in the best position to see the practical implementation of the official quality management systems. This improvement in communication can raise morale and motivation at all levels. If employees' ideas are acted upon as a result of the audit, they feel more committed to make their suggestions work. Equally, audits may raise expectations, and if not acted upon may, in fact, lower motivation and morale.

To assess individuals' performance   A human resources audit can produce an unbiased assessment of each individual's training needs, and more importantly of each individual's self-perceived effectiveness at his or her job. Furthermore, audits can yield normative data enabling individuals to be compared. Many managers dislike the feeling that they are sitting in judgement on their subordinates, and some are concerned that personal feelings may cloud the issue and render their appraisals less than accurate. The human resources audit can help to safeguard the subordinate's position, because any personal dislikes between subordinates and management will not be taken into account, and subordinates can respond honestly without fear of censorship.

To assess the status and capability of company equipment   A human resources audit assists in obtaining an unbiased assessment of the status and capability of equipment throughout the enterprise: its physical condition, its maintenance requirements, its repair and fault history, as well as the need for modified equipment to perform new procedures. It can also help to show how effective the preventive maintenance or condition-monitoring systems are and assess whether or not, in the light of technological advances and competitors' activities, the equipment wastes time and resources (such as manpower, floor space or energy) in use. Most importantly, a human resources audit determines users' attitudes to equipment, be it state-of-the-art or old fashioned. The change of old fashioned, less reliable and less efficient equipment to more modern equipment is frequently and, perhaps surprisingly for some, not accepted as being self-evidently beneficial.

To provide insight into recruitment and selection   By selecting (or rejecting) people with specific preferences, values and potentialities, it is possible both to maintain and to change a culture. Some organizations are very careful to select employees from a particular background knowing that they share common beliefs, attitudes and values. Equally, others attempt to change corporate culture and identity, by recruiting a more heterogeneous group who do not share the same beliefs and values. Audits can demonstrate the homo- or heterogeneity of a department or organization as a whole.

To assist with the assessment of training company staff A human resources audit can provide useful information about training for the personnel who participate. These audits provide information on who has been trained on what, their reactions to courses, and any perceived further training needs.

A bottom-up view of the organization Communication generally flows down an organization more freely and regularly than it flows up. Hence senior managers do not always have their finger on the pulse of working life among the rank and file. A human resources audit can provide a very useful and important feedback mechanism to senior management.

Audits can be used for evaluation If an audit is done before a major change programme is put into place and again at some point afterwards, the effectiveness of the programme as a whole can be established. Thus, a before-and-after measure of its success can be done through the use of a human resources audit. The audit can also be repeated to reveal major trends in values, beliefs, and attitudes over time.

Audits highlight the suitability for innovation and change Human resources audits might signal not only that change is needed, but also what form such change should take in an organization. This detailed and specific knowledge may be quite invaluable. If the organization is in a turbulent market, both internal human resources and external customer audits could be used together most effectively to gather information to guide new policy or strategy development.

Audits show potential fit and misfit in mergers and acquisitions By comparing two companies before a merger or an acquisition, it may be possible to predict the level of difficulty that each may have in adjusting to the other. By auditing similar aspects of the different organizations involved, the nature, extent and implications of their unique characteristics can be examined.

Audits make good economic sense Making decisions based on little, poor or no information is highly risky. Human resources audits do cost money, but can provide a good return on investment if they help the decision-making process. The probability that an audit will provide a good return is increased if it is well prepared, salient issues are correctly analysed, and the resultant data properly interpreted. Audits provide a safe, anonymous means for both unhappy and satisfied employees to express their opinions about all aspects of the organization.

Audits are part of the management measurement trend In all aspects of management there is an increasing trend towards using empirical measurement (Sayle, 1988; Walley, 1974). Human resources audits are part of this sensible movement towards a more scientific approach to management and fact-gathering. Financial audits have been done by accountants for decades. Human resources audits are now also emerging as respectable corporate procedures, providing a professional approach to the evaluation and measurement of organizational problems.

Peer pressure is already extensive to do audits   Pressure from competitors who already conduct human resources audits have provided a stimulus to many organizations to do the same. Added to this, chief executives these days often expect answers to human resources questions that only audits can provide. To answer specific points about employee satisfaction and dissatisfaction, the effect on work-force performance of new policies and procedures, and the response of the company to market developments, organizations are finding more and more that they need to audit their employees.

Audits may help ensure survival   Those organizations that do not audit their human resources regularly may miss out on crucial signs of much needed internal adjustments. Audits can help diagnose a latent problem long before it becomes impossible to deal with.

SOME COMMON MYTHS ABOUT AN AUDIT

For some, the business of assessment, evaluation and auditing is mysterious, even dangerous. Managers brought up in the old traditions often resist any form of data collection by putting forward various spurious, easy-to-knock-down arguments. They include:

- **You can't measure things as abstract as corporate culture or climate**   One argument against human resources audits is that they cannot be relied upon to provide accurate and sensitive measures of such abstract organizational attributes as climate or culture. Research has provided evidence which flies in the face of this viewpoint, however. Human resources audits can, when properly designed, effectively tap into and generate workable operational definitions and measures of aspects of an organization's culture and climate. (See Chapter 2.)
- **You can't tell what information to collect**   Whenever an organization embarks on a human resources audit, it is important that it undertakes preparatory exercises designed to define the nature of the problems or questions to be measured. Many useful clues as to what the audit should address can be obtained through pilot work (initial interviews with key individuals, open-ended discussions with small groups of employees, and so on). To a large extent the purpose of the audit, in

the first place, tends to make it very clear what kinds of information need to be collected.

- **If you can't calculate the benefits of an audit (return on investment), it's pointless even to do it** It is not always easy to demonstrate exactly the direct or immediate financial benefits of a human resources audit, but there are often ways of calculating the cost of *not* doing such an audit. Failed mergers and inadequate performance of acquisitions can often reflect an inability of distinct corporate cultures to work effectively together. An early audit might have identified the problems to come and indicated ways of avoiding them.

- **Auditing can only be used in respect of production and financial matters** It is true that auditing is traditionally associated with financial planning and productivity, but it is not restricted to them. Many organizations are now realizing the importance of systematic assessments of their human resources in the context of monitoring performance and guiding functional internal adjustments designed to improve morale and productivity.

- **Senior people in the organization would not even look at the feedback report from the audit** Chief executives are often overburdened by paperwork. But if the results of a human resources audit are important, and they generally are, few will choose to ignore them. Indeed, an executive summary with some counter-intuitive or myth-breaking findings usually means senior management will read the report from cover to cover. Because the information is so important, top management teams tend to go through audit data in great detail.

- **There are just too many factors that affect an audit to pinpoint anything useful** A good human resources audit can take into consideration practically any factors that relate to organizational satisfaction and productivity. Most audits are multidimensional, measuring employees' perceptions of numerous aspects of corporate functioning. Furthermore, multivariate statistical techniques can measure the individual or combined effects of any major variables that influence audit responses.

- **Audits can exacerbate employee discontent** If done properly, human resources audits can reduce rather than worsen organizational problems. They actually provide a much sought after mechanism to let management know what the staff think. Indeed, employees can safely let off steam through responding to an audit. If employees have not been provided with a constructive mechanism by which to express their discontent and dissatisfaction, it may manifest itself in more serious, destructive ways (absenteeism, turnover, Luddite behaviour).

- **Data from human resources are regarded with scepticism** Management may not always be convinced by the honesty and accuracy of a technique which invites staff to offer personal views. Staff may distrust the motives of management for carrying out an audit, and fail to be convinced that it will improve their own situation. Scepticism can easily be dispelled if the audits are done in a detailed and professional manner. If done by an outside independent consultant who has nothing to gain from the results of an audit, employee scepticism can be much alleviated.

WELL REHEARSED CRITICISMS

Corporate audits are based on questionnaire surveys. Both academics and lay people of various persuasions have attacked and criticized surveys (audits) for a variety of reasons. De Vaus (1986) lists ten criticisms, all of which are relatively easy to rebut.

The most common criticism of surveys can be classified into three categories: philosophical, technique-based and political. These will simply be mentioned here, but will be taken up again in the final chapter.

Philosophically based criticisms

1 Surveys cannot adequately establish causal connections between variables. For example, even though older people are more conservative than younger people we cannot be certain that growing older causes conservatism.
2 Surveys are incapable of getting at the meaningful aspects of social action. Because actions are the actions of conscious people who make choices, have memories, wills, goals and values which motivate behaviour, research must take these into account when developing and evaluating why people behave and think as they do.
3 Surveys just look at particular aspects of people's beliefs and actions without looking at the context in which they occur. Taken out of context it is easy to misunderstand the meaning of behaviour. For example, if a person goes to church regularly it may mean they are highly religious, but it *could* mean they are searching for a religious faith, or they cannot avoid going because of social pressure, or they go because of important contacts at church and so on.
4 Surveys seem to assume that human action is determined by external forces and neglect the role of human consciousness, goals, intentions and values as important sources of action.
5 Survey research is equated with a sterile, ritualistic and rigid model of science centred around hypothesis testing and significance tests, which involves no imagination or creative thinking.
6 Survey research is basically empiricist. That is, it merely collects a mass of facts and statistics and provides nothing of theoretical value.
7 Some things are not measurable – especially by surveys. For example,

a survey researcher would probably have great difficulty in actually measuring the extent to which anybody has power.

Technique based criticisms

8 Surveys are too restricted because they rely on highly structured questionnaires which are necessarily limited.
9 Surveys are too statistical and reduce interesting questions to totally incomprehensible numbers. While many studies are unnecessarily statistical and sterile, the logic involved in these statistical analyses is important and the same logic is widely used in both statistical analyses and more qualitative analyses. It is this logic and the role of creative thinking that will be emphasized in this book. Statistics should be the servant rather than the master of the survey analyst.

'Political' criticisms

10 Survey research is intrinsically manipulative and is described by the Frankfurt Marxists as 'scientistic' and 'technistic'. It is seen to be manipulative in two ways. First, the knowledge it provides about the social world gives power to those in control and this can lead to an abuse of power. Second, survey research leads to ideological manipulation. It does not produce knowledge about reality but is an ideological reflection whose acceptance by 'the public' furthers particular interests.

(pp. 7–9)

De Vaus (1986) was able to refute all of these common, but misplaced interpretations. Most of these objections are the result of ignorance of the method rather than any well thought-out understanding of it. Whilst some of the criticisms are true of poorly designed surveys, they are rarely true of a well constructed survey.

HOW TO DO A COMPANY AUDIT

The company assessment methods on which we will focus are those involving 'soft' data. Soft data are based on subjective impressions and responses of employees as obtained through face-to-face interviews or self-completion questionnaire ratings of events or situations and observations of how they work. It is important to emphasize, however, that any corporate change programme is likely to involve assessment and application of hard data like financial statistics, sales performance charts, and absenteeism figures, as well as soft data, based on employee perceptions.

The significance of soft data has been recognized from the time of the earliest organizational studies (e.g., Elton Mayo's Hawthorne experiments) which found that worker productivity can be affected as much by human as by technical considerations. Human factors can be operationally defined through surveys of employee attitudes, beliefs, values and behaviours which address aspects of specific jobs, work processes, company structure and policies, and the physical work environment. This kind of feedback from employees has been used successfully to restructure the workplace and to improve both productivity and employee satisfaction or morale.

Positive employee perceptions of the work environment are critical to a productive organization. One source has observed that 'whether the organization is labour-intensive or capital intensive, product-oriented or service-oriented, it is the *people* that will cause productivity improvement through their actions and decisions.... In a productive work environment, workers are involved and contribute their efforts and ideas for improvement and feel pride in their accomplishments'.

(*Industrial Relations*, July 21, 1979)

Employee perceptions and opinions are important, but they are in a constant state of flux. We live in a rapidly changing world, and changes in values and outlook take place all the time. Changing social and economic circumstances and demographic profiles alter the shape and character of the working population. The influx of new youthful workers, together with increased numbers of more affluent leisure-orientated older ones, have produced changed views of the world of work (and leisure). Better educated and more informed employees bring new values to the workplace and have different expectations of their employers compared with previous generations.

Company managements need to assess employee attitudes toward a wide variety of subjects in order to understand how people approach their work situation, but often have difficulty identifying the most relevant areas to examine, how to examine them, or indeed what to do with the findings.

Organizational communications, overall satisfaction with the work-place, pay and fringe benefits are generally considered to be the most important subjects in the workplace and are often the focus of employee attitude surveys (Sayle, 1988). While these matters do indeed frequently concern employees (and always do, or should concern management), there may be many other aspects of the work situation that employees are concerned about, but lack appropriate channels through which to put them across. Company audits can play an important part in facilitating such feedback and, at the same time, classify and target areas of concern.

Supervision of a corporate human resources audit, however, is a skilful exercise requiring a high level of professional expertise and organizational commitment. It is first crucially important to gain the commitment of those involved, particularly that of more senior-level managers. It is important also that the project has an agreed timetable, clear definition of who is involved and the nature of their individual or collective responsibilities.

Apparently minor points that are overlooked in the planning stage may turn out to have major significance at a later stage. Rarely is the final report fully considered at the outset. What kind of document is required? How much detail should it contain? Who should receive it? With human resources audits, as with so much else, the quality of the end result depends on how much effort has been invested in it. Some of the characteristics of a good audit are:

- **Knowing what to measure – distinguishing the wood from the trees** An effective human resources audit depends critically on having a clear idea about its aims and objectives. What is the audit going to try to measure? Preliminary stages should concentrate on establishing the main goals of the audit: in short, what has to be audited, and why.
- **Having clear, well thought-through dimensions** It is very important then to be sure about what facets of the organization are to be measured. Some organizations are sorely tempted to suppress questions on pay, appraisal schemes and training, not because they believe them to be irrelevant, but rather because they are anxious about the results.
- **Being user-friendly** Some human resources audits are written in impenetrable management jargon or psychobabble. It takes skill to devise clear, unambiguous, logically constructed questions that tap into all facets of an issue. Audits need to be simple to understand and complete in order to provide useful and valid data. This is especially true if unskilled employees are being asked to complete them.
- **Simplicity and brevity** Audits need to be succinct but comprehensive. To ask 100 questions is not unreasonable, and such an audit may generally take no more than 30–45 minutes to complete. It is important therefore that the most pertinent 100 questions are asked.
- **Being organization-specific** Every audit needs to be tailored to the needs of each organization for which it is intended. All organizations have their own specific meanings for words, their own unique concepts which need to be considered.

The phases of the human resources audit process

The process of developing human resources audit questions, obtaining employee opinions and perceptions, analysing the data, and recommending appropriate action programmes can be carried out either internally by appropriately skilled personnel or by an external consultant. An outside consultant can provide an extra element of independence and confidentiality, and employees may feel more relaxed and able to divulge opinions on sensitive issues. The internal operative, on the other hand, has the advantage of knowing the organization better and being in tune with existing communications channels and management systems. Both, therefore, have certain advantages and disadvantages.

When conducting any audit, it is important to have a plan of action which is broken down into a number of stages.

Stage 1: Pre-audit administration

Prior to distribution of the audit questionnaire, there is an important preliminary stage of development. In this stage, the internal or external consultant opens discussions with management (and unions if appropriate) at the highest level to confirm their decision to conduct an audit and their commitment to follow appropriate courses of action which may eventually be recommended, contingent upon its results. The organization's higher-level management are briefed on how the audit will proceed, with the consultant underlining the necessity for full company commitment to act upon it, and to be seen to act upon it, by employees. The consultant will also begin to clarify the main areas of concern and subjects upon which the audit should focus, through open-ended discussions with higher-level management. This ensures that senior management 'owns' the projects. The ownership of the audit and its results needs to be fully discussed.

Stage 2: Formulating and testing the audit instrument

The next stage takes the developmental phase of the audit a step further. Questions need to be formulated and an audit questionnaire begins to take shape. Organizations might choose to accept a known, published off-the-shelf audit; to adapt an older audit used before in the organization; or to start from scratch and develop their own. Open-ended group discussions with employees elsewhere in the organization help to provide further input concerning the areas to be covered and the form in which the questions should be phrased. A pilot questionnaire should be tested among a small sample of employees at different levels within the company to check applicability, misunderstandings, and ambiguities. This stage is completed with the finalizing of the audit instrument and its agreement with higher-level management. The entire project rests on the fact that the questionnaire is comprehensive, user-friendly, succinct, unambiguous, and relevant.

Stage 3: Audit administration

The third stage involves the administration of the agreed audit questionnaire to those sections of the organization which have been targeted at earlier stages (see Chapter 2 on sampling). The questionnaires are distributed throughout the organization as appropriate and a time limit placed on completion, with an expected date of return clearly indicated. Late returns may need to be chased up to ensure as large a response rate as possible. The questionnaires have then to be collected together and then usually returned to the consultant for the analysis stage.

Stage 4: Audit analysis and interpretation

The completed questionnaires are processed by having codes allocated to answers, most of which will be multiple-choice responses, which are then entered into a computer for statistical analysis. Results are initially printed in terms of percentages of respondents who indicate agreement or disagreement (or whatever other response option is used) to individual items or as mean (average) scores. Items subsumed under a particular heading may also be reported on as total or average scores for the category as a whole. The results can then be presented in tabular form and in graphs or charts. Various departments and levels within the organization can be compared and results statistically analysed. Frequently the data are under-used by simple descriptive statistics. The use of multivariate statistics, such as factor analysis, multiple regression, or canonical correlation can reveal much more interesting things about the organization. Just as the finance sections may use statistical models (and packages) to tease out the underlying patterns and structures in their data, so too can advanced techniques be applied to human resources audit data to capture in a more dynamic fashion, relationships which exist between different categories of perceptions, and to yield predictive models to guide action programmes within an organization.

Stage 5: Recommendations for action

The final stage draws together a plan of action based on the problem areas identified by the audit. A programme of change may be recommended, comprising a number of stages or targets. Further audits may be necessary periodically to check that change targets have been reached.

Employee participation is naturally an important factor in the design and conduct of the audit and resulting change programme. Involving employees at every phase of the process allows them to communicate meaningful information to management through channels not otherwise available. This is a highly effective exercise as it prevents errors being made *before* the audits are done.

Employee interviews early in the process, for instance, are recommended to determine areas of concern and to elicit employee support for conducting the audit. Open-ended interviews with employees can reduce any uncertainty and apprehension they might have about what the audit entails. They can encourage employees to share their ideas about the organization and its future, even though many employees may not be certain they have the 'right' answers. People also communicate much information not simply by what they have to say, but by what they don't say or by the way they react emotionally to particular questions. All this verbal and non-verbal feedback can provide the consultant with valuable input, ensuring that the right questions are used during the main survey phase.

While employee involvement is important in the survey process, management are often disturbed by such techniques as interviews. They feel some pressure because they are unable to see how a company audit, utilizing feedback direct from employees, will assist them in the first place. It is essential, when these feelings arise, that the internal (human resources/personnel) or external (specialist management) consultant can offer reassurance to the company's management. This can, in part, be achieved by explaining to managers what they will get out of the audit. First, it will give the manager measures of managerial effectiveness by providing initial benchmarks of how well the organization is perceived by staff to function in different respects. Thus, intuitive feelings managers may have about problems areas will be either confirmed or disconfirmed. Either way, the feedback will enable management to pinpoint where improvements can be made. Second, the audit process, once custom-built for the company, can be used again. Repeat audits can provide useful trend data, allowing management to gauge whether changes are occurring within the company, and at the rate that is desired. Thus, the audit can identify problems and provide indications about how these problems can be resolved through workable solutions. A third point is that by involving employees in the analysis and solution of problems, it can contribute to their personal and professional growth, which can only be for the good of the organization.

The process of early employee involvement can also set the stage for meaningful change in the audit process. Research has indicated that commitment increases when individuals are involved in their own goal-setting. If individuals are personally involved, they will tend to engage in much more goal-directed activity before becoming frustrated and giving up. On the other hand, if someone else (e.g., their boss) sets the goals all the time, employees may be apt to give up more easily because they perceive these as someone else's goals and not as their own.

Critical action steps – Stage 1

Before the consultant, internal or external, begins the audit process, he or she will need to assign someone as a contact with top management, someone with a depth of knowledge about the organization and its employees. Numerous meetings will be held during the audit process with managers throughout the organization, and it is necessary to have someone responsible for expediting matters.

The steps in Stage 1 assess the needs of management and of employees. They will help the consultant develop an audit instrument that probes areas of concern expressed by each of these groups. This initial phase consists of a series of orientation activities that:

- familiarize the consultant auditor with the organization and its specific needs;
- introduce both management and employees to the audit and explain the ramifications for the organization;
- allow the trades unions to express their concerns and gain an insight into the audit process.

Step 1: Briefing management

Interviews need to be conducted with the management personnel associated with the audit, including the chief executive officer, the personnel or human resources manager, and any staff with responsibility for helping with the audit. These meetings are used to explain the process and to gather information on the specific issues management would like to include in the audit. In addition, it can also be useful for the consultant to arrange a meeting with all people at the executive level, at which he or she explains what the audit will prove, finds out what management's concerns are, responds to questions, and solicits management support and assistance for the audit.

Step 2: Interviewing employees

Interviews should be conducted with a sample of executives, mid-level managers, supervisors, representatives of trades unions, and first-level employees. These interviews are used to define the areas of concern each group or individual would like to include in the audit. At the lower levels interviews with four or eight employees at one time can be more informative than individual interviews; the group members encourage each other to explore new or additional subject areas.

Step 3: Selecting subjects areas

Once the areas of concern have been identified, they should be prioritized and combined in a brief report, which the consultant should present to the management. Management should be encouraged to include all the subjects which concern them in the audit. The final audit instrument, however, should reflect only those areas in which management is willing to accept some change. Soliciting information in an area about which management is intractable is only an exercise in frustration for all concerned. Indeed, if word gets out that management is not prepared to make changes to areas which earlier employee interviews had pinpointed as trouble spots, the net impact of the audit could be distinctly negative. To this extent it is wise to consider the implications of the results (be they positive or negative) before embarking on an exercise.

Step 4: Formulating questions

Audits and surveys by other organizations can help the outside (or inside) consultant begin to find questions appropriate for the audit under preparation. Frequently, the client organization's areas of concern will be similar to ones experienced by other organizations (in the same sector), and if the consultant asks identical questions, cross-comparisons can be facilitated between organizations. Internal consultants may obtain books (such as this one) which provide examples of other audits. The consultant must always remember, though, that the reason for the audit is to improve the client organization, and must therefore select only those questions that fit the concerns of that organization exactly and be expressed in the appropriate terminology. Although questions with a track record of usage in other audits have a background against which they can be judged, no two organizations are ever exactly the same and all audits must, of necessity, be custom-built to fit the idiosyncratic attributes and circum-stances of individual organizations under consideration.

Thus, many questions will be developed out of information obtained in employee interviews. The consultant should select several questions for each area of concern. More questions than necessary should be developed, so that as wide a choice as possible is facilitated from which to select the questions that produce the most effective results in the management review and field testing.

Step 5: Reviewing questions

The large battery of questions (attitudes, behavioural reports, value statements) drawn together by the consultant should then be reviewed with the principal internal contact(s). Leading questions and redundant state-ments should be eliminated. Frequently, a dynamic pilot of the questions with a small group of typical employees will point out any remaining problems. The aim is to select the most sensitive and discriminating items from a large list.

Step 6: Field testing

At least two groups of twelve to fifteen employees should be assembled to field test the proposed questions. These groups should include men and women from different levels in the organization, special interest groups, and minority groups. The test groups complete the preliminary question-naire, and after the consultant collects the answer sheets a discussion should be held with the participants to determine their understanding of the questions and to identify any problems. Questions that produce doubts or confusion should be discarded or modified. Only those questions which can be clearly and unambiguously understood should pass the final screening. This field testing will sometimes provide an early indication of what the final audit results will be like. The rough data are also useful in designing and testing the computer program to be used during the analysis stage.

Step 7: Finalizing questions

The consultant (audit designer) should then develop a final set of questions based on the reaction of management to the proposed questions and the field testing results. The eventual audit instrument will ideally aim to contain around 80–120 items; if the questionnaire is much longer, employees tend not to complete and return the answer sheet in such large numbers. The consultant should present management with a final list of subject areas to be audited and the questions to be used.

Critical actions steps – Stage 2

In this phase of the project, the consultant should develop methods to inform employees of the impending audit and the reasons for it. It is imperative to underscore the questionnaire's confidentiality. In most organizations the employees must be assured that what they say will not cause them problems; they must be reassured of management's trust in them before they will provide information on sensitive issues. The consultant should investigate ways to increase the rate of participation by employees - with internal advertising, for instance. Audit questionnaires should be printed, personalized and distributed to employees, but not before the consultant has worked out a method for return of the forms, such as pre-paid sealed envelopes.

Step 8: Identifying audit groups

The consultant should survey employees by work group or shift, while maintaining the anonymity of the participants. As soon as the questions have been finalized, the consultant should obtain from each major department in the organization a run-down of the work groups. In general, the number in each group should range from 50 to 250 employees. If the survey participation rate is high - over 50 per cent - and the groups are homogeneous, anonymity can be assured with a group size as low as thirty-five. If, however, this is the first time the company has done an audit, or the groups are not homogeneous, the size should be kept to a minimum of fifty.

Step 9: Preparing advertising

Employees should be notified early in the process of the impending audit and the precautions being taken to ensure confidentiality. Company newsletter articles, posters for bulletin boards, and other forms of advertising should be used. Usually employees welcome the prospect of giving feedback 'up-the-organization', and are happy to take part, given sufficient warning and briefing.

Step 10: Preparing the audit form

The consultant should make sure that the audit questionnaire instructions are written clearly, and may design a separate answer sheet. The separate sheet allows employees to keep the questionnaire for further study, which can help to stimulate discussion on the areas of concern before the audit data are published. The design of the answer sheet depends on the methods selected for data scoring analysis. If the data are to be 'machine-scored' to save time, a separate answer sheet could be very beneficial.

Step 11: Distributing questionnaires

When the printed audit forms are in hand, they may be labelled individually so that each employee receives a personalized copy. The employee will place a higher value on the personalized form. On the other hand, some may believe that this ensures the audit is not anonymous and that they can be traced. To have a personalized envelope rather than a questionnaire may overcome this problem. This procedure also provides a means for controlling audit distribution.

The forms should be distributed like any other valuable document. A supply of envelopes will also be needed for the return of the answer sheets, and should be addressed to the consultant. Employees should be asked to return the answer sheets as soon as possible, but certainly within two weeks. Privately, the consultant should allow about a month so that as much data can be collected as possible.

Step 12: Collecting questionnaires

Although there are a variety of different collection methods, the inter-office mail is probably the most effective and efficient means. On the other hand, the employees should have the option of returning their forms by ordinary post. After two weeks, follow-up cards should be sent to employees who have not yet returned their forms (if, of course, they can be identified). Alternatively, some in-house advertising could be used to remind late contributors about filling out their audit.

Critical action steps – Stage 3

This phase of the process is designed to disseminate the initial audit results quickly and to provide management with early information on any strong trends. These steps allow the consultant to probe the data and explore the necessities for individual departments.

Step 13: Analysing data

All the data collected should be entered into a computer file for analysis. Any number of software programs can be used.

A preliminary analysis of the data should be made ready within two weeks of distributing the audit. This may be useful for management in identifying any unusual currents, and may provide information on specific ways to analyse the data when all the results are in. While the data are still being collected, decisions can be made on the types of graphs and charts that will best display the results, as well as what multivariate statistics are required.

Step 14: Developing preliminary conclusions

A print-out of the data should show the percentage of positive, negative and neutral or uncertain responses relating to each question for each work group identified in Step 8. Questions having exceptionally high or low positive response should be identified. Then, a comparison should be made between current survey data and any other relevant data to which the consultant has access. Correlation studies between the various data can be generated and are sometimes informative, but care must be taken not to allow matters to get too technical. Clearly, different people or groups have a preference for how the data are presented. Those who are highly numerate are quite capable of understanding the results from factor analysis, multiple regressions, or canonical correlations which can be run on the data to show in more detail the relationships between the variables.

Step 15: Preliminary reporting

Based on the data collected, the internal or external consultant should prepare a preliminary report for the work groups detailing:

- Response rate – the number of audit answer sheets returned, compared to the number of forms distributed; percentage of positive responses, for each question – the number of positive responses, compared to the total number of responses received.
- Percentage of negative responses for each question – the number of negative responses, compared to the total number of responses received; items that had exceptionally high or low positive responses.

These simple descriptive data will be needed by the follow-up groups in a later stage. The power and speed of computers should mean that more complex multivariate data can be processed very speedily.

Step 16: Briefing management

The consultant should review this report with the CEO and the personnel or human resources director, and point out any general conclusions and any areas of exceptionally high or low results. This is not the final report. It is used only to show management what information will be released to employees for further study.

Step 17: Data printing

The consultant should then prepare this report in a format suitable for printing. The printed copies, containing a few generalizations about the audit results and a description of the process to be used in the final analysis of the data, should be distributed throughout the company as soon as possible. Sharing data early will increase employee trust and encourage employee participation in recommending improvements. To withhold information only causes people to question why they have not heard the results. Rumours are nearly always worse than facts, and employee morale often begins to decline unless something is done as a result of the audit. Providing employees with audit data and information on how improvements will be made is generally enough to cause morale to rise.

Critical action steps – Stage 4

Employees will have to complete the audit forms in the hope that management will make changes in the way the organization is run. Their involvement in the data analysis is important, for their commitment to the organization increases as they involve themselves in their own goal-setting. In Stage 4 two sets of meetings between employee groups and the consultant help to establish a method for analysing the audit results and a process for making recommendations to management. It provides for direct employee involvement in the resolution of their concerns.

Step 18: Establishing follow-up groups

Department heads may choose to select follow-up groups of four to eight employees from various levels in their departments. These employees should be identified several months prior to conducting the audit. Each of these groups should meet with the consultant to discuss their role in the audit process and the processes of goal-setting and action planning. They should be given instructions on how to analyse the audit data when they become available.

Employees taking part in this process become proponents of the audit and help to provide information to other employees as preparation for the final audit results proceeds. They also have the opportunity to broaden their knowledge of the organization and thus to prepare themselves for advancement.

Step 19: Instructing follow-up groups

The consultant should meet with each department head and subsequently with each follow-up group to begin the analysis of the audit data. The groups may then make recommendations and write a short report. These reports should then be directed to the manager who appointed the group. A copy of each report could be included in the final write-up.

Step 20: Critical action

In this phase, the final report is distributed, including the actions planned by the organization as a result of the audit. The report will acknowledge all the groups and individuals within the organization who took part and assisted the audit. It will clarify the areas which need to be addressed in a future programme of change. A slightly different set of stages is shown in Figure 1.1.

These twenty steps are not obligatory, of course, but recommendations to be treated as a check-list for those who commission and run audits. Not all these steps are appropriate, practical or necessary, depending on the nature of the audit and the organization commissioning it. Yet they represent a logical sequence for any auditor to follow.

WHAT TYPE OF AUDIT?

Clearly the single most important question concerns what type of human resources audit the organization most needs. Sayle (1988) has identified three types of audit which vary in their depth and scope.

Internal audit

This is a management audit performed by a company or a department upon its own system, procedures and facilities. The authors may be from the company's own ranks or hired from outside to act on its behalf. The internal audit is a technique whereby the management feels its own pulse and assesses the organization's performance, its needs, its strong points and its failings. These audits address various organizational attributes such as corporate culture, climate, communication systems, and customer care orientation. We discuss each of these types of audit in more detail in later chapters.

Groundwork (pre-audit) and agreement to proceed

Set up

- Set up steering group
- First briefing for organization
- Assemble project team (to devise, administer, analyse audit)
- Plan project
- Decide who receives report; crucially important question

Job analysis

- Interviews
- Questionnaire
- Report

Decide on roles for administration
Audit design

- Set up design teams
- Meet design teams and brainstorm exercises
- Receive first draft
- Go through proposed changes with design teams
- Receive second draft
- Trial of audit among small depts
- Make final changes
- Devise audit ten-day schemes

Choose and/or design material
Design rating forms
Choose target respondents

- Briefing to respondents
- Briefing to respondents' managers

Run questionnaire
Check return rate

- Send reminders
- Determine section response
- Set final closing date

Send questionnaire for data processing and analysis
Inspection of crosstabs/first break of data
Doing appropriate stats analysis to test specific questionnaire

- Factor analysis to determine structure
- Regressional analysis to determine predictions
- Path analysis to determine process

```
Write draft report
• Get feedback for design commitment
• Draft to head of HR/CEO for comments
• Redrafted

Final report written
Results in comprehensible and comprehensive form published
Recommendations for changes made
Changes instituted
```

Figure 1.1 Stages to the development of corporate audit

Self audit

This is a particular type of internal audit performed by an individual upon his or her own system, procedures and facilities in order to assess his or her performance, needs, strengths and failings. This usually involves the completion and analysis of one of the many psychometric tests in this area. Alternatively, a manager may give out questionnaires to all those reporting to him or her to attempt to elicit how they respond to his or her management style.

External audit

External audits are performed by a company upon its own suppliers or sub-suppliers (clients or competitors). The auditors may be either from the company's own ranks or hired from an outside source to act on behalf of the company. This type of management audit is usually performed in order to assess the status of contracts made with the company's suppliers and sub-suppliers, in order to determine whether the company will be receiving what it is paying for.

In some cases, the distinction between the external audit and the internal audit may be blurred - as, for example, when the auditing company considers its suppliers as part of its own organization for the duration of the contract, providing technical guidance and support until the contract is fulfilled. Sayle (1988) categorizes his audits in the form shown in Table 1.1.

This book describes four types of internal audits: culture, climate, communications, and clients/customers. They are all concerned with procedures for the assessment of the personal, subjective, perceptions, feelings and experiences of employees regarding the organization they work for. Although these corporate concepts are related and overlapping, they can be meaningfully differentiated. (See Chapters 3, 4, 5, 6.)

Table 1.1 Management audit type, depth and scope

Type	Auditor organization	Auditee organization	Scope	Depth	Duration
Internal	'Us' = own organization or hired auditor	'Us'	Full, partial or follow-up	Systems or compliance	Weeks
External	'Us' = own organization hired auditor, consortium	Out supplier, sub-suppliers, etc.	Full, partial or follow-up	Systems or compliance	Days for each supplier
Extrinsic	Our customer, customer's customer, etc., regulatory body	'Us', our supplier, sub-suppliers, etc.	Full, partial or follow-up	Systems or compliance	Days

Source: Sayle (1988) Reproduced by permission of publisher

CRUCIAL DECISIONS ABOUT MAKING AN AUDIT

Practitioners and those preparing to do a corporate human resources audit need to answer a number of questions before embarking upon such an exercise. The following points are worth considering.

Do we need an audit?   Is a human resources audit a necessary or relevant course of action, given a careful consideration and definition of an organization's problems and information needs?

What is the objective of the management audit?   Since the prime purpose of any human resources audit is to obtain information, it is important to establish exactly what sort of information management expects the audit to produce. Embarking on an audit without a clear definition of its objectives is dangerous and potentially highly costly. Any audit must define both the terms of reference and aims. It is very unwise to authorize the expenditure of resources for unknown and undefined benefits, thereby giving the auditor a blank cheque. The objective(s) of an audit can be stated in simple terms, and each of these needs to be carefully and unambiguously defined.

What must be the type, depth and scope of the audit?   The type of human resources audit will be determined by the initially stated audit objectives and information to be sought. So far as scope is concerned, pilot-testing on a particular phase of the project will indicate if a large-scale audit exercise is needed. The depth of the audit is directly affected by the risks involved in not having reliable information available for management to use as the basis for its decisions.

When is the audit needed? To obtain management information in advance of key decision points dictates the need for diarized timing, so that the full cost–benefit potential of an audit may be realized. Sensible advance timing should enable proper implementation of any corrective action that the audit reveals as being required. Delay or total failure are thus minimized or totally avoided from the outset. It is essential to plan the audit for the entire work phase envisaged. As indicated earlier, errors detected at such a late stage are extremely expensive and embarrassing to put right.

What are the risks involved if the audit is postponed and major problems then found during its course? These are questions that too few ask, but which all should consider. It is unwise to postpone an audit continually until there is no time left in which to perform it or in which to correct major problems without incurring considerable expense. The question remains as to whether or not it is likely that major problems will come to light during the audit. The answer depends on the previous performance of the 'auditee'. An auditee who has either a poor record or little experience of the product or contract requirements is more likely to suffer from a number of deficiencies, some of which may be major problems. This point must be considered when the audit is scheduled and planned.

Who should perform the audit? There is a range of considerations involved here, apart from the required expertise. That expertise must be provided regardless of the level at which it might be found in the company. The auditor must 'fit' within the organization, which in turn must trust investing in him/her.

Can the audit be combined with some quality control activity to avoid duplication of effort? In order to ensure that particular expertise is available during an audit, it is worthwhile determining whether or not the audit can be timed to coincide with another activity at which specialist personnel from the auditor's organization will be present. 'Piggy-backing' can save a great deal of money; that is an audit can usefully be combined with some other activity like training.

Can audits improve decision making? Audits are fact-finding activities which examine objective evidence in an unbiased manner so as to provide reliable and valid input for decisions. A central purpose of a human resources audit is to obtain correct information that will provide essential input to assist the decision-making process so that quality problems and costs can be prevented or rectified, and avoidable costs be saved. Audits should be fact-finding exercises which can substantially improve the quality of decisions by helping to reduce the risks associated with them. Audits provide management information: the decisions based upon them can only be as good as the information produced. Audits cannot ensure good decision-making, but they can ensure that decision-making is made on the best possible evidence.

In-house or hired auditors?   An organization will inevitably have to consider the value, or otherwise, of employing a permanent staff whose duties will consist solely of auditing. The decision depends upon a number of factors, including the size of the organization, the product or service supplied, the type and number of contracts with which it is involved, and the costs. Large organizations can generally justify and sustain the cost of in-house auditors as a part of their quality assurance department. A major benefit of outside management auditors is their independence – the absence of inbred company habits, and freedom from preconceived ideas.

Are audits too costly?   The benefits of human resources audits discussed here must be weighed against the costs of performing them. During the audit, the auditee of the company normally invests at least twice as much as the auditor. Time is consumed as an audited employee answers questions and produces evidence for the auditor; the consultant's time is also taken up just by being present. Given that a minimum of two of the auditee's people are thus present throughout the audit proceedings, twice as many man hours are involved, assuming that only one auditor is present. Even when more than one auditor is present, the investment made by the auditee must still be respected.

Accordingly, the audit needs to be conducted professionally. For his investment, the auditee is entitled to a good return, some constructive criticism and valuable conclusions from the audit. Incompetent and ill-trained practitioners bring auditing and quality assurance into disrepute. The attitude of many auditors also leads to inadequate results. Some of them revel in their apparent power and abuse the authority vested in them: they are irresponsible.

CONCLUSION

This chapter discussed some of the basic issues concerning corporate audits. Certain criticisms and myths surrounding corporate audits were addressed. We considered the various reasons why (and therefore why not) an organization can and should do audits of various kinds. Once the decision has been made whether to do an audit, further crucial questions were considered such as what type of audit. This chapter has thus set the scene for a detailed discussion first of some technical aspects of measurement, and then of some of the specific types of audits that can be done.

2   Measurement issues

INTRODUCTION

This book is about human resources audits for management. It is concerned with how and what to audit in any organization. This chapter deals essentially with two things. First, it is concerned with the 'science of measurement'. Psychologists have spent most of this century refining the process of psychometrics – ways of measuring individual psychological functioning. Much of management science and organizational behaviour has leaned heavily on this source of expertise, and to a large extent is therefore derivative. But whereas the methods of assessing individuals and organizations might be similar, the resultant instruments or tools, or assessment are not invariably the same, nor in the case of organizations should they be. Management science needs to develop a library of useful measurement instruments to assess organizations in general and which are capable of reflecting the varying nuances and idiosyncrasies of different organizations. Secondly, this book considers four quite different, but often related audits: culture, climate, communications and customers. This begs two questions of why these audits should be studied and used and, equally important, of how they are interrelated.

PSYCHOMETRICS AND ORGANOMETRICS

For over one hundred years psychologists have attempted to devise valid measures of psychological functioning. This activity follows from the old adage that whatever exists, exists in some quantity and can therefore be measured. Psychologists have devised thousands of measures of individual abilities, attitudes and beliefs, and have argued that psychometric testing is far superior to any form of impressionistic assessment. Psychometrics is concerned with the devising of reliable and valid measures of an individual's ability, intelligence, interests and personality. Although test scores can be aggregated, or may involve individuals saying how they behave in teams or groups, the analysis is generally conducted at the level of the individual. Organometrics is also concerned with devising reliable and valid measures, but not of an individual's psychological functioning; rather they are specifically concerned with how to assess the functions and characteristics of organizations. It involves, of necessity, a different level of analysis. Historically, far less work has been done on organometrics than on psychometrics. The two areas are closely related, but have some notable differences. For instance, because most human characteristics are fairly stable over time, a radical shift in their profile at the individual level of analysis is usually considered a mark of unreliability and possibly even of a lack of validity in the original measure. However, some organizations undergo consistent and radical changes, and an organometric measure is unreliable if it fails to detect the real changes that have occurred. As noted in Chapter 1 corporate audits, as organometric tools, can serve to monitor organizational functioning in the service of facilitating organizational change, hence we should expect shifts to occur in the nature of any organizational profile they measure.

Returning momentarily to individual-level assessment, Cronbach (1987) has argued that psychometrics are distinguishable from impressionist assessment by four characteristics. These distinguishing features provide a framework of criteria which can also guide the development of effective organometric measurement.

Definiteness of task   The task set may be definite or vague. A task is said to be structured when everyone interprets it in much the same way. The more latitude that is allowed in a measurement task, the less structure it will generate in the nature of response to its questions. Structuring obtains a definite answer to a question formulated in advance. The less structured technique elicits more diverse responses; and such responses can, in turn, generate further questions as well as providing some answers. Psychometricians set themselves the clear task of getting very clear answers to very specific questions.

Constructed response vs. response choice   The test-taker may be asked to construct a response orally or in writing, or to manipulate objects. An interviewer might ask, 'Are you at ease in social gatherings?' and wait for a reply. The psychometric tester provides alternatives such as 'always', 'often', 'sometimes', 'never'. A series-completion item (7 5 8 6 9 ...) may be open-ended or supplied with answer choices. The choice format makes scoring easy, but the information supplied may be less rich.

Analysis of performance   Psychometric testing concerns itself with the tangible product of the performance – the answer given, the block tower constructed, or the essay written – and only rarely with the process by which the product was produced. When psychometric testers do pay attention to the process, they arm themselves with a record sheet for tabulating what they themselves see, and select in advance the particular aspects of the person's style that will be recorded. Formulating in advance just what variables the observer will attend to is often an unacceptable restriction to the impressionistic psychologist. Numerical scores are pivotal in psychometric interpretations, whereas the impressionist may translate a test performance into a character description without ever counting up a score. When a decision is to be made, the investigator can apply some formal rule to the various facts in the record, or can combine them impressionistically. The psychometric tester prefers impersonal rigour; the impressionist prefers flexibility.

Construct validation Psychometric testers place their trust in interpretations made by an explicit, empirical (often statistical) rule derived from previous groups; they distrust more subjective, individualized interpretations. A psychometric tester accompanies every numerical score with a warning regarding the error of measurement and thus should also attach an index of uncertainty to every prediction. The impressionist is less concerned with formal validation. Validating qualitative interpretations and 'portraits' is much more difficult than validating numerical predictions. In effect, it requires validation of the interpreter.

> In the impressionistic style, the interpreter must be an artist, sensitive to observe and skilful to convey impressions. Some psychologists are presumably better judges of personality than others. The psychometric method seeks procedures that everyone can use equally well. The objective test is a camera pointed in a fixed direction; every competent photographer should get the same picture with it. Thus, psychometric testing aims to reduce measurement to a technical procedure. To the extent that it succeeds, it reduces the need for a 'wise' professional psychologist. The psychometric and impressionistic approaches differ most sharply on the issue of confidence in the psychologist. Advocates of rigor regard the test as an erratic instrument whose unregulated interpretations entangle truth with speculation. Impressionists view the observer as a sensitive and even indispensable instrument. The impressionist does not deny the danger of bias and error. He/she, however, is unwilling to ignore the person's background and present situation – and the meanings he gives to them – as a standard formula for scoring does.
>
> (Cronbach, 1987, p. 43)

There is considerable debate as to the applied usefulness of psychological tests (particularly personality tests) in industry. There are both obvious advantages and disadvantages. As many of these apply to organometrics, they will be considered.

Advantages

• Both psychometric and organometric tests provide numeric information that means individuals or groups and even organizations can more easily be compared on the same criteria. In interviews, different questions are asked of different candidates, and the answers often forgotten. Audits allow for exact comparisons which may be used to test hypotheses about how to manage organizations.

- With data-based records one can trace a person's development over time. In fact, by going back to test audit results kept in a group's file one can actually see if, and by how much, the tests were predictive of later success. This represents a monitoring function of psychometrics and organometrics.

- Tests and audits give explicit and specific results on processes and functioning, rather than vague, ambiguous, coded platitudes that are so often found in reference plans. A percentage or a *sten* score (provided of course that it is valid) makes for much clearer thinking about personal characteristics than impressionistic, evaluative terms such as 'satisfactory', 'sufficient' or 'high-flyer'. Furthermore, regularly-obtained comparative profiles of performance based on standardized, quantifiable indicators from different departments provide much more meaningful data than periodic, idiosyncratic reports by a line manager.

- Tests are fair because they eliminate corruption, favouritism, and self-perpetuation of old-boy, masonic, or Oxbridge networks. Thus, if a person does not have the required ability or experience profile they will not be chosen, regardless of their other 'assets'. Similarly audit results do not hide the fact if morale in some part of the organization is poor, possibly due to the lack of skill or consideration of staff needs on the part of a manager.

- Tests and corporate audits are comprehensive in that they cover all the basic dimensions of personality and ability from which other behaviour patterns derive. Similarly, a good audit is able to assess comprehensively the work-related beliefs and behaviours of the entire organization.

- Tests are scientific in that they are soundly empirically based and built upon proven theoretical foundations. That means they are more likely to be reliable, valid and able to discriminate the good from the average, and the average from the poor. Well constructed organizational audits too can be empirically based. A number already exist, both to assess culture (see Chapter 3), and corporate climate (see Chapter 4).

Disadvantages

- Psychometric tests (indeed all self-report questionnaires) can be faked – that is, people like to put themselves in a good light and receive a good score so that they may be accepted, but this in a way reflects their real personality (some tests have lie scores, to attempt to overcome this). Equally, some people may feel obliged to over-report their dissatisfaction in an organization, in the hope that they will get some reward. But there are ways by using ipsative measures, for instance to prevent this.

- Some people do not have sufficient self-insight to report accurately on their own feelings and behaviour – that is, it is not that people lie but that they cannot, rather than *will* not, give accurate answers about themselves. This is less likely to prove a problem in the case of organizational audits, because the issues discussed and measured are explicit, behavioural, or attitudinal phenomena.

- Tests and audits are unreliable, in that all sorts of temporary factors – test anxiety, boredom, weariness, a headache, period pains – all lead people to give different answers on different occasions (although this is partly true, this factor only makes a small difference). Organometrics, like psychometrics, can be unreliable for similar reasons (a bad day, an unlucky encounter with one's boss), but this problem is not great, and test-related reliability is usually sufficiently high over short periods of time.

- Most importantly, some tests or audits are invalid in that they do not measure what they say they are measuring, and their scores do not predict behaviour over time. For many tests this is indeed their Achilles' heel and they are lamentably short of robust proof of their validity. Whereas this is particularly true of ability, aptitude, intelligence, and personality tests which measure hypothetical constructs, and which may have been insufficiently validated in the context of real world behaviour, it is less true of organometric tests which essentially measure attitudes and beliefs. However, earlier organometric measures need to be validated within the contexts or the environments in which they are to be used.

  Individual-level tests might be able to measure all sorts of dimensions of behaviour, but not necessarily those which are most crucial to the organization. Buying personality tests is like having a set menu, when what managers often need is an à la carte menu from which they can select only what they want. Organometricians have realized this, which perhaps accounts for the fact that there are so few normative corporate surveys. Many argue that every organization requires its own unique measure. Hence, corporate audits tend to be organization-specific.

- Employees have to be sufficiently literate or articulate to complete tests and questionnaires. Many organizations may therefore believe their work-force would not complete them properly, or that they would take up too much time or cause needless embarrassment. It is true that all organizations have their own jargon, short-hand terms, and acronyms, many of which have strong emotional connotations. It is, thus, a double-edged sword: to include these terms in a survey would help face validity, but it might also hinder the establishment of concurrent validity, because organizations cannot be strictly compared.

- Since corporate audits tend to be organization-specific, there are no good norms, at least for the kinds of work-force populations most organizations want to test. This is a serious problem, because without benchmark norms one has no idea as to how good or bad individual or organometric scores are.

  Some individual-level tests are allegedly unfair, and biased towards mainstream racial and socio-demographic groups. Hence white males tend to do better, obtain the most attractive profiles and therefore get selected. Such instruments therefore fly in the face of anti-discriminatory legislation by not being meritocratic, in a practice which has been seen as unethical! This is rarely true of organometrics, since they are used not to determine ability of 'fit' for selection, but rather focus on employee perceptions, attitudes and beliefs. Unless they are very badly constructed it seems difficult to conceive how they could be the cause of systematic bias.

- Interpretation of individual-level tests takes skill, insight and experience, and this can be expensive or unavailable. In the wrong hands, these instruments are dangerous because the profiles they reveal can give rise either to inaccurate or to overly literal interpretations. This is equally true of psychometric and organometric tests. Simple mean scores and descriptive statistics can be misleading, and non-experts may be able neither to do, nor to interpret more revealing multivariate statistical analyses which can be carried out on corporate audit data.

- Freedom of information legislation, for instance in the USA, may mean that candidates or employees are entitled to see and thence challenge the scores themselves, the interpretations placed on the scores, or any corporate decisions made on the basis of the scores. Organometricians should generally feed back all the results to all the employees. Indeed, it is often the case that having sight of the results is a minimal condition offered to respondents in return for completing the questionnaire.

- As individual-level tests (ability and personality) become well known, people could buy copies and practise completing specific forms so that they know the correct or most desirable answers. This happens extensively with GMAT (that is, intelligence and ability testing). Results could thus be envisaged as having to do more with preparation and practice than with the measurement of actual ability. Since so few organometric tests are available in print, or are used in an adapted, off-the-shelf, way this problem rarely occurs. Even if they were available, however, the nature of the desired responses to these forms is such that practice is a relevant concept.

WHAT IS A GOOD TEST?

There are a number of criteria that psychometricians insist on for a good psychometric test. Six or seven criteria are always considered. Many, but not all, apply to organometric tests in the same way.

Reliability

For all sorts of reasons, individual-level test results do not always accurately reflect a person's actual attitudes, motives or interests. Scores from these instruments can vary according to:

- The amount of test anxiety respondents are experiencing and the degree to which that test anxiety might significantly affect the test results. Corporate surveys are, however, much less likely to cause anxiety than intelligence or ability tests.
- Capacity and willingness of respondents to co-operate with the researcher, or to comprehend written test instructions. This can be a problem for both personal and political reasons, some individuals or groups may 'spoil' their responses, or agree disengenuously to certain answers. Although this is relatively rare, it does occur.
- The extent to which respondents have received prior coaching, or clear instructions. This is rarely a problem for corporate auditing.
- The importance respondents attribute to portraying themselves in a good or bad light. This is an important issue for corporate auditing, as well as for individual-level tests, and is dealt with later in this chapter.
- The extent to which respondents are, for lack of a better term, 'lucky', and can 'beat the odds', on a multiple-choice test. Since organometric attitude surveys do not have right or wrong answers, this is unlikely to occur.

The use of the term 'reliability', especially in everyday parlance, is synonymous with dependability and consistency. But in psychological terms, it has a more specific definition, referring to how consistently a test yields the same scores. If survey results are highly affected by the weather, people's moods, the phases of the moon, and so on, it is unlikely that they will give very similar (let alone identical) scores from one time to the next. Just as you would expect two or three dentists to give the same diagnosis, so you should expect two consultants to write the same report based on an attitude survey if it is reliable. By and large most, but by no means all, organometric tests are pretty reliable. That is the correlation (the reliability coefficient) between the scores of people who take the same test twice over a reasonable period of time is quite high. They are usually also internally consistent. But when auditing organizational change, the reliability of instruments may drop – in a period of change, corporate audits are sensitive to shifts in the work environment. This, however, also depends on what is being audited. Because corporate culture is generally stable and resistant to change it may give rise to consistent measures over time. A more volatile aspect of an organization, such as climate, may exhibit a less consistent profile when repeatedly tested.

There are various sources of error that may significantly reduce the reliability of a test and lead to poor consistency. These include:

Test construction   The actual range of questions asked, as well as things such as the wording of tests, actually affects the consistency of people's answers. Inexperienced attitude survey researchers frequently fall into this trap.

Test administration   Such conditions as room temperature, ventilation, noise, and writing surface can all affect results. So can the amount of sleep the testee had the night before, the level of test anxiety, any drugs respondents may be taking, illness, having a period, and temporary worries – these can all cause careless mistakes, misreading of questions and the giving of uncharacteristic answers. Finally, certain characteristics associated with the person handing out the survey (age, sex, physical appearance, professionalism) can subtly alter the nature of the test situation as perceived by the person completing the survey, and hence, his or her actual results. However, these effects have been shown to be very minor.

Test scoring and interpretation   The advent of computer scoring has largely prevented error creeping in here, but some tests still require testers to make an 'expert judgement' as to the correctness of an answer. Without rigorous and standardized training it is possible that different interpretations will be placed on test results by different testers. Psychologists have a number of different ways of assessing the reliability of tests. Essentially there are five different methods:

1   **Test-retest reliability** This is simply the lack of agreement between the scores the same person gets on two different occasions. Organometric tests are frequently used to measure employee perceptions 'before and after' the introduction of an organizational programme; in this sense the fact that surveys do not evidence similar scores, is not an index of the survey's unreliability, so much as evidence of change.
2   **Parallel/alternate forms** This looks at the equivalence of different forms of the same survey designed to be equivalent with respect to things such as content. The primary advantage of using an alternate or parallel form of a test is that the effect of memory for the content of a previously administered form of the test is minimized. It is possible, though difficult, to devise two surveys with differently worded questions, measuring the same thing.
3   **Split-half reliability** This is a measure of the similarity or equivalence

of two halves of the same measure administered once (by looking at the answers to odd versus even questions). This is a useful measure of reliability when it is impractical or undesirable to assess reliability with two tests or to have two test administrations.

4   **Internal consistency** There are various ways to examine the inter-item consistency or homogeneity of a test. This tells whether all the items in the test are measuring a single ability or personality trait.

5   **Inter-scorer reliability** Variously referred to as scorer, judge, observer or interpreter reliability, this refers to the degree of agreement or consistency between two or more scorers. On some occasions, organometric measures, such as those used in assessment centres, require expert observers, or coders to record responses to a task. Inter-scorer reliability refers to the level of agreement between different raters.

Validity

The most important aspect of most tests is the extent to which they actually measure what they claim to measure; that is the meaningfulness of the test score. Essentially the validity of any survey may be evaluated by scrutinizing the content; relating the score obtained on the test to other test scores and measures; and examining how the test relates to or predicts other measures, behaviour or beliefs within the theoretical framework originally devised for the test.

Essentially there are five basic kinds of validity:

Face validity   This concerns whether the survey *looks* as if it is measuring what it says it measures, 'on the face of it'. In other words, do the items on the survey look as if they are tapping the feature the test is purportedly measuring? Although less important, it may contribute to the user's confidence in the survey.

Content validity   This is concerned with how well the survey samples behaviour from the complete set of behaviours from which it could, in principle, sample. Clearly the survey must include effective measures of *all* aspects of the corporate behaviour that it claims to cover. Many corporate audits (particularly organizational culture and climate surveys) are lamentably content invalid because although they claim to do so, they rarely measure *all* the aspects of corporate climate and culture.

Criterion-related validity   There are also various forms of criterion validity which refer to how adequately a survey score can be used to infer an individual's score, standing or behaviour on some other measure. Clearly this criterion needs to be reliable, useful and not contaminated in that it is itself based, in part, on the predictor measures.

Concurrent validity   This refers to the extent to which the survey concurs or agrees with other currently used (and themselves hopefully valid) measures of the same thing. If a simple pen-and-paper test yields the same score as a very expensive interview or assessment centre, it is clearly logical to choose the most economic measure.

Predictive validity   Intelligence is a construct that may be invoked to describe why a student performs well in school, while anxiety is a construct that may be invoked to describe why a psychiatric patient paces the floor. Any researchers investigating a test's construct validity must formulate hypotheses about the expected behaviour of high and low scores on the test. Thus, if a test measures intelligence one would expect high scorers to outperform low scorers on numerous behaviours related to intelligence. In a similar vein, if an instrument supposedly measures corporate climate, an index of predictive validity would be how it relates to job absenteeism, employee turnover, and, where appropriate, high revenue generation. Construct validation may be used to show:

- that a test is homogeneous, measuring a single construct;
- that test scores correlate with some tests, but not others in accordance with the theory behind the test (convergent – discriminant validity);
- that test scores obtained by people from various distinct groups vary as predicted by theory;
- that test scores increase or decrease over time as theoretically predicted.

Because of problems associated with surveys, a multi-trait multi-method approach is frequently recommended. In so doing, researchers attempt to use different methods to measure *different* (but often related) facets that need to be measured.

Dimensionality

This refers to the dimensions or factors that a survey measures. Most psychological tests and organometric surveys are multidimensional because they actually measure various different aspects of psychological or corporate functioning. There are, however, some important issues here:

How many dimensions/factors does the survey have?   Does it have too few or too many? For instance if a survey has only one score for job satisfaction, does this refer to pay, promotion, or appraisal satisfaction? On the other hand, the test may claim to measure a high number of related dimensions, and yet it is doubtful if a relatively simple pen-and-paper test would yield so many scores accurately. Clearly it should measure all the relevant dimensions, but not split hairs.

How are these dimensions related? Are the different dimensions or factors that emerge from a test related to each other (like height and weight), or are they independent of each other (like intelligence and eye colour)? If they are related, how closely are they related, and can we infer the score on one dimension by knowing the score on another? It is usually much easier to understand and use unrelated (orthogonal) rather than related (oblique) factors. Many very long, supposedly multidimensional tests can easily be boiled down to fewer dimensions, unrelated to each other.

Are these dimensions of equal importance? It is often claimed that the many different attributes of organizational functioning can be described in terms of a few basic dimensions, which can be further subdivided into more minor related factors. Higher-order factors are thought to be more basic than lower-order factors. The question remains: does the test measure higher-order, lower-order or mixed factors?

Discriminability

This refers to whether the survey can or has been shown to discriminate between known groups. For instance, if someone claims to have invented a test which can predict good salesmen, is there evidence that the test can discriminate between good, average and poor salesmen on the basis of their annual sales? Equally, can a corporate audit distinguish between departments that have high or low absenteeism, or those with many or few 'high-flyers'?

All audits aim to discriminate the more versus the less happy, contented, effective or performing. Do audits also discriminate on other grounds – for instance, what if the survey in discriminating good salesmen discriminates against left-handers, smokers, females, northerners, and so on? Some surveys may be biased in favour of certain groups, and this fact should be taken into account, particularly if it is designed for use by the whole organization.

The fact that some surveys discriminate between individuals and groups may in itself be very useful in finding good items for a survey. Imagine an organization wants to know what a good salesman is. What it needs to do is to get a large group of salesmen, some of whom are known to be good, moderate and bad, and then find which attitudes, beliefs and behaviour discriminate them. Thus, if good salesmen tend to drink less, marry earlier, be more extrovert, have fewer children, show few signs of neurosis, all these facts can then be used to devise a very useful and valid questionnaire. Just as individual-level tests can be used to discriminate between good and poor performing employees (this ability to make a discrimination is itself a sign of a good test), so likewise a corporate audit can be used to discriminate between good and poor organizations on specific criteria, or between departmental sections in an organization.

Fakeability

People don't always tell the truth in surveys. Some may lie to present themselves in a good light, hoping to appear healthily adjusted, intelligent, or motivated people. Occasionally they present themselves in a negative light to avoid new circumstances for themselves, or in the hope of obtaining improved conditions or terms of employment. Some employees believe that if they incorrectly report extensive job dissatisfaction, this will motivate their employers to increase pay or provide some other equivalent benefit.

What can be done about faking behaviour? Essentially four things:

- **Use a lie scale** Many, but not all questionnaires, have a lie scale in them. Lie scales usually contain items of very high social desirability: 'Have you ever broken or lost something belonging to someone else?'; 'Do you always wash your hands before a meal?'; 'Have you ever cheated at a game?' The total lie scale can be calculated and if the person has a score well above a certain level, it may be assumed that they may also be giving a false impression on many other items.
- **Correlating items with measures of social desirability** Another way to detect lying is to look at the social desirability of every item. This can be done by asking people to rate each item or by correlating their full test results with the test of the general tendency to show social desirability. This, at least, pinpoints the areas of social desirability where people are most likely to lie.
- **Having a faker's profile or template** Another useful way to catch fakers is to obtain the typical profile of someone faking good or bad. You do this by actually inviting different groups of people to fake good or fake what they think is the most desirable answer (specifically not give an honest answer). From these people you can derive a fake-good template or profile which you can use to detect fakers.
- **Use warnings** It has been found that people will be more honest if simply told to be so. Stress the importance of honesty, the first answer to come into the head, and the necessity of not lying.

Three additional points need to be made. First, many survey respondents believe that response honesty is tested by checking internal reliability – that is whether respondents tend to give the same answer to the same sort of question. In fact this is not standard practice, but it does no harm for respondents to believe that this is what happens. Secondly, respondents may lie less when computer scoring is involved, because they feel their actual responses are not handled by people or seen by others. Thirdly, when respondents lie they tend to move one or two points away from their true scale position (like a 45-year-old claiming to be 42, or a 58-year-old claiming to be 53), so this has the effect of compressing the range of the scale, rather than actually getting completely different answers. People disagree about what is the best answer, and thus they do not all fake in the same way.

Norms

This refers to the average or mean responses for different categories of respondents such as corporate groups (e.g., departments), organizations, sectors of industry, or the entire working population. It is customary to standardize surveys on large representative population groups. The survey may also be given to specific groups, depending on what the test is measuring: e.g., mental patients for tests of neuroticism, managerial groups for tests of occupational interests and ability. Survey samples among different groups should be sufficiently large to be representative of the category of people they are designed to represent. From these norms it may be possible to examine:

- National differences – typical differences between people from different countries.
- Gender differences – the extent to which males and females typically have different scores on various scales.
- Age differences – whether people in different age bands (20–29, 30–39) tend to have different scores.
- Class differences – typical differences or indeed similarities between people of the same or different social class, however, mentioned.
- Departmental differences – typically different organizational departments such as marketing, human resources, or accounts, have very different perspectives on the organization. Thus, each may have quite different norms.

Good norms are crucial, because they tend to be the yardstick against which results can be interpreted. For instance, you need to know what a score of, say, 13 on a dimension means. The norms will tell you whether it is high or low, for men or women, older or younger people, for successful or unsuccessful organizations, for public or private corporations, and so on. Clearly if a test only has female norms, or norms based on students, it may be much less useful for use on typical male employees. Corporate audit development should invest in good comprehensive normative studies, since failure to do so may severely limit the usefulness of a test. Norms provide the all-important sector benchmarks against which to judge one's own results.

Much more could, and has been, written about psychometrics. It is now a sophisticated social and statistical science, but many people neither trained nor competent in the area practice it for commercial gain.

Many psychological tests have been devised, and a growing number are concerned with the world and experience of work. Indeed Cook *et al.* (1981) subtitled their book on occupational questionnaires 'A compendium and review of 259 measures and their uses'. They classified these occupational psychology measures under eight headings which gives an indication of the scope of these measures: overall job satisfaction (17 measures), specific satisfaction (29 measures); alienation and commitment (16 measures); occupational mental health and ill-health (34 measures); job involvement and job motivation (12 measures); work values, beliefs and needs (29 measures); perception of the job, work role, job context and organizational climate (80 measures) and leadership style and perception of others (32 measures).

Ultimately, nearly all psychometrics is about the assessment of individual differences. Though scores on individuals are frequently summated for research purposes, the scores derive from individuals' perceptions of some range of phenomena.

If psychometrics is the science of psychological testing and assessment, it may be time that management scientists and those involved in organizational behaviour set about developing the sister science of organometrics. This would be the science of organizational assessment in that it would aim to provide reliable and valid measures of whole organizations. Organometrics might involve the cumulative or additive scores of individuals, but it may also involve assessing the *Gestalt* of the organization itself. In all aspects of organizational functions, there is a growing trend towards accountability and evaluation, but many organizations have not felt equipped to audit and evaluate their various aspects, because they lack both the tools and the skills. Organometrics has much to learn from psychometrics. The statistical base and measurement criteria will probably be much the same, but the focus will be different from a number of points of view. Unlike many psychometric tests, the aim of all organometric tests is to collate the opinions of different individuals. Furthermore, they nearly always concentrate on explicit behaviours or perceptions in the workplace, as opposed to the individual's private life.

SAMPLING

Who should receive and complete the corporate audit? In small groups and organizations the answer is simply everyone. This, of course, may prove to be impracticable in large organizations. In the latter context, organizations have to ask who should be chosen to participate, and why? This question gives rise to sampling issues. The terminology here is important.

A *census* is obtained by collecting information about each member of a group. All the members of a group are called a *population*. A *sample* is obtained by collecting information about only some members of the population. Samples can reflect the populations from which they are drawn with varying degrees of accuracy. A sample which accurately reflects its population is called a *representative* sample.

To ensure that a sample is representative of the population it is crucial that certain types of people in the population are not unsystematically excluded from the sample. There are two broad types of samples: *probability* and *non-probability* samples. A probability sample is one in which each person in the population has an equal chance (or probability) of being selected, while in a non-probability sample some people have a greater chance than others of selection. The surest way of providing equal probability of selection is to use the principle of random selection. This involves listing all members of the population (this list is called a *sampling frame*) and then, in effect, 'pull their names out of a hat'.

It is unlikely, however, that any sample will be perfectly representative. By chance alone there will be differences between the sample and the population. These differences are due partly to sampling error. The important thing is that the characteristics of most randomly selected samples will be close to those of the population. Since most random samples produce estimates close to the true population figure, we can use probability theory to help estimate how close the true population figure is likely to be to the figure obtained in the sample (called a sample estimate). A statistic called the *standard error* is used for this purpose.

Probability samples are preferable because they are the more likely to produce representative samples and enable estimates of the sample's accuracy. There are four main types of probability samples. The choice between these depends on the nature of the research problem, the availability of good sampling frames, money, the desired level of accuracy in the sample, and the method by which the data are to be collected.

Simple random sampling (SRS)

One of the problems of SRS is that it requires a good population-sampling frame. While these may be available for some organizations such as schools, churches and unions, adequate lists of population membership are often not available for larger population surveys of multinationals. In addition, where a population comes from a large area, as in national surveys, and where data are to be collected by personal interviews, the cost of SRS is prohibitive. It would probably involve interviewers travelling long distances just for one interview. To survey a large area it is best to use either another sampling strategy, or another method of collecting the data such as mail questionnaires or telephone surveys. In other words, SRS is most appropriate when a good sampling frame exists and when the population is geographically concentrated, or the data-collection technique does not involve travelling.

Systematic sampling

Systematic sampling is similar to SRS and has the same limitations, except that it is simpler. To obtain a systematic sample, work out a sampling fraction by dividing the population size by the required sample size. For a population of 80 and a sample of 10, the sampling fraction is $1/8$: we will select one person for every eight in the population.

Given a sampling fraction of $\frac{1}{8}$ we simply select every eighth person from the sampling frame. The only problem is working out where to start. Since the sampling fraction is $\frac{1}{8}$ the starting point must be somewhere within the first eight people on the list.

Apart from the problems systematic samples share with SRS, they can encounter an additional one: periodicity of sampling frames. That is, a certain type of person may recur at regular intervals within the sampling frame. If the sampling fraction is such that it matches the interval, the sample will include only certain types of people, and systematically exclude others.

Stratified sampling

Stratified sampling is a modification of SRS and systematic sampling designed to produce more representative – and thus more accurate – samples, but this comes at the cost of more complicated procedure. It has similar limitations to these methods. To be representative the proportions of various groups in a sample should be the same as in the population. Because of chance (sampling error) this will not always occur. For example, we might get too many middle-class people, or too many people from one particular group. Sometimes this may not matter, but if the characteristic on which the sample is unrepresentative is related to the focus of the study then we may get distorted results. For example, in a study on organizational behaviour, a sample in which young people are under-represented would produce misleading overall figures about voting intention, because young people tend to vote differently from older people.

Stratified sampling helps to avoid this problem. To use this method we first need to select the relevant stratifying variable(s). A stratifying variable is the characteristic on which we want to ensure correct representation in the sample. Having selected this variable we will order the sampling frame into groups according to the category (or strata) of the stratifying variable and then use a systematic sampling procedure to select the appropriate proportion of people within each stratum. For example, we may wish to survey the entire organization to determine attitudes towards a national issue. We might stratify by age, rank, and date of joining the organization to ensure proper proportions from each department. To do this we need to know the department of each worker and then order the sampling frame so that workers from the same department are grouped together. Then we can draw a systematic sample.

Some sampling frames will automatically stratify at least roughly. An alphabetically arranged list will guarantee that people whose names begin with X or Z are sampled in their correct proportion. Membership lists in which people are ordered according to length of membership would automatically stratify for this. Staff lists of organizations may be ordered in terms of seniority or employment category. Ordered lists will normally produce better samples than unordered ones. The main difficulty of stratifying samples, apart from those shared with SRS and systematic sampling, is that information on the stratifying variable is often unavailable.

The problem with all the sampling techniques considered so far is that they are of limited use on their own when sampling a geographically dispersed population with whom we want to conduct face-to-face interviews. They are also of no direct help when drawing a sample in which no sampling frame is available. When conducting large area surveys (e.g. national or even just city wide) both these problems exist. Multi-usage cluster sampling is an attempt to overcome these difficulties.

Multi-usage cluster sampling

This technique of obtaining a final sample really involves drawing several different samples (hence its name) and does so in such a way that the cost of final interviewing is minimized.

The basic procedure is first to draw a sample of groups. Initially large areas are selected, and then progressively smaller groups within the larger ones are sampled. Eventually we end up with a sample of small work groups, and use a method of selecting individuals from the selected work group.

The general principle is to maximize the number of initial clusters chosen, and consequently only to select relatively few individuals or units within each cluster. The reason for this is that it is important that different departments or divisions are included. If only one or two sections were selected we could end up with a very unrepresentative sample. By maximizing the chance for variety initially, we increase the chance of maintaining representativeness at later stages. The problem is that as the number of clusters chosen initially increases, so do the research costs later on. In the end a compromise between cost and sampling error has to be made.

One way of minimizing the effect of reducing clusters on representativeness is to use stratification techniques. Thus when selecting sections of the organization, put them into various strata (e.g. location, size, age groups, composition, etc.) and then randomly select from groups within the strata.

There are difficulties in applying these techniques to determine sample size. Apart from requiring that we can specify the degree of precision needed, we must also have a rough idea of how people are going to answer the question (how they will split in terms of answering yes or no). The problems with this are twofold – we often do not have this information, and surveys often have more than one purpose. On one key variable of interest there may be an anticipated split of 80/20, but on another it may be closer to 50/50. For such multi-purpose surveys it seems best to play safe and determine size on the basis of the variables on which there is likely to be greatest diversity within the sample.

Non-response

For a variety of reasons, people selected in a sample may not finally be included. Some will refuse, others will be difficult to contact, and others will prove to be problematic interviewees. Non-response can create two main problems: unacceptable reduction of sample size, and bias in representativeness. How can these problems be dealt with? First, employ techniques designed to reduce non-response. These include paying attention to methods of collecting data, careful training of interviewers, use of interpreters, and calling back to trace respondents at several different times of the day and week. Second, we can draw an initial sample that is larger than needed. Even assuming good technique, we may still experience about a 20 per cent non-response rate, so we might draw an initial sample that is 20 per cent larger than we expect to end up with.

This, however, does nothing to avoid the problem of bias. Problems can arise if non-responders are different in crucial respects to responders. Even increasing the sample size will do little to produce the correct proportions of various groups if some types systematically fail to respond. The difficulty is not so much the bias itself, since once discovered there are statistical techniques for minimizing its influence on the analysis (see page 196), but in working out what the bias is to begin with and to what extent it occurs. Once this is known, suitable allowances can be made. There are three main ways of obtaining information to enable adjustments for bias.

• Use what observable information can be picked up about non-responders. Where contact is made but people refuse to participate, any biographical information which is already known about them or can be gleaned, may help to identify who they are.
• Some sampling frames can provide useful information. For example, if official records provided the sampling frame for members of an organization, we could identify characteristics of non-responders by using information in the records such as sex and age, and depending on the organization we might learn about income, education and so forth.
• If characteristics of the population from which the sample is drawn are known, we can simply compare the characteristics obtained in the sample with those of the population. Any differences indicate the areas of bias, and the extent of the differences indicates the degree of bias. With this information adjustments can be made during analysis to neutralize the effect of non-response bias.

Non-probability sampling

There are often situations where probability sampling techniques are either impractical or unnecessary. In such situations the much cheaper non-probability techniques are used. These techniques are appropriate when sampling frames are unavailable or the population is so widely dispersed that cluster sampling would be too inefficient. For example, it would be very difficult to obtain a random sample of homosexuals, tax-evaders, or cannabis users. Any attempt to do so would either be so expensive that we would end up with a sample too small for meaningful analysis, or the rate of dishonesty and refusal would produce such a bias that the sample would not be representative, despite probability sampling methods.

In the preliminary stages of research, such as testing questionnaires, non-random samples are satisfactory. On occasions researchers are not concerned with generalizing from a sample to the population, and in such cases representativeness of the sample is less important. Instead they may be interested in developing scales (see Chapter 7) or in a tentative, hypothesis-generating, exploratory look at patterns. Some research is not all that interested in working out what proportion of the population gives a particular response, but rather in obtaining an idea of the range of responses or ideas that people have. In such cases we would simply try to get a wide variety of people in the sample, without being too concerned about whether each type was represented in its correct proportion.

Purposive sampling   This is a form of non-probability sampling where cases are judged as typical of some category of cases of interest to the researcher. They are not selected randomly. Thus a study of union attitudes in a work-force might, in the absence of a clearly defined sampling frame or population, select some typical members from a number of typical work groups. While not ensuring representativeness, such a method of selection can provide useful information.

Political polling often uses purposive sampling. Here districts within an electorate are chosen because their pattern has in the past provided a good idea of the outcome for the whole electorate. Or key electorates which generally reflect the national pattern (i.e. they are typical) are paid attention. While not using probability sampling techniques, such a method can provide cheap and surprisingly efficient predictions. Thus organizations can get to know which groups' attitudes best reflect those of the organization as a whole.

Quota sampling   This is another common non-probability technique aimed at producing representative samples without random selection of cases. Interviewers are required to find cases with particular characteristics: they are given quotas of particular types of people to find. The quotas are organized so that in terms of the quota characteristics the final sample will be representative. To develop quotas one must decide which characteristics to use to ensure that the final sample is representative. By then finding out the distribution of this variable in the population, appropriate quotas can be set accordingly. Thus if 20 per cent of the population is aged between twenty and thirty, and the sample is to comprise 1,000 individuals, then 200 of the sample (20 per cent) should be in this age group. If twenty people were doing the interviewing and each had identical quotas of fifty, each interviewer would find ten people in this age group (20 per cent of fifty). Quite complex quotas can be developed so that several characteristics (e.g. sex, age, marital status) are employed simultaneously. Thus, an interviewer would be assigned a quota for unmarried females between twenty and thirty years, married females between twenty and thirty years, and for each other combination of the three quota variables (Moser and Kalton, 1971, p. 129).

Quota techniques are non-random because interviewers can select any cases which fit certain criteria. This can lead to bias, as interviewers will tend to select those who are easiest to interview and with whom they feel most comfortable (e.g. friends). Another difficulty is that accurate population proportions may be unavailable. Finally, since random sampling is not used, it is impossible to estimate the accuracy of any particular quota sample.

Availability samples   These are also common, but must be used with caution and only for specific purposes. They are the least likely of any technique to produce representative samples. Using this approach, anyone who will respond will do. Surveys where newspapers ask readers to complete and return questionnaires printed in the paper, or where TV stations conduct 'phone-in' polls, are examples of such samples. While these techniques can produce quite large samples cheaply, their size does not compensate for their unrepresentativeness. This type of sample can be useful for pilot testing questionnaires or exploratory research to obtain the range of views and develop typologies, but must not be used to make any claim to representing anything but the sample itself. Sampling is clearly an important issue. The bigger, more complex and more geographically distributed the organization, the more carefully the sampling frame for the audit needs to be designed.

THE SCIENCE OF PERCEPTION

Nearly all audits – whether they are of culture, climate, communications or customer care – are dependent on employees' self-reports on how they perceive the organization they work for. This means that the data are subjective and for some managers seem therefore less reliable than hard, objective data such as sales figures, production levels, absenteeism reports and so on. Yet there is a growing body of research which shows that the impact of organizational structural and technological features on individual workers is mediated by their individual perceptions. Indeed, it could be argued that this subjective 'perceived' reality is more important than any objective measures available.

As Rousseau (1988) has pointed out, these perceptions tend to be treated in one of three ways:

1   As intervening variables between the actual organization (e.g., its climate, culture, etc.) and the individual response of its employers.
2   As a surrogate or substitute for an objective indicator of the organization's health, as none exists.
3   As a genuine useful, predictive measure of how employees actually experience the work-place.

Rentsch (1990) has noted that consensually-shared perceptions (i.e., those found in audit responses) represent the way in which an organization's employees make sense of organizational policies, practices and procedures.

The question is often raised as to whether 'climate or culture analysis' is merely a different name for 'attitude survey'. The two share a common mode of data collection – people are asked to report their reactions to their organization's working conditions, management systems, etc., in answer to a series of questions – but from that point on, some very significant differences distinguish them.

First, the sample for an attitude survey normally starts at the bottom of the organization and works up, usually one or two levels, sometimes a little higher. But a corporate assessment programme, embodying a climate or culture audit starts at the top of the organization, usually with the chairman, chief executive, managing director or other leader, and works its way down through other organization levels.

Because each type of audit addresses itself to different organizational characteristics, the nature of the questions asked tends to be different in each case. Furthermore, the language used in corporate assessment programmes and modes of questioning often needs to vary across the different levels of the organization. For example, a climate survey may ask about the clarity of corporate goals, a topic largely inappropriate for the production floor level. Therefore, because the two groups typically surveyed are dissimilar, the issues being investigated are distinct.

Second, attitude surveys grew out of a reaction to 'scientific management', which viewed human beings as little more than units of production, and out of fascination with the findings of the original Hawthorne studies and some of the early laboratory studies on leadership. These early studies were concerned quite specifically with the effect of physical conditions and the work group on productivity. The thrust of this movement was to encourage worker satisfaction, which in turn would lead to greater production. Thus, many attitude surveys deal with employee satisfaction and focus upon supervision–subordinate and work-group interaction, which are most influential on satisfaction. Although the implications of the studies are far-reaching, the value of the Hawthorne studies for managers lies in its discoveries concerning individuals, groups, individuals-in-groups, and organizational design.

Individual differences   The Hawthorne Studies emphasized the time-honoured maxim that individuals are all different and that these differences can have a significant impact on managerial behaviour. The interview programme demonstrated the complexity of attitudes, and how overt behaviour may differ from attitudes. This is why a manager may be frustrated by the fact that new wage incentive or vacation policy may be perfectly acceptable to one person, and totally rejected by another.

Groups After the findings of the Hawthorne Researchers were publicized, the importance of group processes was realized. For one thing, during various stages of the experiments it became evident that informal groups, not prescribed by the organization, can, and do, exert great influence on individuals. Group pressures can cause individuals to work more or less, to accept or resist change, and to behave in a variety of ways that may differ from their own personal preferences. The implication becomes quite clear that groups will influence behaviour. Therefore, managers would do well to concentrate on developing group norms that reinforce organizational goals, thus using the group in a positive motivational sense.

Individuals-in-groups Formal groups are those required and established by the organization such as production and sales units. Employees also belong to informal or social groups that are not prescribed by the structure. A group of 'old-timers' who have worked together for a long time may form a social group who eat or spend their free time together. The same is true of 'newcomers' or recent employees. Such groups may be quite important in the formation of individual attitudes and in influencing work behaviour.

Organization design The implications of the studies for the formal design of organizations are perhaps a little more subtle. Probably the most significant finding has to do with the organization as a social system. Although the structure of an organization appears very fixed and formal, in reality there is an 'organization' that does not show up on the chart. This social organization includes all the social groupings and power alliances that exist in all structures. Even though such things are not required for accomplishing goals, they are fundamental in understanding the personality of the organization and the individuals who comprise it.

The audits suggested in this book have not evolved from the human relations or employee survey school, but from a concept of enterprise management and a focus upon organizational performance. They are based on the idea that employee attitudes and perceptions can be scientifically and accurately audited. For an organization to be justified it must have a mission, and to accomplish that mission, it must have a strategy, whether articulated or not, and people organized in some kind of structural relationship. These elements are related by a series of processes such as planning, decision-making, performance measurement, and so on. The experience of these elements – strategy, structure, process and people – causes people to hold certain views about the organization – its climate – and to share certain values which comprise its culture.

From this point of view, climate analysis is far from the measurement of employee satisfaction. It is truly the measurement of the state of managerial health of the organization from the perspective of those who should know best – the employees themselves.

OVERLAP BETWEEN CONCEPTS

An obvious problem associated with the four management audits considered in this book is the overlap between them. This is particularly true of the distinction between corporate culture and climate. Prevailing systems and modes of communication within organizations and the implementation of customer service programmes represents manifestations of existing or changing organizational culture and climate. Hence there have been various attempts to distinguish the two.

Rentsch (1990) argued that the issue was qualitative:

The qualitative approaches traditionally used to study meaning in culture research may provide a richer, more comprehensive view of meanings in organizations than does the questionnaire approach preferred by climate researchers. Moreover, culture researchers may actually be measuring a different kind of meaning than climate researchers. Climate questionnaires directly assess descriptions, indirectly assess patterns of relationships among these descriptions, and do not assess organizational members' interpretations of events. Culture research focuses on assessing the sense-making meaning of events. The data used in culture research may better represent meaning as it is discussed in climate theory, but the qualitative methods of culture researchers lack the objectivity and comparability of the quantitative methods of climate researchers.

(p. 666)

French, Kent and Rosenzweig (1985) defined the relationship between organizational culture and organization climate by making a distinction between the actual situation (i.e. culture) and the perception of it (climate). The cultural variables are 'the prevailing patterns of values, myths, beliefs, assumptions and norms', and may be taken to be relatively stable and long in the making. The climate variables are the 'relatively persistent set of perceptions held by members concerning the characteristics and quality of organizational culture'. These writers defined the organizational climate as a 'set of measurable properties of a given environment, based on the collective perceptions of the people who live and work in that environment, and demonstrated to influence their motivation and behaviour'. The way in which motivation is affected is that the rewarding of people's needs is conducted through the filter of their perceptions.

Ashforth (1985) argued for a distinction between culture and climate based on the fundamental role of social unit norms in culture and individual descriptive beliefs in climate. The disciplinary bases for climate and culture differ. Climate developed primarily from the Lewinian social psychology of person/situation interaction, while culture emerged from symbolic interactionism. Interactionism requires a social unit and shared experience and thus an individual alone cannot possess a culture, though his or her work group or organization can. A key element of culture is consensus or shared values and beliefs, and not all social units have a culture. Organizations that are new, in transition, or that have conflicting structures and role conflicts, might lack common beliefs, values and behavioural norms among members. Moreover, the intensity or strength of a culture is reflected in group member consensus; some organizations have strong cultures, which shape behaviour, and others have weak cultures which have less impact on members' actions. Although many individuals might not consciously experience a culture in their organization, most individuals will experience its climate, that is a managerial or environ-mental context which they can describe. Normative beliefs are by-products of group memberships; climate, however, can often be highly idiosyncratic, with many different climates residing within a single organization.

Normative beliefs specify what individuals think are appropriate behaviours for themselves and others in a particular social context. They are created through a history of social interactions and group dynamics which informs individuals regarding what it takes to be accepted as a group member. Normative beliefs are individual interpretations of the behav-ioural norms that characterize interacting social groups. These norms can develop and change over time, and can be difficult to control. They are also shared by members of a social unit and are thus a major feature in the construct of culture.

Rousseau (1988) has argued that culture in an organizational context has two features pertinent to its assessment: direction and intensity. Direction refers to the actual content or substance of the culture, exemplified by (though not limited to) the values, behavioural norms, and thinking styles it emphasizes, while values attached to achievement, failure and risk can reflect the direction of behavioural norms. Cultures that vary in direction support different behavioural norms, and have different degrees of influence on organizational members. Intensity is a function of consensus regarding appropriate and inappropriate behaviour, as well as the consistency between behavioural norms and formal structures such as reward systems and hierarchies.

Rousseau (1989) notes that there are striking similarities between climate and culture in the organizational literature:

- Consistency or consensus is required to characterize a unit having a climate or a culture.
- Belief of individual cognitions and interpretations are primary elements in each.
- Each is historical, enduring, and resistant to change.
- Each has a tendency towards differentiation with members in different units of a larger organization demonstrating distinctive sets of beliefs.

Also she provides a useful table of cultural definitions all predicting the rise of interest in the topic (Table 2.1).

Table 2.1 Differing organizational cultural definitions

Kroeber and Kluckholm (1952)	Transmitted patterns of values, ideas and other symbolic systems that shape behaviour.
Becker and Geer (1970)	Set of common understandings expressed in language.
Van Maanen and Schein (1979)	Values, beliefs and expectations that members come to share.
Ouchi (1981)	Set of symbols, ceremonies and myths that communicate underlying values and beliefs of the organization to its employees.
Louis (1983)	Three aspects: some (1) content (meaning and interpretation) (2) peculiar to (3) a group.
Siehl and Martin (1983)	Glue that holds together an organization through shared patterns of meaning. Three component systems: context or core values, forms (process of communication, e.g. jargon), strategies to reinforce content (e.g. rewards, training programmes).
Uttal (1983)	Shared vales (what is important) and beliefs (how things work) that interact with an organization's structures and control systems to produce behavioural norms (the way we do things around here).

Source: Rousseau (1989). Reproduced by permission of the publisher.

Whereas culture has emerged as the explanation of choice for many researchers because of the potential for rich detail it offers, climate has been a vehicle of summary description. Use of qualitative methods to study culture yields details which often are not explicitly linked to a particular level or frame of reference, and are unlikely to be tested for consistency across units. In contrast, consensus is a key issue in climate research.

The blurring of climate and culture has been an issue especially significant to researchers concerned with climate. Based upon the notion of symbolic interactionism, Ashforth (1985) distinguishes between shared assumptions (culture) and shared perceptions (climate) and argues that culture 'informs' climate (p. 842) by helping individuals to define what is important and to make sense of their experiences. Whether a member describes a boss who fails to communicate clearly as cold and unfeeling (a personality-based attribution) or as doing his or her job (in an organization which rewards people for operating on a 'need to know' basis) can be largely a function of the world-view one comes to hold from talking with other employees and accepting the norms. Thus, we might expect organizations with strong cultures to have member consensus in description of it. Increasing concern over the origins of both climate and culture and ways in which one reinforces the other is evident in the current organizational literature. To date, there is little empirical research examining the two together. Striking differences between climate and culture also appear:

- Climate is descriptive, culture is largely normative.
- Climate is a summary description and culture research operationalizes the construct in as rich detail.
- Climate exists in all organizations (at least at the individual level); but many organizations have no culture (strong norms may be absent).
- All individuals in an organizational setting experience a climate. Not all individuals are part of a culture.
- Climate is attached to individual perceptions. To understand its effects, levels of analysis shift upward to collectivities. Culture is a group or social-unit phenomenon. To understand its processes, level of analysis shifts downward to individuals.

(Rousseau, 1988, pp. 151–2)

From these contrasts and comparisons, two conclusions can be drawn:

1 There are sufficient similarities between the concepts of climate and culture for research on one to inform us about the other.
2 The differences between the two are sufficient to maintain their distinctiveness in conceptualization and operationalization.

(Rousseau, 1988, pp. 151–2)

More recently Dastmalchian *et al.* (1991) have attempted another distinction between culture and climate:

The relations between climate and culture are likely to be asymmetrical. The influence of climate on culture is easier to conceive of (that is, the individual perception-based concept influencing the group-based one), than vice versa. To illustrate this point (and more generally the difference between the two concepts), we can make use of the meteorological metaphor of climate discussed earlier, and of an anthropological metaphor of culture. In any geographical region, climate and culture could coexist. Climate, viewed in this way, is likely to have a profound and continuing effect on culture; for example different climates would contribute to the development of different habits, customs, and beliefs – and, more importantly, to the means by which those assumptions are expressed and transmitted. The impact of culture on a region's climate, however, has traditionally been more problematic to identify (though of course current events in different cultures are altering this, such as through massive deforestation and the destruction of the ozone layer, which are both impacting on climate)....

We admit that depending on the position that one takes, and the paradigm and metaphors that one subscribes to, additional explanations as to the relationships between organizational cultures and climate can be developed. For example, Payne referring to Tagiuri and Litwin's (1968) work, stressed that:

> far from obvious is the differentiation [of climate] from other common terms referring to what surrounds the individual such as *environment, ecology, milieu, culture, atmosphere, situation, setting, behaviour setting, conditions....* What the term provides ... is a synthetic, molar concept of the environment: a kind of middle-range concept instead of a middle-range theory.
>
> (Payne, 1971, pp. 143–4)

Payne and Pugh, using a geographical analogy to explain the basis of the relationships between organizational context/structure and climate, pointed out that:

> the organizational context and structure variables are the hills and rivers or physical features of the geographical area. Climate dimensions such as progressiveness and development, risk taking, warmth, support, and control correspond to temperature, rainfall, and wind velocity which have been generated by the interactions of physical features with the sun's energy. Social systems' equivalent energy sources are people who also create and are part of the climate. Although both physical and social climates may affect their respective structures, the context and structure of a social system are more stable than its people, whose energies may not always be spent in predictable cycles.
>
> (Payne and Pugh, 1976, p. 1,127)

In other words, if one agrees with the above view, one is likely to conclude that organizational culture (assuming it is defined as a part of the organizational context) does affect climate.

Further, if one accepts the concept of organizational culture as a 'root metaphor' for understanding and analyzing organizations (Smircich, 1983), in that a 'cultural model' of organization replaces open-system models (Pondy and Mitroff, 1979), one is bound to see the internal features of the organization (including climate) as being embedded within the whole cultural milieu. The research questions will then become those relating to a discovery and an understanding of how the organizational life is possible, rather than prediction, generalizability, and causality.

(pp. 49–50)

It is clear from the various attempts to distinguish culture and climate that these are overlapping concepts. The former is currently a more fashionable concept than the latter, and hence, may account for its popularity.

CONCLUSION

This chapter has been concerned with measurement issues, specifically the relatively new science of organizational perceptions or organometrics. It was argued that organometrics (the assessment of organizations) is relatively similar to psychometrics (the assessment of individuals), and that the former could learn a great deal from the latter. Devising valid and reliable measures of an organization's culture, climate, communications, and customers is an important task and needs to be done by those with organometric training.

3 Corporate culture

INTRODUCTION

A number of research preoccupations and themes of organizational thought have come together to influence the development of the concept of corporate culture. For over a decade this original anthropological concept has been considered, debated and discussed by researchers, business gurus, newspaper and magazine writers, and line managers. Quite how or why this concept became so popular at this present time, and the need to measure corporate culture, have many different explanations.

Attempts to explain the marked success of Pacific-rim countries and Japan in matching and exceeding American and European levels of productivity, quality, innovation and service have tended to point up the importance of values shared by Japanese management and workers as an important determinant of their success. These values, it has been argued, result in behavioural norms that demonstrate a commitment to quality, problem-solving and co-operative effort in greater degree than is generally the case in comparable organizations outside Japan.

In more recent years, researchers in western countries who have investigated and set out to list the definable characteristics of economically successful companies both within Europe and North American countries have pointed to certain aspects of culture, such as the strength and pervasiveness of core values as an element and, it is claimed, a significant element in their success. Thus, it is assumed that the values and behavioural norms which are part of a company and which both define and drive it are a significant part of its economic success.

Partly stimulated by this work and by increasing international competition to capture new markets and maintain old ones, the emphasis on quality (which can be defined as working to a standard above the norm) and customer service has highlighted the importance of people aspects in organizations. We will return in more detail to the subject of customers in Chapter 6, when we discuss customer audits. Responsiveness to needs of customers, however, requires a commitment that goes beyond the routine set rules and procedures, and a minimum, if predictable, level of performance. This commitment requires the internalization and inculcation of appropriate values, not just compliance with external dictates on which more coercive methods of control and motivation depend.

For nearly a decade now, in management circles, corporate culture has been in vogue. Numerous books, articles and papers have appeared on this topic, and it is now widely adopted in both professional and academic circles. It has been used to predict and explain a great variety of behaviours in organizations, both successful and unsuccessful, and many large and small organizations have attempted what they call 'culture change programmes'. Previous fashions over the last fifty years in management science include: 1950s – scientific management; 1960s – organizational structure; 1970s – corporate strategy; 1980s – corporate culture. Precisely how long this concept will remain so popular is unclear, as is the concept which will replace it. At present it remains actively discussed and analysed in industrial/organizational (I/O) academic circles and equally debated in board meetings. It has taken a long time for some managers and management scientists to realize that 'soft' human resource issues may play such an important part in any organization's success (or failure).

It should not be thought, however, that the application of this anthropological concept to management is particularly new, as references to it date back at least thirty years. Industrial/organizational psychologists have tended to use related terms like climate, values, norms and beliefs, rather than culture. However, factors such as the influence of sociology and anthropology on management science and the comparative rise of far eastern organizations (especially the Japanese) combined with the comparative decline of American economic and organization success has meant concepts like culture have been seen to be a part-explanation for success, and hence, explain why 'culture' is such a popular topic now. Smircich and Calas (1987) provide three explanations for the popularity of the concept. First, shifts in the perspective of business managers realizing that national and corporate culture may be more important than strategy in determining organizational efficiency. Second, shifts in organizational and communication theory to a 'softer', more radical approach that conceptualizes organizations as socially constructed, investigates the symbolic nature of management and looks at the unique use of language within organization. Third, shifts in the human sciences from positivistic explanation to constructivist understanding, which emphasizes the importance of subjective perception of employees.

According to Graves (1986) many highly questionable myths surround the concepts of corporate culture: 'The culture of a large organization is always different from that in a small one' (false); 'The culture in a participative organization is different from one in a non-participative organization' (true); 'The culture is a well-articulated organization is always different from that in a badly articulated one' (false). Precisely upon what data Graves drew up this list is unclear, but it is the case that the concept is surrounded by myth.

Graves (1972) attempted to specify the origin of culture, which may give one an insight into definition:

1. The culture is a product of the context – the market in which the organization operates, the legal constraints, and so on.
2. The culture is a product of the structures and functions to be found within the organization. A centralized organization will have a different culture from a decentralized one.
3. The culture is a product of people's attitudes to their work; it is the product of the individual psychological contracts with the organization.

Each of these separate approaches has at some time been combined with each of the others. Each approach, however, suffers from the disadvantage that it treats culture as objective, as if everyone in the world would be able to observe the same phenomenon, whereas this is patently not the case. 'Outsiders' do not have the same sense of culture as 'insiders'. It therefore becomes necessary to look for another explanation.

(p. 172)

THE PROBLEM OF DEFINITION

Culture is a core concept in many of the social sciences. One of the most complete definitions of culture which has been developed in recent years was formulated by Kroeber and Kluckhohn (1952) after an exhaustive historical examination of relevant literature:

Culture consists of patterns, explicit and implicit, of and for behaviour acquired and transmitted by *symbols*, constituting the distinctive achievement of human groups, including their embodiment in *artifacts*; the essential core of culture consists of traditional (i.e.: historically derived and selected) ideas and especially their attached *values*; culture systems may, on the one hand, be considered as products of action, on the other as conditioning elements of further action.

(p. 181)

This definition is well rehearsed, but Eldridge and others have attempted to produce a clearer, more comprehensive definition. Thus Crombie (1974) noted:

Culture ... is a characteristic of all organizations through which, at the same time, their individuality and uniqueness is expressed. The culture of an organization refers to the unique configuration of norms, values, beliefs, ways of behaving and so on that characterize the manner in which groups and individuals combine to get things done. The distinctiveness of a particular organization is intimately bound up with its history and the character-building effects of past decisions and past leaders. It is manifested in the folkways, mores, and the ideology to which members defer, as well as in the strategic choices made by the organization as a whole. The individuality or cultural distinctiveness of an organization is attained through the more or less constant exercise of choice, in all sections and levels.... The character of organizational choice is one of the major manifestations of organizational culture.

(pp. 89–90)

Eldridge and Crombie (1974) drew attention to three dimensions of culture, following the work of Angyal: depth, or vertical dimension; breadth, or lateral co-ordination of the contributing parts; and the progression dimension, which refers to co-ordination through time. They elaborated as follows:

The depth dimension is exemplified in the formulation and adoption of policies, programmes, procedures and practices that represent the basic values and strategic commitments of the organization as a whole – the inducement of behaviour at the 'surface', in the day-to-day organization functioning.

(p. 96)

The construct of culture has caused much confusion. While there are multiple definitions, they tend to be vague and overly general. This confusion is exacerbated by the various disciplines interested in this topic (anthropology, sociology, psychology) which while increasing richness, do not necessarily increase clarity. Hence, occupational psychologists and organizational behaviour specialists could be accused of 'muddying the waters', rather than disambiguating the concept.

Whilst it may be seen as a somewhat pointless etymological exercise, it is worthwhile considering how various researchers and reviewers have understood specifically the concept of organizational or corporate culture. There have been a number of ways at arriving at a useful, clear, working definition. Some have attempted to specify the *dimensions* of culture (Schein, 1990; Hampden-Turner, 1990); others have concentrated on the *functions* of corporate culture (Williams *et al.*, 1989; Graves, 1986); while there has been a serious effort to taxonomize culture (Deal and Kennedy, 1982); and of course there have been a host of attempts to simply define it succinctly (Gonzalez, 1987).

There is no shortage of definitions for corporate culture. Consider:

a historical transmitted pattern of meanings embodied in symbols, a system of inherited conception expressed in and developed by their knowledge about attitudes towards life.... Culture is the fabric of meaning in terms of which human beings interpret their experience and guide their actions.

(Geertz, 1973, p. 78)

Culture is the best way we do things around here.
>   (Bower, 1966, cited in Deal and Kennedy (1982))

Culture is a system of informal rules that spells out how people are to behave most of the time.
>   (Deal and Kennedy, 1982)

Culture can now be defined as (a) a pattern of basic assumptions, (b) invented, discovered, or developed by a given group, (c) as it learns to cope with its problems of external adaptation and internal integration, (d) that has worked well enough to be considered valid and, therefore (e) is to be taught to new members as the (f) correct way to perceive, think and feel in relation to those problems.
>   (Schein, 1990, p. 110)

Cooke and Rousseau (1988) were even more enthusiastic and comprehensive in the search for definitions. Schneider (1987) considered the problems of multinational companies that are frequently interested in promoting a strong and coherent corporate culture (to improve control co-ordination and integration of their subsidiaries) in local national cultures where the underlying basic assumptions are different. According to Schneider, culture involves both underlying assumptions about the world and human nature. These assumptions include views of the relationship with nature and of human relationships. The relationship with nature reflects several dimensions: control over the environment; activity vs. passivity, or doing vs. being; attitudes towards uncertainty; notions of time; attitudes towards change; and what determines 'truth'. Views about the nature of human relationships include: the importance of task vs. relationships; the importance of hierarchy; the importance of individual vs. group. For example, some cultures, often Western, view man as the master of nature, which can be harnessed and exploited to suit man's need; time, change and uncertainty can be actively managed. 'Truth' is determined by facts and measurement. Other cultures, often eastern, view man as subservient to or in harmony with nature. Time, change and uncertainty are accepted as given. 'Truth' is determined by spiritual and philosophical principles. This attitude is often referred to as 'fatalistic' or 'adaptive'.

Assumptions regarding the nature of human relationships are also different. The importance of relationships over task, of the hierarchy, and of the individual versus the group are clearly different not only between the East and West, but also within western cultures. In eastern cultures, for example, importance is placed on relationships over task, on the hierarchy, and on the group or collective. By contrast, in western cultures, the focus is more on task, on the individual, and the hierarchy is considered to be of less importance. However, there is variance between the US and Europe, as well as within Europe (East and West).

Sackmann (1989) has pointed out, quite correctly, that culture is a word with different meanings, analysed for different purposes. She contrasted its use by anthropologists, organizational theorists and actual managers. The latter two were much more similar than the former. Thus, anthropologists see the criteria for membership of a culture as unconditional, and managers see it as conditional on an exchange relationship; anthropologists expect life-long membership, while managers see it as short to intermediate; anthropologists see cultures as essentially stable, and managers see it as essentially unstable.

Sackmann (1990) has expanded on the perspective of organizational culture as a variable. She argues that the use of culture as a variable is based on three major assumptions:

1 Culture is one of several organizational variables.
2 This variable 'culture' consists of a finite and patterned set of components which are visible and manifest in artefacts as well as collective behaviour and, in fact, culture *is* these artefacts.
3 Culture serves several functions which contribute to the success of organizations.

Organizations have or develop in addition to other products, the product 'culture', which is itself composed of sub-products such as artefacts, symbols and collective verbal and non-verbal behaviour. A common definition of culture within this perspective is 'the way we do things around here' (Deal and Kennedy, 1982). Other products include 'myths, sagas, language systems, metaphors, symbols, ceremonies, rituals, value systems and behaviour norms' (Shrivastava, 1985, p. 103). More concrete and recognizable examples of artefacts are the logo of a firm, the architecture of buildings, existing technologies and machinery or tools, the interior design and the use of a work setting, documents and products, the organization chart, the typical and expected clothing of employees, and existing status symbols such as company cars, reserved parking, or furniture. Verbal examples can be seen in language in general, and speeches, jargon, humour, stories, sagas, legends and myths in particular. Non-verbal behaviours include interpersonal behaviours such as the typical way of approaching each other (e.g. shaking hands), gestures, and dress codes, as well as existing forms and functions of rites, rituals and ceremonies such as personal birthday wishes from the boss, congratulations for long tenure, the Friday afternoon 'beer bust', celebrations of company anniversaries or the company Christmas party.

These components form together the product of culture, whose major importance is seen in its attributed functions. It is assumed that culture serves predominantly two functions which contribute to organizational success or prevent it. These functions are internal integration and co-ordination. Culture represents the 'social glue' and generates a 'we-feeling', thus counteracting processes of differentiation which are an unavoidable part of organizational life. Organizational culture offers a shared system of meanings which is the basis for communications and mutual understanding. If these two functions are not fulfilled in a satisfactory way, culture may significantly reduce the efficiency of an organization.

Most emphasis is placed on the integration function of culture, the consistency among its sub-components and the general consensus about acceptance of these sub-components. As a result, cultures can be evaluated and designated 'good' or 'bad'. A 'good' culture is consistent in its components and shared amongst organizational members, and it makes the organization unique, thus differentiating it from other organizations. Such a culture is created primarily by an organization's leader(s) and/or founder(s) who can also influence, imprint or change this culture – that is, they can control it.

Within the perspective, the management of culture is not seen as problematic. Culture is manageable in terms of a culture-controlling management and follows the formulated strategy. One only has to identify the presently existing culture, that is, its components, and then change it (the culture) or them (its components) toward the desired culture, or 'close the culture gap'. But Sackmann (1990) is sceptical about such an approach:

> The problems of the culture-controlling management are rooted in the underlying assumptions of the perspective. First, it is assumed that a management of culture is initiated and exerted by the leaders of an organization to 'glue' the organization together. A cultural value engineering is advocated where the leaders are able to and do prescribe and sanction a specific pattern of homogeneous values. Second, equating culture with one of several organizational variables implies an unproblematic 'making' and control of culture. It remains, however, unclear which ones are the *relevant* dimensions of culture to be managed and controlled. Third, it is questionable if human behaviour can be prescribed and predicted in a planned change effort. And fourth, the assumption of a stable culture is rather problematic.
>
> (p. 11)

Later, even more critically, she concludes:

> The management of culture is the least problematic when conceptualized from the 'culture-as-a-variable' perspective. Culture as one of several organizational variables is manipulated, managed, changed and controlled by top management and/or the leader(s). They use indirect and direct means to manage the existing culture toward the desired culture which is prescribed by the anticipated strategy. Such a culture is homogeneous, integrative, strong, rich or participative – depending on the author – and leads to organizational success. Unfortunately, no empirical evidence supports these statements of dreams. A critical analysis of the underlying assumptions questions the feasibility of such a

culture-controlling management. First, human systems do not follow deterministic laws such as machines. Second, top management and leaders are not omnipotent. Even if they act in the firm belief that they control their employees like puppets, the strings in their hands may not be attached. In other words, values and other mind matters cannot be dictated and the result of intended actions cannot be predetermined. Third, cultural manifestations do not allow direct inferences regarding underlying assumptions and cultural knowledge. And fourth, it remains unclear which ones are *the* relevant dimensions of culture which need to be managed. A cynic may wonder why the concept of culture is needed within the variable perspective. Frequently, it could be substituted by other concepts, such as organizational climate or the 'value analysis' within some conceptions of strategy. The potential power of the concept of culture is not used or realized within this perspective.

(p. 23)

Not all would agree with this analysis, yet it is made so forcefully that it demands a reply from the culture-as-dimension school of thought.

DIMENSIONS, FACTORS, DISTINCTIONS

Another way to understand corporate culture is to make various distinctions, or, spell out the factors or dimensions underlying the culture. For instance, Schein (1990) has listed seven dimensions of organizational cultures after he provided a definition. Schein argues that these seven dimensions provide the basis for an interview that can reveal some of the more hidden, implicit facets of corporate culture (Table 3.1).

This list is potentially useful, not only because it provides possible markers for the measurement of corporate culture, but also because it attempts to anchor dimensions in clearly stated opposites. Hampden-Turner (1990), on the other hand, preferred to list a dozen characteristics of corporate culture:

- Individuals make up the culture.
- Cultures can be rewarders of excellence.
- Culture is a set of affirmations.
- Cultural affirmations tend to fulfil themselves.
- Cultures make sense and have coherent points of view.
- Cultures provide their members with continuity and identity.
- A culture is in a state of balance between reciprocal values.
- A corporate culture is a cybernetic system.
- Cultures are a pattern.
- Cultures are about communications.
- Cultures are more or less synergistic.
- Only cultures can learn.

This list, for that is all it is, is a series of well-known assertions about culture, but does not seem to help either in the description or understanding of corporate culture.

Table 3.1 Dimensions of corporate culture

	Questions to be answered
1. The organization's relation to its environment.	'Does the organization perceive itself to be dominant, submissive, harmonizing, searching out a niche?'
2. The nature of human activity.	'Is the "correct" way for humans to behave to be dominant/proactive, harmonizing, or passive/fatalistic?'
3. The nature of reality truth.	'How do we define what is true and what is not true; and how is truth ultimately determined both in the physical and social world?'
4. The nature of time.	'What is our basic orientation in terms of past, present, and future, and what kinds of time units are most relevant for the conduct of daily life?'
5. The nature of human nature.	'Are humans basically good, neutral or evil, and is human nature perfectible or fixed?'
6. The nature of human relationships.	'What is the "correct" way for people to relate to each other, to distribute power and affection? Is life competitive or co-operative? Is the best way to organize society on the basis of individualism or groupism? Is the best authority system autocratic/paternalistic or collegial/participative?'
7. Homogeneity vs. diversity.	'Is the group best off if it is highly diverse or if it is highly homogeneous, and should individuals in a group be encouraged to innovate?'

Source: Schein (1990). Reproduced by permission of publisher.

According to Deal and Kennedy (1982) corporate culture has a number of specific elements: a widely shared philosophy in the business environment; shared values, e.g.: 'The consumer is important; things don't just happen, you have to make them; we want to make employee interests our own'; specific rites and rituals; and a primary (but informal) means of communication. In their highly popular and readable book they offer, most helpfully and insightfully, examples of how these elements or markers can be seen in the various cultures they describe. For Meek (1988), corporate culture has much more to do with internalizing shared beliefs and behavioural norms. He notes that culture is different from corporate structure, but clearly related to it, and that highly symbolic corporate behaviours survive in organizations' memories and legends. Also corporate cultures have elaborate work patterns and procedures and pay inordinate attention to titles and formalities.

Gonzalez (1987) points out another list of observations. Culture is a set of symbols and meanings people use to organize their ideas, interpret their experiences, make decisions, and ultimately guide their actions. Culture is 'taken for granted', in that there are shared assumptions about how work is done and how people relate to one another. Culture is a pattern of assumptions that a given group has invented, discovered or developed to learn to behave at work. Finally, culture is important because it has a direct impact on motivation, satisfaction and morale.

The model developed by Schein (1985) helps to organize the pieces of the culture puzzle. According to Schein's model, culture is represented at three levels:

1   Behaviours and artefacts.
2   Beliefs and values.
3   Underlying assumptions.

These levels are arranged according to their visibility, such that behaviour and artefacts are the easiest to observe, while the underlying assumptions need to be inferred. While behaviour and artefacts may be observable and beliefs and values can be articulated, their meaning may not be readily comprehensible. To understand what the behaviour or beliefs actually mean to the participants/employees, the underlying assumptions have to be brought to the surface or made manifest, which is most difficult as this level of culture is considered to be taken for granted and thus beyond awareness.

More recently Schein (1990) has noted:

For our purposes it is enough to specify that any definable group with a shared history can have a culture and that within an organization there can therefore be many subcultures. If the organization as a whole has had shared experiences, there will also be a total organizational culture. Within any given unit, the tendency for integration and consistency will be assumed to be present, but it is perfectly possible for coexisting units of a larger system to have cultures that are independent and even in conflict with each other.

Culture can be defined as:
(a) a pattern of basic assumptions;
(b) invented, discovered, or developed by a given group;
(c) as it learns to cope with its problems of external adaptation and internal integration;
(d) that has worked well enough to be considered valid and, therefore;
(e) is to be taught to new members as the;

(f) correct way to perceive, think, and feel in relation to those problems.

The strength and degree of internal consistency of a culture are, therefore, a function of the stability of the group, the length of time the group has existed, the intensity of the group's experiences of learning, the mechanisms by which the learning has taken place (i.e.: positive reinforcement or avoidance conditioning), and the strength and clarity of the assumptions held by the founders and leaders of the group.

(p. 11)

Essentially all these attempts to define and describe organizational culture have led to a position where certain areas of agreement and disagreement are acknowledged.

Agreement over the concept of culture

• It is difficult to define (even a pointless exercise).
• It is multidimensional, with many different components at different levels.
• It is not particularly dynamic and ever changing (being relatively stable over short periods of time).
• It leads to significant misunderstandings (that are unexpected) when cultures meet.
• Culture shock or moving into a different corporate culture is real, painful and debilitating.
• It represents a group solution to certain problems which may be adaptive or maladaptive; positively or negatively related to productivity.
• It takes time to establish, and therefore change, a corporate 'culture'.
• It is in many senses intangible but has numerous observable artefacts.
• It is clearly linked to implicit beliefs and values underlying behavioural norms.

Disagreement over the concept of culture

• What are the exact components/facets of corporate culture: i.e., what makes something part of corporate culture and what not part of culture?
• How to categorize/dimensionalize culture: what typology to use; which dimension to apply; what terminology we should use.
• How national, ethnic, corporate, departmental gender (etc.) cultures overlap, interact, and influence each other.
• How, when, or why corporate culture can be changed.
• Whether to celebrate corporate departmental culture differences, or work towards eliminating them.

- Whether it is possible to bridge already established departmental or corporate cultures.
- How organizational corporate culture differs from organizational climate.
- Who, when, and how 'forms' or establishes a culture.
- Whether some cultures are adaptive and others maladaptive: what is the healthiest, most optimal, or desirable culture.

Inevitably, there remains more disagreement than agreement. This is not necessarily a bad thing, as disagreement frequently encourages people to seek more fruitfully for the answers to the academic and applied problems. Another approach is to spell out some of the more important issues on which people from different national and corporate cultures actually differ.

The issue of the definitive list of dimensions of corporate culture has not, and will not, be resolved. Though there remains much overlap between different lists and concepts, as yet there is no consensus.

THE ORIGINS OF CORPORATE CULTURE

How is it that so many individuals within an organization share basic attitudes, behaviour patterns, expectations and values? In other words, how does a culture form, and how is it maintained?

First, organizational culture may be traced, at least in part, to the founders of the company, or to those who strongly shaped it in the recent past. These persons often possess dynamic personalities, strong values, and a clear vision of how the organization should be. Since they are on the scene first, and/or play a key role in hiring initial staff, their attitudes and values are readily transmitted to new employees. The result is that these views become the accepted ones in the organization, and persist as long as the founders are on the scene, or even longer. Classic examples are monastic orders which follow closely, even dogmatically, their founders' rules. Given the length of time over which cultures get established, the reasons why people do things may well be forgotten.

Second, organizational culture often develops out of, or gets changed by, an organization's experience with its external environment. Every organization must find a niche and an image for itself in its sector and in the market place. As it struggles to do so, it may find that some values and practices work better for it than others. For example, one organization may gradually acquire a deep, shared commitment to high quality, while another company may find that selling products of moderate quality, but at attractive prices, works best for it. The result: a dominant value centring around price leadership takes shape. This organization's culture is shaped by its interaction with the external environment, which may be in a state of flux. Hence, the pressure to change culture to 'fit' the external environment is constant, particularly in turbulent times.

Third, culture develops from the need to maintain effective working relationships among organization members. Depending on the nature of its business, and the characteristics of the person it must employ, different expectations and values may develop. Thus, if a company needs rapid and open communication between its employees, informal working relationships and open expressions of view probably will come to be valued within it. In contrast, very different values and styles of communication may develop in other organizations working in other industries with different types of personnel. Just as groups go through a well-known sequence in their development, remembered as forming, storming, norming and performing, so do corporate cultures. Indeed it is the development of behavioural norms that is at the very heart of culture.

For Schein (1990), culture is created through two main factors. First, norm formation around critical incidents – particularly where mistakes have occurred. The lessons learnt from important corporate events (often crises) are crucially important factors in the formation (or change) of culture. Second, identification with leaders particularly: what leaders pay attention to, measure and control; how leaders react to critical incidents and organizational crises; deliberate role modelling and coaching; operational criteria for the allocation of rewards and status; operational criteria for recruitment selection, promotion, retirement, and excommunication. The role of unique, visionary leaders cannot be understated. Understanding the factors that lead to the establishment of corporate culture is important because they also serve to highlight the factors that need to be concentrated on, when changing that culture.

CLASSIFYING AND CATEGORIZING CULTURE

In order to compare and contrast, evaluate and predict it is clearly important that one is first able to classify or taxonomize organizational cultures. Categorization is the beginning of science; what follows this all-important stage is an understanding of the processes and mechanisms that account for the origin and maintenance of culture. Various attempts have been made at this natural history task. First, however, it is perhaps important to try to understand the advantages and disadvantages of the quest as a whole.

Advantages of classification systems for corporate culture

• It is possible to compare and contrast cultures so as to be able to predict (and control) areas of misunderstandings/friction before they occur.
• Empirical data of groups, clusters or types may yield counter-intuitive findings that simple guesswork would not show. In other words, there

may be good reasons why two superficially similar types do not 'fit' together at a deeper level.

- It may be useful to prepare a behavioural culture atlas for a traveller from one organization to another. Only a scheme or category system could facilitate this.
- Theories of classification can be tested by gathered empirical data. In this sense they can be discarded, revised, or maintained.
- It helps people become aware of their own culture and how it differs from others. It serves to make the implicit, explicit and help the whole audit process.
- It specifies the areas of training that become necessary for the culture traveller within and across organizations and culture. Like the periodic table for the chemist or the map for the explorer, a typology of culture allows more interesting and important work to be done.

Disadvantages of classification systems for corporate culture

- Classification systems are only as good as the evidence/data upon which they are based, and that is frequently poor: hence the taxonomics are weak, commonsensical, or wrong.
- Different statistical techniques yield different dimensions, and it is not certain which is most useful. There is no agreement upon the particular way of treating the data, yet each reveals a rather different problem.
- Very 'broad brush' approaches (that offer a small number of distinguishable types) can be insensitive, missing out on the really interesting and important dimensions. In fact they may be dangerous, giving an illusion of knowledge, which is often incomplete or incorrect.
- Classifying culture does not tell you either the consequences of differences or similarities, or how to fix them. This knowledge may be implied, but it is not necessarily provided.

There are various different ways to classify culture which can be fitted into the matrix shown in Table 3.2. The difference between theoretical and empirical is that the former is 'top-down', based on previous research, conceptional distinctions and theories (and does not rely on current research), whereas the latter is 'bottom-up', being theoretically void, or naive with hope that data collected will yield the basic dimensions of culture.

Table 3.2 Modes of culture classification

Culture classification	Theoretical	Empirical
Geographical		
Economic		
Historic-linguistic		
Religio-political		
Values		
Organizational classification		
Product		
Size		
Structure		

Without doubt, however, it is Hofstede's work which has attracted most recent interest and critical acclaim. It was his aim to describe national culture as parsimoniously as possible by extracting the most fundamental underlying dimension.

There are various studies to show that national and organizational cultures are interlinked. This in itself is not surprising; indeed, common sense would predict it. However, due to the very different methodologies and approaches, there is not yet any standard taxonomy of the stages within an organization and the extent to which they affect each other.

From his extensive data base collected throughout IBM, Hofstede (1980) developed four 'dimensions' of culture – power distance, uncertainty avoidance, individualism, and masculine/feminine – against which he was then able to plot forty different nationalities. His study showed that within one multinational organizational culture there can be marked differences based on national norms. Various researchers have proposed using Hofstede's dimensions to select and carry out culturally sensitive interventions in overseas organization development.

Hofstede's dimensions may be defined as follows:

1 **Power distance** The extent to which the less powerful members of institutions and organizations accept that power is distributed unequally.
2 **Uncertainty avoidance** The extent to which people feel threatened by ambiguous situations, and have created beliefs and institutions that try to avoid these.

3 **Individualism/collectivism** This dimension reflects an ethic position of the culture in which people are supposed to look after themselves and their immediate family, or a situation in which people belong to in-groups or collectives which are supposed to look after them in exchange for loyalty.

4 **Masculinity/femininity** A situation in which the dominant values in society are success, money and possessions. A situation in which the dominant values in society are caring for others, and the quality of life.

National characteristics in terms of these dimensions can be applied to organizations (Table 3.3).

The advantages of Hofstede's four-factor theory is that if allows empirical comparison of countries to determine differences in the four indices so that statistical predictions can be made.

There are, of course, many ways of diagnosing or describing corporate culture. One approach is to contrast the outsider's and insider's perspectives. Thus, from the outside, an observer could note:

- The physical setting – inside and outside buildings (the buildings, style, logo).
- What the company says about itself through press releases, adverts, etc.
- The way the company greets strangers, (formal/informal; relaxed/busy; elegant/nondescript), inducts new people.
- The history of the company: stories about why the company is a success; what kind of people it attracts, the nature of an average day.
- How people spend their time, both whilst at work but also how they choose to interact after work.

From the inside it may be equally possible to highlight features of corporate culture:

- By understanding the career path progression of employees.
- By noting how long people stay in middle management jobs.
- By examining the content of what is being discussed or written about in meetings, memos, etc.
- Examining anecdotes and stories that pass through the cultural network.

Naturally there have been many attempts to classify and codify culture. Interestingly, nearly all these attempts have resulted in the description of four types (Handy, 1980).

Table 3.3 Four dimensions of corporate culture

1. The power distance dimension (POW)	
LOW (Australia, Israel, Denmark, Sweden, Norway)	HIGH (Phillipines, Mexico, Venezuela, India, Brazil)
• Less centralization • Flatter organization pyramids • Smaller wage differentials • Structure in which manual and clerical workers are in equal jobs.	• Greater centralization • Tall organization pyramids • More supervisory personnel • Structure in which white-collar jobs are valued more than blue-collared jobs.

2. The masculinity/feminity dimension (MAS)	
LOW (Sweden, Denmark, Thailand, Finland)	HIGH (Japan, Australia, Venezuela, Italy, Mexico)
• Sex roles are minimized. • Organizations do not interfere with people's private lives. • More women in more qualified jobs. • Soft, yielding, intuitive skills are rewarded. • Social rewards are valued.	• Sex roles are clearly differentiated. • Organizations may interfere to protect their interests. • Fewer women in qualified jobs. • Aggression, competition, and justice are rewarded. • Work is valued as a central life interest.

3. The individualism/collectivism dimension (IND)	
LOW (Venezuela, Columbia, Taiwan, Mexico, Greece)	HIGH (United States, Australia, Great Britain, Canada, The Netherlands)
• Organization as 'family'. • Organization defends employee interests. • Practices are based on loyalty, sense of duty, and group participation	• Organization is more impersonal. • Employees defend their own self-interest. • Practices encourage individual initiative.

4. The uncertainty avoidance dimension (UNC)	
LOW (Denmark, Sweden, Great Britain, United States, India)	HIGH (Greece, Portugal, Japan, Peru, France)
• Less structuring of activities. • Fewer written rules. • More generalists. • Variability. • Greater willingness to take risks. • Less ritualistic behaviour.	• More structuring activities. • More written rules. • More specialists. • Standardization. • Less willingness to take risks. • More ritualistic behaviour.

Source: Adapted from Hofstede (1981)

Deal and Kennedy's taxonomy of corporate culture

According to Deal and Kennedy (1982), the following four quite different types of corporate culture are identifiable.

Tough-guy macho culture

- A world of risk-taking individualists, eager for immediate feedback.
- Frequently construction, management consultancy, venture capital, media, publishing, sports (high-risk, quick return).
- High-risk, high-gain philosophies abound.
- Heroes are survivors who win high stakes.
- The chance-like nature of success in this world means many superstitions, 'comfort blanket' rituals exist.
- Very short-term oriented.
- Unlikely to learn from failures, set-backs.
- The culture fosters immaturity and distrust of colleagues.

Work hard – play hard culture

- The culture encourages people to maintain a high level of relatively low-risk activity.
- Frequently real-estate, computer companies, automotive distributors, door-to-door sales operation.
- Success comes with persistence, so this is most rewarded.
- Client/customer centred, aimed at meeting a need and filling it.
- Heroes are friendly, carousing, super sales people.
- Rites and rituals revolve around energetic games and contests, meetings.
- The action-oriented culture is ideal for people who thrive on quick tangible feedback.
- But quality is sacrificed for quantity.
- There may also be a lack of thoughtfulness and attention.
- They can get fooled by success because of little long-term planning.
- High energy enthusiasts drift into cynicism when the quick-fix existence loses its meaning.
- The culture requires great respect and cultivates young people.

Bet-your-company culture

- The culture is a high-risk, slow feedback existence with less pressure but 'slow-drip water torture'.
- Frequently banks, mining companies, large-system business, architectural firms, computer-design companies, actuarial insurance companies.

- They are often ponderous, deliberate companies where good ideas are given a proper chance to show success.
- Decisions are slow, consultative, but top-down.
- Heroes can cope with long-term ambiguity, and are those who respect authority and technical competence and rely upon it.
- These organizations move with awesome slowness.
- These cultures are vulnerable to short-term fluctuations and cash-flow problems.

Process culture

- This is the classic bureaucracy – a world of little feedback, where it is difficult to concentrate on outcome, so people concentrate on process.
- Frequently government, local government, utilities, some banks and insurance companies, heavily regulated industries.
- It is characterized by excessive reliance on memos by people trying to 'cover their ass'.
- Protectiveness and caution are natural responses to the absence of feedback.
- Heroes are orderly, punctual, attend to detail.
- Sport/play is important – which sport, how often, who with.
- Special language and jargon abound.
- Greeting rituals may be peculiar to this company.
- Co-worker rituals – tough guys score points off each other; workers/ players drink together, betters mentor each other; process people discuss memos.

This fourfold classification was one of the first in the area and has attracted considerable interest, if not research.

Williams, Dobson and Walters' taxonomy of power, role, task and people cultures*

Williams *et al.* (1989) also identify four (rather different) cultures:

1 **Power orientation** Power-orientated organizations attempt to dominate their environment and those who are powerful within the organization strive to maintain absolute control over subordinates. They buy and sell organizations and people as commodities, in apparent disregard of human values and general welfare. They are competitive and have voracious appetites for growth. Within the organization, the law of the jungle often seems to prevail among executives as they struggle for personal advantage.
2 **Role orientation** Such organizations would more typically be described

*Reproduced by permission of publisher.

as bureaucracies. There is an emphasis upon legality, legitimacy and responsibility. Conflict is regulated by rules and procedures. Rights and privileges are defined and adhered to. There is a strong emphasis upon hierarchy and status. Predictability of behaviour is high and stability and respectability are often valued as much as competence.

3 **Task orientation** In such organizations, structures, functions and activities are all evaluated in terms of their contributions to organizational goals. Nothing is allowed to get in the way of task accomplishment. If individuals do not have the skills or technical knowledge to perform a task, they are retrained or replaced. Authority is based upon appropriate knowledge and competence. Emphasis is placed on a rapid and flexible organization. Collaboration is sought if this promotes goal achievement. Task and project groups are common.

4 **People orientation** This type of organization exists primarily to serve the needs of its members. Authority may be assigned on the basis of task competence, but this practice is kept to a minimum. Instead, individuals are expected to influence each other through example and helpfulness. Consensus methods of decision-making are preferred. Roles are assigned on the basis of personal preference and the need for learning growth.

Another American group (Schein, 1985) have isolated four rather different corporate cultures:

Power culture

- Leadership resides in a few, and rests on their ability.
- People motivated by rewards and punishments (and association with strong leaders).
- Good power cultures have strong, just, firm, fair leaders.
- Bad power cultures have corrupt, fear-inducing leaders.
- Can be good for entrepreneurial and start-up organizations.
- Problems arise when the size and complexity of organizations increase.

Role culture

- Power is balanced equitably between the leader and bureaucratic structures.
- Roles and rules are clearly defined, and 'contracts' are established.
- Values are order, dependability, rationality and delegation.
- Little supervision is needed.
- These cultures work well in stable environments.
- They can be impersonal, against innovation and change, and tend to make members feel entrusted.

Achievement culture

- Stresses personal, intrusive motivation and commitment where people can 'do their own thing'.
- The attempt to evoke passion, commitment and the sense of a 'calling'.
- People voluntarily 'line up' behind exciting, noble goals.
- These cultures value action, excitement and impact.
- High demands are made on people's energy and time.
- However, the culture is difficult to sustain, and people are prone to burn-out and disillusionment.
- There is more common vision to organize the work, than subjection to discipline and procedures.

Support culture

- Here support is voluntary and relationships are characterized by mutuality.
- People contribute out of a sense of commitment and solidarity.
- Found in the military, foreign service, ex-pat communities, union organizers, start-up teams.
- There is reciprocal caring and trust, and concern for others' welfare.
- A strong feature is extremely strong motivation in the service of the group; a willingness to make sacrifice.
- A weakness is a tendency to avoid conflict; consensus is over-valued and there is some favouritism.

Graves (1986) also specifies four culture types. The language and imagery change, but obviously the four 'standard' types are recognizable. They are:

Graves' taxonomy of culture*

Barbarian

- Anti-bureaucratic, ego-driven culture that rejects procedures and formality.
- Warriors (workers) are workaholics, mavericks, pop-star individualists.
- Leadership is charismatic and groups are unstable.
- There is an atmosphere of perpetual ferment.
- Members share the experience of the thrill of the switchback, the euphoria of high life and the bitterness of despair.
- Character types are 'fixers' in strong battle, truculent in defeat and contemptuous of a settled life.

*Reproduced by permission of publisher.

Monarchical

- Contempt for formalization and bureaucracy and planning, yet loyalty and doggedness are highly praised.
- Heavily dependent on the skills of the leader.
- In this culture, succession can be a serious problem.
- Promotion comes from within and the quality of leadership is variable.

Presidential

- In the democratic culture the elected leader embodies the needs and aspirations of all the people in the organization.
- The leader is sustained by subordinates, who know his term is short and his influence limited.
- The leader needs to give clear messages to prevent people drifting into sub-groups.
- Bad cultures of this type tend to be reactive rather than proactive, living off internal momentum.

Pharaonic

- A culture with a passion for order, status and ritual.
- The culture is changeless but shadowy, healthy but false.
- Individualism is accepted but the pre-eminence of the system is maintained.

Like all other authors in this area, Graves (1980) offers no evidence for the categories, nor does he explain how he came to choose this particular categorizing system.

Is it possible to have a culture-free classification system? Jamieson (1981) has noted the need for a conceptual 'meta-language' to be able to compare and contrast organizations but questions whether this is possible, although desirable.

Despite the overall similarity of these disparate systems, there remains no overall agreement as to what the basic categories of culture are. These first attempts to describe the major types are no more than interesting intuitions which may prove validated. Few of these theorists have attempted the more interesting questions of how these cultures arise or how they are maintained.

ATTITUDES TO CULTURAL DIFFERENCES

Discovering cultural differences (whether they are ethnic, gender, religious, corporate or linguistically based) is frequently an unpleasant experience, and people react in rather different ways. This occurs when individuals

Table 3.4 Comparisons of corporate culture taxonomies

1. *Tough-guy culture* Risk-taking Individualistic	1. *Power culture* Entrepreneurial Ability values	1. *Barbarian* Ego-driven Workaholic	1. *Power-oriented* Competitive Responsibility to personality rather than expertise
4. *Work/play hard* Persistent Sociable	2. *Achievement* Personal Intrinsic motivation	2. *Presidential* Democratic Hierarchical	2. *People-oriented* Consensual Rejects management control
3. *Bet your company* Ponderous Unpressurized	3. *Support culture* Mutuality Trust	3. *Monarchical* Loyalty Doggedness	3. *Task-oriented* Competency Dynamic
4. *Process culture* Bureaucratic Protective	4. *Role culture* Order Dependable	4. *Pharaonic* Ritualized Changeless	4. *Role-oriented* Legality Legitimacy Pure bureaucracy

Authors

Deal and Kennedy (1982)	Schein (1990)	Graves (1980)	Harrison (1972) Handy (1980)

Dimensions

(High/Low) Speed of feedback (Slow/Fast)	Individualistic- collectivistic	Anti-Bureaucratic Managerial – Ego Drive	(High/Low) Centralization (High/Low)

move from one organization to another; when a merger or take-over occurs, and/or when companies become multinational and expand to different countries, territories and region. Essentially people (notably senior management) tend to assume one of the various positions detailed below:

Chauvinistic imperialists 'Ours is the best way [management structure and style] and others should learn our ways.' Differences are fairly minimal and due to *their* ignorance. Chauvinistic imperialists believe their way of doing things is more sensible, adaptable, natural (especially efficient and profitable), and hence should be learnt by others.

Ashamed post-colonialist 'Theirs is the best, most natural way of managing a business, dealing with people: and ours is the worst, most exploitive way.' Others have the best solution and we are/were arrogant and wrong. This reaction is to reject a traditional way of doing things totally and whole-heartedly and to embrace, rather uncritically, the culture of another group or organization.

Ignoramuses   'Cultural differences don't really exist and are emphasized by people who have ulterior [political] motives.' This response is to deny the presence of culture and may be due to extreme defensiveness or short-sightedness.

Relativists   'Every culture does things differently and has its share of the truth.' Nearly every aspect of corporate and national culture varies, and they are essentially incomparable. Some people seem so overwhelmed by the number, type, origin and consequences of corporate and national culture differences that they are quite unable to deal with them.

Vacillators and marginals   'All cultures are valid in some respects and the trick is to find which has the best answer to the problem.' This reaction argues that cultures tend to be completely right or wrong on the specific topics and that it is difficult to predict which is which and when. People with this perspective try to mix and match the bits of various cultures they like the most.

Mediators   'The most sensible approach is to choose the most sensitive, veridical and appropriate aspect of cultural tradition and attempt to live them out.' This approach represents a sensitive mix, rather than a homogenization.

Hybrid creators   'We should try to create a new hybrid culture that best meets our needs and that is adaptive and healthy.' This most radical and perhaps naive approach suggests that one should start from scratch and develop a new culture. To what extent this is possible and desirable is rarely discussed.

WHAT IS THE MAJOR IMPACT OF CORPORATE CULTURE ON ORGANIZATIONS?

Clearly, corporate culture generates strong but subtle pressures to think and act in a particular way. Thus, if an organization's culture stresses such values as service to customers, participative decision-making, and a paternalistic attitude towards employees, individuals within the company will tend to adopt these values in their own behaviour. If, in contrast, an organization's culture involves maximizing output, centralized decision-making, and 'going by the book', individuals' actions will often reflect these attitudes and values.

Corporate culture also actually relates to performance, though many argue there is not compelling evidence for a clear link between culture and performance. One view is that in order to influence performance, organizational culture must be strong (basic aspects of the culture are strongly accepted by most employees), and must also possess certain key traits (e.g. humanistic values, concern about quality, and innovativeness of products).

But according to Baron and Greenberg (1990) there are three reasons why this relationship is far from clear. First, much of the research on this issue has erroneously assumed that organizations possess a single, unitary culture. Therefore, the findings reported may apply only to some groups of employees (often top management, in the companies studied). Second, serious questions remain about the measures of cultural strength (qualitative and quantitative) used in these projects. Different researchers have adopted different definitions; thus, it is not clear that the same variable was being assessed in all cases. Third, none of the studies conducted to date have included appropriate comparison groups. To demonstrate that possession of certain types of culture contributes to corporate success, it is necessary to show that such cultures are indeed characteristic of highly productive organizations, but not of less successful ones. To date, no clear data have been reported on this issue. Certainly there are various ways of measuring the impact of culture on organization and individuals.

One learns about corporate culture through the process of organizational socialization. Looking at the bombed House of Commons, Churchill said, 'We shape our buildings and afterwards they shape us,' implying a sort of environmental determinism. The same may be true of corporate culture. Organizations develop or build a culture which afterwards shapes how people 'learn the ropes' or 'speak the language' in an organization. They do so through organizational socialization, which is the process through which individuals are transformed from outsiders into participating effective members of organizations. Baron and Greenberg (1990) have identified three quite distinctive steps:

1 **Getting in: anticipatory socialization** Before individuals actually join an organization, they usually know quite a bit about it. Such information, which is the basis for expectations concerning what the organization and their specific job will be like, is obtained from several sources. In many cases, it is provided by friends or relatives already working for the organization. These individuals provide a wealth of information which strongly colours the perceptions and expectations of new recruits. Second, individuals often acquire information about an organization from professional journals, from magazine and newspaper articles, from its annual reports, and other formal sources. Third, and perhaps most important, potential employees gain such information from the organization's recruitment procedures. Since competition for top-notch employees is always intense, successful recruitment of such persons usually involves a skilled combination of salesmanship and diplomacy. Recruiters tend to describe their companies in glowing terms, glossing over internal problems and emphasizing positive features. The result is that potential employees receive an unrealistically

positive impression about what working in it will be like. When they actually arrive on the job and find that their expectations are not met, disappointment, dissatisfaction, and even resentment about being misled can follow. Such reactions, in turn, can contribute to high rates of turnover, low organizational commitment, and other negative outcomes.

2 **Breaking in: the encounter stage** The second major stage in organizational socialization begins when individuals actually assume their new duties. During this stage, they face several key tasks. First, they must master the skills required by their new jobs. Second, they must become oriented to the practices and procedures of the organization. This often involved unlearning old habits or behaviours and acquiring new ones, for co-workers quickly become tired of hearing a new recruit say, 'That's not how we did it where I worked before.' Third, new members of an organization must establish good social relations with other members of their work group. They must get to know these people and gain their acceptance. Only when they do, can they become full members of the team. It is during the encounter stage, of course, that formal training and orientations programmes are conducted. These are designed to help individuals accomplish the tasks described above.

3 **Settling in: the metamorphosis stage** Some time after an individual enters an organization, he or she attains full member status. Depending on the type and length of the training programme used, this entry may be marked by a formal ceremony, or may be quite informal. In the former case, individuals may attend a dinner, reception, or graduation exercise at which they exchange their temporary, provisional title (e.g., trainee, apprentice) for a more permanent one. Alternatively, they may receive a concrete sign of their new status (e.g., the key to the executive washroom, a pass to the executive dining room, a permanent identity badge). In other cases, especially when training has been shorter or informal in nature, full acceptance into the work group may not be marked by any specific ceremony. Instead, it may be acknowledged by informal actions, such as being invited to lunch by co-workers, or being assigned a seat at their dining table in the dining room.

For Schein (1990) it is more interesting to understand how culture is *preserved* through socialization. For him there are seven dimensions along which organizational culture socialization processes vary:

1 **Group versus individual** The degree to which the organization processes recruits in batches, as in boot camp, or individually, as in professional offices. This may be partly associated with the size of the organization.

2 **Formal versus informal** The degree to which the process is institutionalized and formalized, as in set training programmes, or is handled

informally through apprenticeships, individual coaching by the immediate superior, or the like.

3 **Self-destructive and reconstructing versus self-enhancing** The degree to which the process destroys aspects of the self and replaces them, as in boot camp, or enhances aspects of the self, as in professional development programmes. Clearly, few organizations attempt the dramatic strategy of the army, but some do attempt a fairly radical change policy, whereby the induction process attempts to shake individuals into a new approach.

4 **Serial versus random** The degree to which role models are provided, as in apprenticeship or monitoring programmes, or are deliberately withheld, as in sink-or-swim kinds of initiations in which the recruit is expected to devise his or her own solutions.

5 **Sequential versus disjunctive** The degree to which the process consists of guiding the recruit through a series of discrete steps and roles, versus being open-ended and never letting the recruit predict what organizational role will come next. Few organizations presumably *aim* to be disjunctive, but it does occur by chance.

6 **Fixed versus variable** The degree to which stages of the training process have fixed timetables for each stage, as in military academies, or rotational training programmes, or are open-ended, as in typical promotional systems where recruits are not advanced to the next stage until they are 'ready'. The latter is of course more demanding, and may be part of a secondary selection procedure.

7 **Tournament versus contest** The degree to which each stage is an 'elimination tournament' where one is out of the organization if one fails, or a 'contest' in which one builds up a track record or batting average.

But the clearest way to examine the effect of culture on an organization is to see what occurs when two cultures collide in a merger. Buono, Bowditch and Lewis (1985) examined the merger of two banks, before and after the merger, and the resultant culture. Using in-depth interviews, observations and archival data they built up a picture of the subjective and managerial culture of the two banks. Table 3.5 shows the categories used, and it is extremely apparent that there are major differences between the two. The authors also did a climate survey before and after the merger, looking at such things as organizational commitment management and supervision practice, job security, etc. The merger led to some interesting issues, such as who and from which bank to retain, and to what extent new hybrid factors/cultures needed to be invented. The post-merger survey indicated that Bank B employees felt significantly less alienated and less negative after the merger than did former Bank A employees.

Table 3.5 Subjective and objective organizational cultures of Banks A and B

	Bank A	Bank B
Subjective culture		
Managerial culture		
CEO style	Participative	Authoritarian
	Egalitarian	Elitist
	'Good guy'	'Bad guy'
	'Buddha'	'Dennis the menace'
	Externally oriented	Internally oriented
Locus of power	Bureaucratic	Personal
Management style	Anticipatory	'Management by crisis'
General orientation	People oriented	Task oriented
Heroes	V.P. human resources, first woman bank officer	Prior CEO, treasurer
Mecca	Branches	'CEO's office'
Myths	'Fat cats/lazy personnel'	'Lean and mean' 'Hell hole'
When new job duties emerge	New people are hired, highly specialized employees	Responsibility is delegated, 'jack of all trades'
Community involvement	High	Low
Objective culture		
Employee eating facility (main office)	Plush restaurant-like	Spartan, cafeteria-like
Branches	High quality appearance (spare no expense)	Functional appearance (avoid embellishment)
CEO's office	Isolated, view of external environment	Centralized, view of internal working environment

Source: Buono, Bowditch and Lewis. Reproduced by permission of publisher.

This paper has attempted to outline some of the issues involved in the study of organizational cultures and the problems that emerge when two cultures are forced together by a merger. The objective and subjective aspects of a given culture greatly influence the behaviours, satisfactions, and expectations of organizational members. Although individuals may not fully realize this influence during 'normal' organizational functioning, when the culture is threatened it becomes quite salient in people's minds. Since subjective culture evolves over time as a product of shared experience, when attempting to merge two firms, the greater the number of these shared experiences that can be reproduced within a period of time, the faster a repertoire of symbols and shared meanings will develop with which the merged group of members can begin to identify, and a new culture can begin to take hold. There is a clear need for those involved with mergers or acquisitions to explicitly consider the central facet of organizational culture much more fully.

(Buono, Bowditch and Lewis, 1985, p. 498)

Research done by Laurent shows that senior to middle level executives of different nationalities have differing preferences of organizational structure (Laurent, 1983). The statement he found had the most variance was 'it is important for a manager to have at hand precise answers to most of the questions that his subordinates may raise about their work.' The results ranged from 10 per cent agreement for Swedish managers, to 66 per cent agreement for Italian managers. If these are typical responses, then there are clear indications about the kind of organizational structure each nationality would prefer. The Italian end of the spectrum would probably assume a more hierarchical structure with less room for flexibility and delegation than the Swedish.

Laurent's study also showed that within one multinational, managers tend to become three times more nationalistic at the attitudinal level, although they learnt to blend behaviourally with the corporate norm. One feature of both Laurent's and Hofstede's studies was that in neither case was the questionnaire developed with the idea of eliciting the dimensions and organizational types that were later drawn out. The result is that in all but two categories, the dimensions against which different nationalities are being compared are the results of grouping together only three or four seemingly related questions. In both studies the questions were of a general nature, and therefore possibly more prone to generating cultural differences.

The particular issues that Schneider (1987) sees as leading to the possibility of a clash between national and corporate culture include:

Planning and staffing

- Should planning be: formal vs.informal?
  short vs. long term
  explicit vs. implicit?
- Is planning pointless (i.e. no one but God can know the future)?
- Can we control the future?

Career management

- This approach assumes that people can be evaluated, measured and assessed fairly, dispassionately and comprehensively.
- It assumes that the past predicts the future.
- It assumes that skills can be matched to jobs, the latter of which do not change and are clearly specifiable. Also that some skills are more valued than others (arts vs. science; specialist vs. generalist).
- The approach assumes and expects geographic mobility of the work-

force; and that relocation is acceptable and desirable.

- The assumptions that promotions are desirable and are criteria of success are not always valid or fair.

Appraisal and compensation

- This assumes that objectivity is possible and important.
- This assumes that feedback is important and ignores the problem of 'face saving', common in the Far East.
- Appraisal feedback is used for correction and change of individual behaviour, but the assumption is that individuals have actual control over their outcomes.
- Management by objectives (MBO) has various stated assumptions (goals can be set, measured, negotiated).
- Tying performance to reward is individualistic, and ignores the contribution of groups.
- Incentives for some breaks the egalitarian spirit of communities or groups.

Selection and socialization

- Corporate training sessions, particularly if highly ritualized, are viewed cynically.
- Expatriate managers are often seen as birds of passage.

In other words, where cultural values clash, all sorts of extremely important issues surface, some of them extremely fundamental.

Evan (1978), attempting to ascertain the impact of culture on organizations, was highly critical of the current literature. He set out a seven-point programme for future research (pp. 107–9):

1   A multinational, or better still, a multicultural research team is necessary to eliminate as many unconscious cultural assumptions and biases as possible on the part of the researchers themselves.
2   A multidisciplinary team is essential in order to measure how much of the variance in the structure and performance of organizational systems is attributable to cultural variables, as compared with other variables such as psychological, structural, inter-organizational, and societal.
3   One of the principal problems confronting a research team would be to adapt or construct research instruments, such as those mentioned above, which will tap cultural variables with a high level of reliability and validity.
4   The research instruments measuring cultural variable would be used, first on a representative sample of the population of a society, and second on a representative sample of the members of one or more

organizations in order to measure 'societal culture' as well as 'organizational subculture'.

5 In designing sample surveys, at least two modes of cross-societal comparisons would be used: first, intra-systemic comparisons, i.e., matching domestic or national firms with those of foreign subsidiaries, distinguishing wholly owned subsidiaries from joint ventures, and controlling for various structural and industrial characteristics; and second, intra-organizational comparisons, i.e., subsidiaries of the same company and of comparable size, function, and technology in different societies.

6 In addition to sample surveys, at least two other complementary research methods would be desirable: laboratory and field experiments, in order to test major causal hypotheses, suggested and supported by sample surveys to test the impact of cultural values on organizational behaviour and organizational system performance.

7 Berrien's (1970) nine principles, which he labels 'A super-ego for cross-cultural research', should guide the entire research process. They deserve to be quoted:

The best cross-cultural research is that which: (1) engages the collaborative efforts of two or more investigators of different countries, each of whom is (2) strongly encouraged and supported by institutions in their respective countries to (3) address researchable problems of a common concern not only to ... science ... but (4) relevant to the social problems of our times. Such collaborative enterprise would begin with (5) the joint definition of the problems, (6) employ comparable methods, (7) pool data that would be 'owned' by the collaborative jointly who are free to (8) report their own interpretations to their own constituents but (9) obligated to strive for interpretations acceptable to the world community of scholars.

(Berrien, 1970, pp. 33–4)

ASSESSING AND MEASURING CORPORATE CULTURE

There are good theoretical and practical reasons for measuring corporate culture; however, although there is considerable superficial overlap in defining and conceptualizing culture, precisely how it is assessed remains hotly debated. Part of the problem surrounds whether to assess subjective beliefs, 'unconscious assumptions', attitudes and expectations, or more observable phenomena like agreed heroes, rites, rituals and behavioural norms. Measurement of artefacts, patterns of behaviour, and behavioural norms is frequently done quite differently from the way one might or could measure attitudes, beliefs values, and fundamental (often unquestioned) assumptions. Distinctions between objective versus subjective, superficial versus deep, accessible versus inaccessible, conscious versus unconscious have not been helpful, nearly always because one pole of the dimension is frequently thought of as good and the other bad.

The role of the unconscious (the idea that culture exists at an unconscious level), the uniqueness of organizations (and their lack of comparability), as well as the often rehearsed epistemological and ethical debates, means that the issue of measurement is fraught with ambiguity. Frequently this debate is between the *emic/insider* perspective, which believes culture to be highly subjective, idiosyncratic, unique, requiring non-standardized, sensitive, interactive probing (by observation and interview) and cannot be properly studied by apron research constructed categories and scales, and the *etic/outsider* tradition of psychometrics and survey research, which seeks to compare and contrast organizations on standard measures.

While zealots advocate the use of one exclusive methodology over all other, eclectics advocate the case for multiple methods. Rousseau (1992) has offered a review of some of the currently used and psychometrized culture inventories which documents aspects of culture measured, focus, dimensions, levels, and format as well as traditional psychometric criteria like realiability and validity (consensual, construct, criterion-related). For many, the psychometrics criteria were either non-existent or poor, so there is serious doubt regarding traditional measurement criteria. They also seemed very variable in what they measured:

- **Norms diagnostic index** (Allen and Dyer, 1980) measures seven behavioural norms.
- **Kilmann-Saxton culture gap survey** (Kilmann and Saxton, 1983) measures four behavioural norms in a 2 x 2 framework.
- **Organizational culture profile** (O'Reilly, Chatman and Caldwell, 1988) measures nine categories of value.
- **Organizational beliefs questionnaire** (Sashkin, 1984) measures ten values shared by organizational members.
- **Corporate culture survey** (Glaser, 1983) measures Deal and Kennedy's (1982) four types of shared values and beliefs.
- **Organizational culture inventory** (Cooke and Lafferty, 1989) measures behavioural norms categorized into twelve scales reflecting a circumplex model.
- **Organizational values congruence scale** (Enz, 1986) measures the similarity of twenty-two individual values to those of top management.

Rousseau (1990) pointed out that these various self-report measures have been used to investigate important questions such as: Is there intra-unit agreement on organizational values and behavioural norms? What influences do dominant cultures relate to other organizational processes or outcomes? Is culture related to other organizational characteristics and processes? What influences do cultures have on individual outcomes? How idiosyncratic are cultural elements to specific organizations?

Two examples of instruments are given:

Diagnosing organizational ideology (Roger Harrison)

Organizations have patterns of behaviour that operationalize an ideology a commonly held set of doctrines, myths, and symbols. An organization's ideology has a profound impact on the effectiveness of the organization. It influences most important issues in organization life: how decisions are made, how human resources are used, and how people respond to the environment. Organization ideologies can be divided into four orientations: power, role, task, and self. The items below give the positions of the four orientations on a number of aspects of organizational structure and functioning and on some attitudes and beliefs about human nature.

Instructions. Give a '1' to the statement that best represents the dominant view in your organization, a '2' to the one next closest to your organization's position, and so on through '3' and '4'. This is a measure of the *existing* organization ideology. Then go back and again rank the statement '1' through '4', this time according to your desires in the preferred organization you would like to work in.

1 A good boss is:
(a) Strong, decisive and firm, but fair. He is protective, generous, and indulgent to loyal subordinates.
(b) Impersonal and correct, avoiding the exercise of his authority for his own advantage. He demands from subordinates only that which is required by the formal system.
(c) Egalitarian and capable of being influenced in matters concerning the task. He uses his authority to obtain the resources needed to complete the job.
(d) Concerned with, and responsive to, the personal needs and values of others. He uses his position to provide satisfying and growth-stimulating work opportunities for subordinates.

2 A good subordinate is:
(a) Compliant, hard-working, and loyal to the interest of his superior.
(b) Responsible and reliable, meeting the duties and responsibilities of his job, and avoiding actions that surprise or embarrass his superior.
(c) Self-motivated to contribute his best to the task and is open with his ideas and suggestions. He is, nevertheless, willing to give the lead to others when they show great expertise or ability.
(d) Vitally interested in the development of his own potentialities, and is open to learning and to receiving help. He also respects the needs and values of others, and is willing to help and contribute to their development.

3 A good member of the organization gives first priority to the:
(a) Personal demands of the boss.
(b) Duties, responsibilities and requirements of his own role, and to the customary standards of personal behaviour.

  (c) Requirements of the task for skill, ability, energy, and material resources.

  (d) Personal needs of the individuals involved.

4 People who do well in the organization are:
(a) Shrewd and competitive, with a strong need for power.
(b) Conscientious and responsible, with a strong sense of loyalty to the organization.
(c) Technically effective and competent, with a strong commitment to getting the job done.
(d) Effective and competent in personal relationships, with a strong commitment to the growth and development of people.

5 The organization treats the individual as:
(a) Though his time and energy were at the disposal of persons higher in the hierarchy.
(b) Though his time and energy were available through a contract with rights and responsibilities for both sides.
(c). A co-worker who has committed his skills and abilities to the common cause.
(d) An interesting and worthwhile person in his own right.

6 People are controlled and influenced by the:
(a) Personal exercise of economic and political power (rewards and punishments).
(b) Impersonal exercise of economic and political power to enforce procedures and standards of performance.
(c) Communication and discussion of task requirements leading to appropriate action motivated by personal commitment to goal achievement.
(d) Intrinsic interest and enjoyment to be found in their activities and/or by concern, and caring for the needs of the other persons involved.

7 It is legitimate for one person to control another's activities if:
(a) He has more authority and power in the organization.
(b) His role prescribes that he is responsible for directing the other.
(c) He has more knowledge relevant to the task.
(d) The other accepts that the first person's help or instructions can contribute to his learning power.

8 The basis of task assignment is the:
(a) Personal needs and judgement of those in authority.
(b) Formal divisions of functions and responsibilities in the system.
(c) Resource and expertise requirements of the job to be done.
(d) Personal wishes and needs for learning and growth of individual organization members.

9 Work is performed out of:
(a) Hope of reward, fear of punishment, or personal loyalty toward a powerful individual.
(b) Respect for control obligations backed up by sanctions and loyalty toward the organization of system.
(c) Satisfaction in excellence of work and achievement and/or personal commitment to the task or goal.
(d) Enjoyment of the activity for its own sake and concern and respect for the needs and values of the other persons involved.

10 People work together when:
(a) They are required to by higher authority or when they believe they can use each other for personal advantage.
(b) Co-ordination and exchange are specified by the formal system.
(c) Their joint contribution is needed to perform the task.
(d) The collaboration is personally satisfying, stimulating or challenging.

11 The purpose of competition is to:
(a) Gain personal power and advantage.
(b) Gain high-status positions in the formal system.
(c) Increase the excellence of the contribution to the task.
(d) Draw attention to one's own personal needs.

12 Conflict is:
(a) Controlled by the intervention of higher authorities and often fostered by them to maintain their own power.
(b) Suppressed by reference to rules, procedures, and definitions of responsibility.
(c) Resolved through full discussion of the merits of the work issues involved.
(d) Resolved by open and deep discussion of personal needs and values involved.

13 Decisions are made by the:
(a) Person with the higher power and authority.
(b) Person whose job description carries the responsibility.
(c) Persons with the most knowledge and expertise about the problem.
(d) Persons most personally involved and affected by the outcome.

14 In an appropriate control and communication structure:
(a) Command flows from the top down in a simple pyramid, so that anyone who is higher in the pyramid has authority over anyone who is lower. Information flows up through the chain of command.
(b) Directives flow from the top down and information flows upwards within functional pyramids which meet at the top. The authority and responsibility of a role is limited to the roles beneath it in its own pyramid. Cross-functional exchange is constructed.
(c) Information about task requirements and problems flows from the centre of the task activity upwards and outwards, with those closest to the task determining the resources and support needed from the rest of the organization. A co-ordinating function may set priorities and overall resource levels based on information from all task centres. The structure shifts with the nature and location of the tasks.
(d) Information and influence flow from person to person, based on voluntary relationships initiated for purposes of work, learning, moral support, enjoyment, and shared values. A co-ordinating function may establish overall levels of contributions needed for the maintenance of the organization. These tasks are assigned by mutual agreement.

15 The environment is responded to as though it were:
(a) A competitive jungle in which everyone is against everyone else, and those who do not exploit others are themselves exploited.
(b) An orderly and rational system in which competition is limited by law, and there can be negotiation of compromise to resolve conflicts.
(c) A complex of imperfect forms and systems which are to be reshaped and improved by the achievements of the organization.

(d) A complex of potential threats and support. It is used and manipulated by the organization both as a means of self-nourishment, and as a play-and-work space for the enjoyment and growth of organization members.

Figure 3.1 Harrison's organizational ideology questionnaire
Source: Harrison (1972). Reproduced by permission of the publisher.

The questionnaire is then scored as in Table 3.6.

Table 3.6 Scoring frame for Harrison's organizational ideology questionnaire

Sums of ranks	Individual and group profiles			
	Power orientation	*Role orientation*	*Task orientation*	*Self orientation*
Existing organization ideology				
Participant's preferred organization ideology				
Tally of lowest scores of the group members				
	Power orientation	*Role orientation*	*Task orientation*	*Self orientation*
Existing organization ideology				
Participant's preferred organization ideology				

Source: Harrison (1972). Reproduced by permission of publisher.

This questionnaire is about CORPORATE CULTURE which is the commonly held beliefs, attitudes, and values that exist within an organization. Put more simply, corporate culture in *your* organization is 'the way we do things around here'.

Please think about how people behave in your organization, and the expectations people have of you. What are the policies and practices work colleagues expect you to follow and believe in? Then read each question and indicate the importance attached to those beliefs and values.

The higher the number you circle, the more important and valued that set of behaviours are by the *company*. The lower the numbers, the less

importance your organization attaches to these values.
IN YOUR ORGANIZATION, TO WHAT EXTENT DO PEOPLE ENDORSE EACH OF THE
BELIEFS AND VALUES LISTED BELOW:

A Task dimension

1 Initiative-taking orientation   *Great extent   Not at all*

1 It is vital for business success to
keep up with new development.   7 6 5 4 3 2 1
2 Try to avoid doing things in the
same, predictable ways.   7 6 5 4 3 2 1
3 Successful organizations generally
keep one step ahead of the rest.   7 6 5 4 3 2 1
4 New ideas and procedures should
always be treated with caution.   7 6 5 4 3 2 1
5 People should always look for new
ways of solving problems.   7 6 5 4 3 2 1 [   ] I

2 Risk-taking orientation

6 Never act on anything before
thinking things out carefully.   7 6 5 4 3 2 1
7 Always try to avoid risky decisions. 7 6 5 4 3 2 1
8 Don't take unnecessary chances.   7 6 5 4 3 2 1
9 It often pays to stick your neck out
once in a while.   7 6 5 4 3 2 1
10 Caution is the best policy.   7 6 5 4 3 2 1
11 Nobody got anywhere without
taking a chance every once in a
while.   7 6 5 4 3 2 1 [   ] RA

3 Performance quality orientation

12 Even the simplest jobs should be
done well.   7 6 5 4 3 2 1
13 Quality comes before quantity.   7 6 5 4 3 2 1
14 If a job is worth doing, it is worth
doing well.   7 6 5 4 3 2 1
15 You should always take time to do
things right.   7 6 5 4 3 2 1
16 Those who know their business
well will succeed.   7 6 5 4 3 2 1
17 Always try to pursue a standard of
excellence.   7 6 5 4 3 2 1
18 Always try to be right.   7 6 5 4 3 2 1
19 Never settle for half measures
when doing a job.   7 6 5 4 3 2 1 [   ] PQ

4 Strategic planning

20 Treat rules as more important than
ideas.   7 6 5 4 3 2 1
21 Always explore the alternatives
before acting.   7 6 5 4 3 2 1

22 It is essential to think ahead.   7 6 5 4 3 2 1
23 A successful organization always
    knows where it is going.   7 6 5 4 3 2 1
24 Too much attention to planning can
    slow you down.   7 6 5 4 3 2 1
25 You can never spend too much
    time planning ahead.   7 6 5 4 3 2 1 [   ] SP

B Interpersonal dimensions

1 Power orientated

26 You have to play politics to get on.   7 6 5 4 3 2 1
27 Successful people are those who
    are loyal to their boss.   7 6 5 4 3 2 1
28 You need to be firm and decisive to
    survive.   7 6 5 4 3 2 1
29 Subordinates should be
    hard-working and loyal.   7 6 5 4 3 2 1
30 Control is all-important.   7 6 5 4 3 2 1
31 People in authority have more
    clout.   7 6 5 4 3 2 1
32 You have to be hard and tough to
    get on.   7 6 5 4 3 2 1 [   ] P

2 Achievement orientated

33 Success comes to those who
    believe in getting the job done.   7 6 5 4 3 2 1
34 Personal commitment to attaining
    goals is of utmost importance.   7 6 5 4 3 2 1
35 Successful people take on
    challenging tasks.   7 6 5 4 3 2 1
36 Getting the right results comes first. 7 6 5 4 3 2 1
37 Always strive for better ways of
    achieving goals.   7 6 5 4 3 2 1
38 Be the first to reach your targets.   7 6 5 4 3 2 1
39 Everyone likes a winner.   7 6 5 4 3 2 1 [   ] A

3 Co-operation orientation

40 Success comes to those who get
    on with others.   7 6 5 4 3 2 1
41 You've got to look out for yourself
    first and foremost.   7 6 5 4 3 2 1
42 Always try to get on with your
    colleagues.   7 6 5 4 3 2 1
43 Working together is important.   7 6 5 4 3 2 1
44 Always look for constructive ways
    of overcoming problems.   7 6 5 4 3 2 1
45 Teamwork comes first.   7 6 5 4 3 2 1
46 It doesn't usually pay to 'rock the
    boat'.   7 6 5 4 3 2 1 [   ] C

4 Supportive orientation

47	Show concern for the needs of others.	7 6 5 4 3 2 1
48	Always try to help your colleagues.	7 6 5 4 3 2 1
49	Warmth among colleagues helps get the job done.	7 6 5 4 3 2 1
50	People are more important than things.	7 6 5 4 3 2 1
51	People should be told when they have done well.	7 6 5 4 3 2 1 [____] (S)

5 Communication orientation

52	People at work need encouragement.	7 6 5 4 3 2 1
53	Ideas should flow freely.	7 6 5 4 3 2 1
54	Line management should take care over what they say to subordinates.	7 6 5 4 3 2 1
55	Open communication is best.	7 6 5 4 3 2 1
56	Everyone in an organization should be kept informed.	7 6 5 4 3 2 1
57	Communication needs to be carefully controlled.	7 6 5 4 3 2 1
58	Policy decisions should always be based on sound information.	7 6 5 4 3 2 1
59	Only communicate on a 'need-to-know' level.	7 6 5 4 3 2 1 [____] (R/C)

6 Rewards orientated

60	People need regular rewards.	7 6 5 4 3 2 1
61	Rewards should go to those who are committed to their work.	7 6 5 4 3 2 1
62	Promotion goes to those who wait.	7 6 5 4 3 2 1
63	People shouldn't always expect special rewards for doing their job well.	7 6 5 4 3 2 1
64	Rewards should follow quickly on performance.	7 6 5 4 3 2 1
65	Good workers deserve rapid promotion.	7 6 5 4 3 2 1
66	Rewards for effort should not be too easily given.	7 6 5 4 3 2 1 [____] (R)

7 Moral orientation

67	Happy workers are more productive.	7 6 5 4 3 2 1
68	A healthy team spirit is important to a successful organization.	7 6 5 4 3 2 1
69	Friendly managers seldom gain the respect of their subordinates.	7 6 5 4 3 2 1
70	People are best motivated with friendliness.	7 6 5 4 3 2 1

71 An organization which takes care of
    its employees can expect them to
    work well.   7 6 5 4 3 2 1 [   ] (M)

C Individual-level orientation

1 Autonomy orientation

72 Final decisions should always be
    checked with superiors.   7 6 5 4 3 2 1
73 It is best to give individuals the
    freedom to do things in their own
    way.   7 6 5 4 3 2 1
74 Good workers accept goals without
    question.   7 6 5 4 3 2 1
75 Strict management procedures
    build a tight ship.   7 6 5 4 3 2 1
76 Superiors should never be
    challenged.   7 6 5 4 3 2 1
77 Giving workers a major say in how
    they do their jobs improves
    performance.   7 6 5 4 3 2 1 [   ] (AU)

2 Self-expression orientation

78 Always question others' decisions. 7 6 5 4 3 2 1
79 Be spontaneous.   7 6 5 4 3 2 1
80 Always try to improve your
    understanding of your job.   7 6 5 4 3 2 1
81 Employees should be helped to
    realize their full potential.   7 6 5 4 3 2 1
82 Workers should be encouraged to
    be enthusiastic about their work.   7 6 5 4 3 2 1
83 Order and discipline are essential
    to business success.   7 6 5 4 3 2 1
84 Workers would normally do best to
    concentrate on the jobs they are
    given.   7 6 5 4 3 2 1 [   ] (SE)

3 Diversity orientation

85 Employees should concentrate on
    mastering just a few clearly-defined
    duties and responsibilities.   7 6 5 4 3 2 1
86 Job variety builds a happy
    work-force.   7 6 5 4 3 2 1
87 Employees can benefit their
    organization by trying different jobs. 7 6 5 4 3 2 1
88 Workers work best if they are given
    different things to do.   7 6 5 4 3 2 1
89 It is essential that work is
    interesting.   7 6 5 4 3 2 1 [   ] (D)

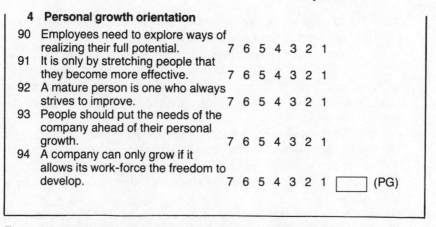

4   Personal growth orientation

90 Employees need to explore ways of realizing their full potential.   7 6 5 4 3 2 1

91 It is only by stretching people that they become more effective.   7 6 5 4 3 2 1

92 A mature person is one who always strives to improve.   7 6 5 4 3 2 1

93 People should put the needs of the company ahead of their personal growth.   7 6 5 4 3 2 1

94 A company can only grow if it allows its work-force the freedom to develop.   7 6 5 4 3 2 1   (PG)

Figure 3.2 Furnham and Gunter's corporate culture questionnaire

Some indication of the usefulness of these measures may be examined by looking at studies which have used them. Consider two studies using Cooke and Lafferty's organizational culture inventory. The inventory was not designed to sample domains of interpersonal and task-related styles that might be promoted by an organization, nor exhaustively to tap the variety of socially derived cognitions that constitute culture. Instead, it is intended to enable respondents to clarify their own experiences of their organization's culture with respect to these specific styles, to compare their perceptions to the aggregated perceptions of co-workers, and to understand how their own thinking styles might be affected by organizational norms.

The twelve types are set out below:

1 A *humanistic-helpful culture* characterizes organizations that are managed in a participative and person-centred way. Members are expected to be supportive, constructive, and open to influence in their dealings with one another. (Helping others to grow and develop; taking time with people.)

2 An *affiliative culture* characterizes organizations that place a high priority on constructive interpersonal relationships. Members are expected to be friendly, open, and sensitive to the satisfaction of their work group. (Dealing with others in a friendly way; sharing feelings and thoughts.)

3 An *approval culture* describes organizations in which conflicts are avoided and interpersonal relationships are pleasant – at least superficially. Members feel that they should agree with, gain the approval of, and be liked by others. (Making sure people accept you; 'going along' with others.)

4 A *conventional culture* is descriptive of organizations that are conservative, traditional, and bureaucratically controlled. Members are

expected to conform, follow the rules, and make a good impression. (Always following policies and practices; 'fitting into the mould'.)

5 A *dependent culture* is descriptive of organizations that are hierarchically controlled and non-participative. Centralized decision-making in such organizations leads members to do only what they are told and to clear decisions with superiors. (Pleasing those in positions of authority; doing what is expected.)

6 An *avoidance culture* characterizes organizations that fail to reward success but nevertheless punish mistakes. This negative reward system leads members to shift responsibilities to others to avoid any possibility of being blamed for a mistake. (Waiting for others to act first; taking few chances.)

7 An *oppositional culture* describes organizations in which confrontation prevails and negativism is rewarded. Members gain status and influence by being critical, and thus are reinforced to oppose the ideas of others and to make safe (but ineffectual) decisions. (Pointing out flaws; being hard to impress.)

8 A *power culture* is descriptive of non-participative organizations structured on the basis of the authority inherent in members' positions. Members believe they will be rewarded for taking charge, controlling subordinates and, at the same time, being responsive to the demands of superiors. (Building upon one's power base; motivating others in any way necessary.)

9 A *competitive culture* is one in which winning is valued and members are rewarded for outperforming one another. People in such organizations operate in a 'win-lose' framework and believe they must work against (rather than with) their peers to be noticed. (Turning the job into a contest; never appearing to lose.)

10 A *competence/perfectionistic culture* characterizes organizations in which perfectionism, persistence, and hard work are valued. Members feel they must avoid all mistakes, keep track of everything, and work long hours to attain narrowly-defined objectives. (Doing things perfectly; keeping on top of everything.)

11 An *achievement culture* characterizes organizations that do things well and value members who set and accomplish their own goals. Members of these organizations set challenging but realistic goals, establish plans to reach these goals, and pursue them with enthusiasm. (Pursuing a standard of excellence; openly showing enthusiasm.)

12 A *self-actualization culture* characterizes organizations that value creativity, quality over quantity, and both task accomplishment, and individual growth. Members of these organizations are encouraged to gain enjoyment from their work, develop themselves, and take on new and interesting activities. (Thinking in unique and independent ways; doing even simple tasks well.)

A London consultancy, Sheppard and Maslow, have usefully attempted to translate the organizational messages and results of the different corporate cultures (Figure 3.3).

1 Helpful

Messages	*Outcomes*
We value you as a person.	High satisfaction
Be supportive and helpful to others.	Low staff turnover
We welcome your ideas and	Involvement in problem-solving
suggestions.	Positive relations with clients
Take time with people.	Pride in service/products
We support your training,	
development and career planning.	
Participate in decision-making.	

2 Affiliative

Messages	*Outcomes*
Treat one another in a friendly way.	Excellent communication
Openly sharing information,	Positive feelings about organization
opinions, feelings.	May be too little emphasis on
Communication channels are open.	productivity
People are more important than	Co-operation
things.	
Co-operate.	
Be constructive in relationships.	

3 Approval

Messages	*Outcomes*
Please others.	Superficially pleasant climate
Be positive.	Quiet frustration
Don't point out problems.	Quick responses to requests and
Acceptability, not quality of	demands
decisions and goals.	Long-term goals, priorities driven out
Submerge your differences.	of sight.
Watch out how your job impacts on	Not working to full capacity
other people.	Live with problems
	Appearance of smooth running

4 Conventional

Messages	*Outcomes*
Conform.	Dissatisfaction
Follow the rules and procedures.	Comfort for some
Maintain the status quo.	Rules get in the way of the job
Don't rock the boat.	In the way of customer satisfaction
Avoid risks and conflicts.	Problems when work or methods
	become outdated

5 Dependent

Messages	*Outcomes*
Do only what you are told.	Absenteeism and turnover
Clear all decisions with superiors.	Strain from having to behave

Only share info with subordinates
on a 'need-to-know' basis.
Don't think of yourself.
Don't take the initiative

differently from personal style
Resistance to change
Can't respond to non-routine
problems

NB Where there are complex interdependencies, dependent norms are
fine but must be complemented with satisfaction styles for maximum
co-ordination; adaptation; satisfaction.

6 Avoidance

Messages
You'll be punished for mistakes.
Be reliable and consistent.
Your errors will be noticed.
Don't take risks.
Don't expect rewards for success.
Don't try to change things.

Outcomes
Managers abdicate, procrastinate,
and don't delegate
Low motivation
Lack of planning
People pass the buck
Low ambition
Conflicting orders
People don't know what is expected
of them

7 Oppositional

Messages
Confront and criticize others' ideas.
Point out people's weaknesses.
Question what people say.
Look for problems and mistakes.

Outcomes
Conflicting orders from above
Adversarial relationships
Low co-operation
Low interpersonal support

NB May be created inadvertently by getting sub-units to compete for
resources/failure to integrate their goals/improper co-ordination.

8 Power

Messages
Be loyal.
Be hard and tough.
Build up your power base.
Control others.
Do what the boss says.
Don't question authority.

Outcomes
Rigid control
Limits on upward communication
Rigid structure
Reduced willingness to subordinates
Tension
All levels give orders
Inconsistent messages

9 Competitive

Messages
Outperform your peers.
Be a winner.
Compete not co-operate.
The job is a contest.

Outcomes
Unrealistic standards
Inconsistent demands
Frustration
Inconsistent quality

10 Perfectionistic

Messages
Monitor everything.
Work hard.

Outcomes
Impossible standards
Appearance of efficiency

Never make a mistake. Be persistent. Keep things organized. Attend to detail. Prove your competence.	Extra-long hours Personal and family life suffers Hard work but not fulfilling potential
11 Achievement *Messages* Enjoy your work. Take on new, interesting activities. Innovate. Develop yourself. Be positive. This whole task is yours. Your work has important impact.	*Outcomes* High satisfaction Attractive to quality recruits Low staff turnover Truly democratic teamwork Adaptive to change We can rely on each other

Figure 3.3 Sheppard and Maslow's corporate culture inventory

Four factors characterize a team-oriented, satisfaction-oriented culture:

- **Achievement** Members set challenging but realistic goals, establish plans to reach these goals, and pursue them with enthusiasm.
- **Self-expression** Members value creativity; quality over quantity, and individual growth.
- **Humanistic/helpful** Members are supportive and constructive, participative, and open to influence in their dealings with one another.
- **Affiliative** Members place a high priority on constructive interpersonal relationships; are friendly, open, and sensitive to the satisfaction of their work group.

Research by Cooke and Rousseau (1988) indicates that organizations characterized by chief executives as excellent or ideal (i.e., for implementing successful organizational strategies), take the form of satisfaction cultures. Security-oriented cultures involve the use of organizational sanctions to promote particular behaviour patterns, and often are more behaviour-inhibiting (e.g., risk-avoiding), in contrast to satisfaction cultures which tend to be behaviour-amplifying (e.g., risk-seeking). Cooke and Rousseau (1988) found that the security-oriented styles fall into two empirical groupings: People/Security and Task/Security.

People/Security

Beliefs are characterized focusing on control in interpersonal relations, under the following four dimensions:

- **Approval** Conflict is avoided and interpersonal relationships are superficially pleasant. Members believe they agree with, gain the approval of, and are liked by others.

- **Conventional** Conservative, traditional, and bureaucratically controlled. Members believe they must conform, follow the rules, and make a good impression.
- **Dependent** Hierarchically controlled and non-participative. Decision-making is centralized, and members believe they must do as they are told, clearing all decisions with their superiors.
- **Avoidance** Emphasis is on punishment of mistakes, not rewards for success. Negative reward systems lead to shifting responsibilities to others and avoiding any possibility of being blamed for a mistake.

Task/Security

Beliefs are characterized focusing on control in task-related activities:

- **Oppositional** Confrontation prevails and negativism is rewarded. Members gain status and influence by being critical and opposing the ideas of others.
- **Power** Descriptive of non-participative organizations structured on the basis of hierarchy and position authority. Members are rewarded for taking charge, controlling subordinates, and being responsive to their own superiors.
- **Competitive** Winning is valued and members are rewarded for outperforming one another. Members operate in a win-lose framework and believe they must work against (rather than with) their peers to be noticed.
- **Perfectionistic** Perfectionism, persistence, and hard work are valued. Members believe they must avoid all mistakes, keep track of every detail, and work long hours to attain narrowly defined objectives.

Cooke and Rousseau (1988) showed clear evidence that there was agreement within the organizations, significant differences across organizations, and that subculture differences occur across hierarchy levels. They were able to draw up the profile of an excellent organization, one with security-oriented norms, and an 'ideal' culture profile. This scored high on satisfaction styles and low on people and task/security styles.

In another study Rousseau (1990) was able to show them that certain cultural norms were actually related to actual performance on the job, as well as employees' perception of role clarity, role conflict, overall satisfaction, and propensity to stay in the organization. Earlier Rousseau (1989) examined security-oriented cultures in great detail and found these 'high rehability' organizations to have strong norms that support hierarchical referral, avoid conflict, and tend to be behaviour inhibiting and associated with employee dissatisfaction and role conflict.

CONCLUSION

The corporate culture concept, issue, and debate is here with us for some time to come. While it will no doubt lose its popular appeal as it gets replaced by yet another 'solution' to all management problems, it has uncovered enough of a hornets' nest among academics from different disciplines and epistemological perspectives to fuel argument and research for many years to come.

Just as there is no shortage of definitions of culture, so there has been a sudden increase in measures that attempt to ascertain corporate culture. Certainly the majority of these new organometric measures tap into similar dimensions, but it remains unclear as to whether they are able to describe all the many features of culture in all companies.

4   Corporate Climate

INTRODUCTION

Administrators or managers are well aware that actual *atmospheric* climate (i.e. the weather) can, and does, greatly affect their organizations. Many organizations have been either partially or totally destroyed by climatic disturbances such as storm and flood. *Organizational* climate also affects organizations and can be potentially just as devastating to their survival as atmospheric climate. However, the two climates do not affect the same resources of the organization. Whereas atmospheric climate acts primarily upon the *physical* resources of the organization, organizational climate acts upon the *human resources* (the personnel) of the organization.

People problems have always been, and probably always will be, the most difficult and time-consuming problems with which administrators or managers must deal. To cope with personnel problems that they face almost daily, it is helpful for managers to understand the perceptions which employees hold of different aspects of the organization. Managers should have as much knowledge as possible of the factors that significantly influence the behaviour of the people in their organization. One such factor, or set of factors, with which they should be familiar is organizational climate – the psychological atmosphere of all departments and sections in an organization.

Organizational psychologists have become increasingly interested in organizational climate because of the significant relationships exhibited between this construct and job satisfaction and job performance. In fact, the concept of organizational climate is now well established in the management literature: it has been around for over thirty years, and well over a dozen reviews of research in this field have appeared. An organization's climate can be made manifest through appropriate corporate audits which collate the individual views of an organization's employees to produce a perceptual profile of the organization. As interest in organizational climate has grown, a number of definitions have appeared in the literature over the last few years which are discussed in the next section.

As we will see, one view of organizational climate envisages it as a feature of the organization that people, regardless of where they work, experience daily. Furthermore, this type of 'psychological' climate has just as vital an impact on individuals in the work-place as does the atmospheric climate in respect of people's general moods and activity. In fact, organizational climate may prove to be one of the primary factors in job satisfaction and job performance in organizations. According to some writers it is a moderator variable between the structure and process in an organization and major employee outputs. In essence, this implies that the structure of the organization and the daily procedures and processes influence and establish a climate which, in turn, affects performance and employee satisfaction. Climate here is seen as a moderator variable.

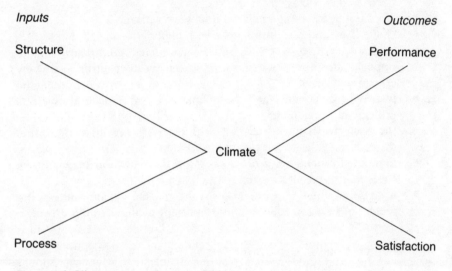

Figure 4.1 Climate as a moderate variable

The creation of a healthy, motivating organizational climate is mainly the result of leadership behaviour and style. For many years, however, the establishment of a desirable climate was a hit-or-miss matter. Nobody could be sure what led to climate change, or indeed, resistance to change, and nobody could get a clear enough understanding of the 'atmosphere' of an organization to be able to trace changes in it. The internal climate of an organization encompasses the nature of the organization's communications networks, reward systems, leadership style, goal-setting techniques, and other factors. In asking about an organization's climate, we are really asking how effective that organization is in mobilizing its human resources. Climate is the focus of a complex set of forces within an organization which impinge upon those who work in it. A knowledge of climate variables enables management to harness those forces toward the accomplishment of organization goals.

Mullins (1989) has argued that:

A healthy organizational climate might be expected to exhibit such characteristic features as;

- the integration of organizational goals and personal goals:
- a flexible structure with a network of authority, control and communications, and with autonomy for individual members;
- styles of leadership appropriate to particular work situations;
- mutual trust, consideration and support among different levels of the organization;
- recognition of individual differences and attributes, and of people's needs and expectations at work;
- attention to job design and the quality of working life;
- challenging and responsible jobs with high performance standards;
- equitable systems of reward based on positive reinforcement;
- opportunities for personal development, career progression and advancement;
- justice in treatment, and fair personnel and industrial relations policies and practices;
- the open discussion of conflict, with emphasis on the settlement of differences without delay or confrontation;
- democratic functioning of the organization with full opportunities for genuine consultation and participation;
- a sense of identity with, and loyalty to, the organization and a feeling of being needed and an important member of the organization.

In addition to arrangements for carrying out organizational processes and the execution of work, management has a responsibility for creating an organization climate in which people are motivated to work willingly and effectively. If organizational climate is to be improved, then attention should be given to the above features.'

(pp. 489–90)

HISTORY AND DEFINITION

The term 'organizational climate' began to achieve popularity in the late 1960s. Taguiri (1968) notes various synonyms of the term, such as 'atmosphere', 'conditions', 'culture', and 'ecology'. Some writers have attempted a formal definition of the term. Gilmer (1966) writes:

By organizational climate we mean those characteristics that distinguish the organization from other organizations and that influence the behaviour of people in the organization....

It is, in effect, what we react to ... the context of stimulation and confusion where we work.... Climate affects not only the behaviour of individuals but also how organizations themselves interact.

(p. 57)

Such definitions stress the essence, the core of the organization as an organism, perceptible by insiders, but also relevant to outsiders. Climate, however, should refer to the quality of the organization's *internal* environment, especially as experienced by the *insider*.

Forehand and von Gilmer (1964) offered a more exhaustive definition that goes beyond the idea that the beholder of the climate is a member of the organization. Organizational climate, they state, is 'the set of characteristics that describe an organization and that (a) distinguish the organization from other organizations, (b) are relatively enduring over time, and (c) influence the behaviour of people in the organization.' (p. 362) Forehand and von Gilmer chose these defining properties 'in the effort to focus discussion upon features of organizational variation that are amenable to specification, measurement, and incorporation into empirical research' (p. 362).

Taguiri (1968), however, has complained that this definition still gives excessive attention to the organization as a whole and places insufficient emphasis on the perceptions of the individual members of the organization. He preferred to lay greater stress on the idea that organizational climate suggested that the environment is interpreted by the members of the organization to have a certain quality to which they are sensitive and which, in turn, affects their attitudes and motivation. He notes that Forehand and von Gilmer's (1964) definition also insufficiently distinguishes, in the phrase 'the set of characteristics', between the *attributes* or variables that are used to describe the organization, and the *value* of these attributes. Accordingly he would rather define it as follows:

Organizational climate is a relatively enduring quality of the internal environment of an organization that (a) is experienced by its members, (b) influences their behaviour, and (c) can be described in terms of the values of a particular set of characteristics (or attributes) of the organization.

Taguiri (1968) believed 'it was difficult to give a general, formal definition that is not trivial or nearly useless because it encompasses too much.' It is possible, however, to delimit the concept in many ways by arbitrarily ascribing to it certain attributes, chosen from the many that seem to have been assumed as its properties in the various uses we have examined.

- Climate is a molar, synthetic concept (like personality).
- Climate is a *particular* configuration of situational variables.
- Its component elements may vary, however, while the climate may remain the same.
- It is the *meaning* of an enduring situational configuration.
- Climate has a connotation of continuity, but is not as lasting as culture.

- Climate is determined importantly by characteristics, conduct, attitudes, expectations of other persons, by sociological and cultural realities.
- Climate is phenomenologically external to the actor, who may, however, feel that he contributes to its nature.
- Climate is phenomenologically distinct from the task for both observer and actor.
- It is in the actor's or observer's head, though not necessarily in a conscious form, but it is based on characteristics of external reality.
- It is capable of being shared (as consensus) by several persons in the situation, and it is interpreted in terms of shared meanings (with some individual variation around a consensus).
- It cannot be a common delusion, since it must be veridically based on external reality.
- It may or may not be capable of description in words, although it may be capable of specification in terms of response.
- It has *potential* behavioural consequences.
- It is an indirect determinant of behaviour, in that it acts upon attitudes, expectations, and states of arousal which are direct determinants of behaviour.

As early as 1960, Gellerman saw the climate as the 'personality' of organizations. Gellerman (1960) listed five steps for analysing the character of a company. First, identify the people in the organization whose attitudes count. Second, study these individuals and determine their goals, tactics, and blind spots. Third, analyse the economic challenges facing the company in terms of policy decisions. Fourth, review the company history, giving particular attention to the careers of its leaders. Fifth, integrate the total picture with the aim of extracting common denominators instead of adding up all the parts to get a sum.

Von Haller, Gilmer and Deci (1977) recognized the usefulness of describing companies in terms of human personalities. Hence they talked of Upward Mobiles; Indifferent, Ambivalent. They believed that climate like culture, can be ascertained from small as well as big things: the office memo, the company logo, etc.

Attempting to define or operationalize the concept, many researchers quote Forehand and von Gilmer (1964) whose definition of climate referred to its ability to distinguish between organizations, to be enduring over time, and to influence employees' behaviour in organizations, as noted above. However, the concept proved ambiguous, nebulous, and controversial. The main problems in the conceptual clarification concerned whether climate should be conceived in terms of the objective (physical or structural) features of the organization, or the subjective (perceptual) reaction to the organization. Hence, Guion (1973) argued that a perceived climate concerned both the attributes of an organization and those of the perceiving individual, and that as most often conceived, climate was simply an alternative label for affective responses to an organization, like job satisfaction. James and Jones (1974) suggested the term 'psychological climate' be used to emphasize the fact that it is the aggregated cognitive interpretations of an organizational work-force which arise from

Table 4.1 Climate definition chronology

Forehand and von Gilmer (1964)	Characteristics that (1) distinguish one organization from another, (2) endure over time, and (3) influence the behaviour of people in organizations. The personality of the organization.
Findlater and Margulies (1969)	Perceived organizational properties intervening between organizational characteristics and behaviour.
Campbell *et al.* (1970)	A set of attitudes and expectancies describing the organization's static characteristics, and behaviour–outcome and outcome–outcome contingencies.
Schneider and Hall (1972)	Individual perceptions of their organizations affected by characteristics of the organization and the individual.
James and Jones (1974)	Psychologically meaningful cognitive representations of the situation; perceptions.
Schneider (1975)	Perceptions or interpretations of meaning which help individuals make sense of the world and know how to behave.
Payne, Fineman and Wall (1976)	Consensus of individuals' descriptions of the organization.
James *et al.* (1978)	Sum of members' perceptions about the organization.
Litwin and Stringer (1978)	A psychological process intervening between organizational characteristics and behaviour.
Joyce and Slocum (1979)	Climates are (1) perceptual, (2) psychological, (3) abstract, (4) descriptive, (5) not evaluative, and (6) not actions.
James and Sell (1981)	Individuals' cognitive representation of proximal environments ... expressed in terms of psychological meaning and significance to the individual ... an attribute of the individual, which is learned, historical and resistant to change.
Schneider and Reichers (1983)	An assessed molar perception or an inference researchers make based on more particular perceptions.
Glick (1985)	('Organizational climate') – a generic term for a broad class of organizational, rather than psychological, variables that describe the context for an individual's actions.

Source: Rousseau (1988). Reproduced by permission of publisher.

experience in the organization, and provide a representation of the meaning inherent in the organizational features, events, and processes (Schneider, 1983a, 1983b; Kozlowski and Farr, 1988).

Rousseau (1988) has provided a useful chronology of climate definitions that enables one to compare and contrast different conceptions.

Rousseau notes:

The lack of boundaries differentiating what climate is, from what it is not is troublesome – and may in fact be 'suppressing' research on climate by causing researchers to focus on either specific perceptions of context exclusively (eschewing any mention of the climate concept as in the case of motivation and leadership research) or to reject its relevance to the study of organization.

None the less, climate as a concept clearly does have specific boundaries that differentiate it from both other characteristics and other perceptions. Two consistent defining attributes of climate persist through its various conceptualizations: it is a perception and it is descriptive. Perceptions are sensations or realizations experienced by an individual. Descriptions are a person's reports of these sensations. Whether individual differences or situational factors explain large or minute amounts of variance in these descriptions varies from one notion of climate to the next, and is more an empirical than a definitional one....

It is in the distinctions between different types of *beliefs* where the nature and operation of climate can perhaps be best understood. Beliefs are the result of an individual's attempt to make sense of a set of stimuli, a situation, or patterns of interactions between people. There are cognitions, the result of information processing, but beliefs are more than perceptions *per se* (such as sights and sounds). In a sense, perceptions are simply informational cues that are registered or received. Beliefs are the result of active cognitive processing.... Initiated by perceptions, beliefs result from the interpretation and organization of perceptions into an understanding of the relationship between objects, properties and/or ideas. Self-report measures of molar constructs such as climate involve interpretation....

(p. 142)

An important but related issue concerns the amount of consensus within an organization concerning the perceived climate. Pace and Stern (1958) suggested a two-thirds agreement, but Guion (1973) has argued that agreement should be 90 per cent for the concept of climate to be invoked. Payne (1990) has argued that the concept of organizational climate is invalid, because people in different parts of the organization have radically different perceptions of the organization (hence, the perception is not shared) and that where perceptions are consensually shared, only in small groups, they are not representative of the climate of the whole organization. Thus, for Payne (1990) it is possible to have departmental but not organizational climates.

This conceptual muddle has become worse with the introduction of the concept of corporate or organizational culture which Schein (1990) defined as:

(a) a pattern of basic assumptions, (b) invented, discovered, or developed by a given group, (c) as it learns to cope with its problems of external adaption and internal integration, (d) to be taught to new members as the correct ways to perceive, think, and feel in relation to those problems.

(p. 111)

Yet as we saw in Chapter 3, the definition of corporate culture is equally unclear.

There are as many, if not more, problems associated with the concept of corporate culture as there are with corporate climate. One way to circumvent, rather than overcome, the conceptual issues, is to talk of *employee perceptions*, rather than of culture or climate. Naturally, employee perceptions differ within an organization as a function of seniority, department, and so forth, and those perceptions influence, and are influenced by organizational behaviours. But because the term 'climate' has been used in the past, it shall be returned to here to examine the current literature.

The second major theoretical problem concerns the effect of climate (or employee perception) on organizational behaviour. Climate may be conceived of as an independent, dependent, moderator, or epiphenomenal variable. If climate is conceived of as an independent variable, as for instance in the work of Campbell *et al.* (1970), it is assumed that organizational climate itself directly influences (causes) various work outcomes which can be both positive, like productivity, satisfaction and motivation, and negative, like absenteeism, turnover and accidents. Others have considered climate as a dependent, outcome variable that is the result, and not the cause, of organizational structure and processes. In this sense, climate may be a useful index of an organization's health, but not a causative factor of it. A third and perhaps more common approach has been to see climate as a moderator variable, in that climate may be the indirect link between two organizational outcomes. Thus, climate may be the moderator variable between job satisfaction and productivity. Various untested but heuristically satisfying models consider climate as one of a number of powerful moderator variables (Litwin and Stringer, 1968). Finally, some researchers believe that climate is epiphenomenal, neither a direct cause nor an effect variable, but one that emerges in some form in all organizations, while having no influence on the organization itself. It therefore consists of employee perceptions which, although interesting, are not directly relevant to the functioning of the organization.

There are many models which use the concept of climate (Litwin and Stringer, 1968; Bonoma and Zaltman, 1981) but very few specify the exact relationship between climate and other organizational processes or products. Few theorists or researchers have acknowledged that climate may be *both* an independent and a dependent variable, simultaneously. Few studies have tested any longitudinal path-analytic models, to find out what major factors influence climate and which are influenced by it. Yet this would seem to be a potentially important and relevant theoretical and empirical avenue to pursue.

THE PERCEPTUAL NATURE OF CLIMATE

In asking about an organization's climate, we are really asking how effectively that organization is mobilizing its human resources. A knowledge of climate variables enables management to harness those forces toward the accomplishment of organizational goals.

The emphasis on the perceptual nature of organizational climate raised several questions which Campbell *et al.* (1970) considered relevant. A major issue concerned the importance of the *actual* situation versus the *perceived* situation in determining behaviour and attitudes in organizations. A second question concerned relationships between *objective* and *perceptual* factors, especially in terms of determinants and accuracy of such perceptions.

In an attempt to answer these questions, Campbell *et al.* (1970) postulated that different levels of situational and individual variation operated at different levels of explanation. This notion was based on Indik's (1965) linkage model which stated that the linkage between an objective, independent organization variable (participation in an organization) is mediated by two sets of processes, namely, the organization processes related to size (e.g., amount of communication, task specialization) and the psychological processes of the members (e.g., felt attraction, satisfaction with performance). Organizational climate was viewed as a situationally-determined psychological process, in which organizational climate variables were considered to be either causative or moderator factors for performance and attitudes.

Campbell and Beatty (1971) defined organizational climate as a 'summary variable intended to represent ... perceptual filtering, structuring, and description of numerous stimuli, impinging on an employee from the domain we so casually refer to as "the situation"' (p. 1) Organizational climate was considered a perceptual measure that described the organization and was different from attitudinal, evaluation, and need satisfaction variables. Moreover, perceptions of organizational climate were thought to influence the valences attached to certain outcomes, the instrumentalities for these outcomes, and expectations for various strategies to achieve these outcomes.

It seems that the reliance on perceptual measurement may be interpreted as meaning that organizational climate includes not only descriptions of situational characteristics, but also individual differences in perception and attitudes. This is somewhat confusing, since the use of perceptual measurement introduces variance which is a function of difference between individuals and is not necessarily descriptive of organizations or situations. Therefore, the accuracy and/or consensus of perception must be verified if accumulated perceptual organizational climate measures are used to describe organizational attributes (Guion, 1973).

Johannesson (1973) addressed the question of accuracy and/or consensus of perception when he investigated relationships between perceptually measured organizational climate and variables from the job attitude literature. Results of his study demonstrated that 'by and large, organizational climate as measured in this study failed to add new or different variance to commonly identified satisfaction factors' (p. 141).

The relationship between perceived organizational climate and job attitudes found by Johannesson has been seen as indicating that perceived organizational climate is more a function of individual attributes than of organizational attributes (Guion, 1973). However, it may also be the case that both perceived organizational climate and job attitudes *covary* because of similar differences in situations, and that ascertaining only the relationships between organizational climate and job attitudes may lead to erroneous conclusions. Herman and Hulin (1972) demonstrated that differences in job attitude measures (satisfaction and some perceived environment items) were more directly accounted for by organizational structural groupings than by individual characteristics, although the number of individual characteristic variables was quite limited (e.g., age, tenure, and education). These studies demonstrated that the degree to which perceived climate is based upon individual differences in job attitudes (or vice versa) rather than differences in individuals' perceptions of situations requires additional empirical validation of the accuracy and/ or consensus of the organizational climate data.

The uniqueness of the variables and/or constructs underlying perceived organizational climate has been questioned from another standpoint. House and Rizzo (1972) compared scores on nineteen items from the Organization Description Questionnaire which is designed to measure organizational climate, with two role theory scores (role ambiguity and role conflict), a satisfaction score, and five leadership scores (initiating structure, tolerance of freedom, consideration, production emphasis, and predictive accuracy). Using an adaptation of the multitrait-multimethod matrix, they concluded that many Organization Description Questionnaire climate scores measured the same constructs as the role, satisfaction, and leadership scores:

The review of the perceptual measurement–organizational attribute approach has raised a number of conceptual and empirical points. First, if perceived organizational climate is to be used to measure an organizational attribute, the accuracy of the perception should be stressed. The question of accuracy would appear to require multiple sources of situational measurement for validation purposes. Moreover, the question of consensus of agreement among perceivers is also major. The requirement for purely perceptual measurement does not permit a differentiation between such diverse but importantly different situations as: (a) inconsistent or capricious leader behaviour, (b) leader behaviour adapted to individual needs, (c) differences in perception caused by perceivers having different opportunities to observe leader behaviour, (d) differences in perception related only to individual characteristics, and (e) instrument error. Thus, it must again be stated that different sources of measurement of organizational climate are needed, thereby appearing to negate the requirement or stipulation for purely perceptual measurement. Second, if organizational climate is seen as encompassing some situational variables such as leadership, autonomy, and formalization, but not other situational variables such as size, shape, and span of control, the criterion for differentiation is not at all clear. Level of explanation is not a viable criterion because measures such as formalization are organizational in the same sense as size, shape, and so on.

Of additional concern is the possibility that the perceptual measurement–organizational attribute approach may inherently include a logical inconsistency. On one hand it proposes to measure organizational attributes which have been shown to vary across levels of explanation (e.g., total organization, subsystem and group; or from a related standpoint, causal and process variables), while on the other hand it is considered a psychological process which operates at a level of explanation separate from objective organizational characteristics and organizational processes. This seems to confound stimulus conditions while perceptually measured organizational climate represents a set of responses to the organizational characteristics and processes. The psychological process level of explanation places emphasis on the characteristics of responses, namely individual differences which may or may not be congruent with stimulus conditions. Thus, it appears inconsistent to require the same set of organizational climate data to be accurate measures of organizational stimuli and simultaneously to be representative of the response-oriented psychological process level of explanation.

(p. 173)

DIFFERENT TYPES OF CLIMATE

The conceptual issue of the extent to which climate perceptions have to be consensually held to warrant the definition of climate, has led some writers to solve the problem by specifying or defining different types of climate. Rousseau (1988) has conceptually differentiated between four types.

Psychological climate   This is essentially unaggregated individual percep-tions of environments: how individuals organize their experience of the environment. Individual differences play a substantial role in creating these perceptions, as do the immediate or proximal environments in which the individual is an active agent. Psychological climate is shaped by factors including individual thinking styles, personality, cognitive processes, structure, culture, and social interactions. These perceptions need not agree with those of other individuals in the same environment to be meaningful, since: (a) an individual's proximal environment may be unique (e.g., when only one person does a particular job); and (b) individual differences play a substantial role in these perceptions.

As Rousseau notes, the major problem with this definition is how to differentiate cognitive style from climate perceptions. In other words, is self-reported climate more a function of the individual's personality and cognitive structures than of the actual organization itself? For instance, do neurotics always perceive the organization as threatening, irrespective of the actual threats present?

Aggregate climate   This is individual perceptions averaged at some formal hierarchical level (e.g., work group, department, division, plant, sector, organization). Aggregated climates are constructed, based on membership of individuals in some identifiable unit of the formal (or informal) organization and within-unit agreement or consensus in percepts. The rationale behind aggregating individual data to a unit level is the *a priori* assumption that certain organizational groups or collectivities have a climate and that these can be identified through tests of significant difference between units. One might also infer that this aggregation of individual perceptions is justified because perceptual agreement implies a shared meaning. However, no research to date has justified this assumed connection between aggregated perceptions and interpretation.

It is, of course, both an empirical question and an empirical task to aggregate individual perceptions. Consensus can be defined empirically (in terms of range, standard deviations, etc). But Rousseau (1988) notes that:

> Some questions persist: (1) Does aggregate climate explain responses that psychological climate does not? (2) Does it have surplus meaning beyond individual perceptions? (3) Are its relations with other variables

different from those of other climate types? If aggregated climate is a real unit-level phenomenon, individuals should have fewer discon-firming experiences and their interactions with other members should serve to shape and reinforce a common set of descriptors comparable to a social construction of reality. But since interaction among unit members is not considered a requirement for consensus, there need be no social or group dynamics underlying that consensus.

(p. 145)

Collective climates   These emerge from agreement between individuals regarding their perception of behavioural contexts. However, in contrast to aggregated climate, collective climates need not overlap formal units and are identified by taking the individual perceptions of situational factors and combining these into clusters reflecting similar climate scores. Personal and situational factors have been considered as predictors of cluster member-ship, but findings indicate that personal factors such as management and work experience, length of time in current post, and age, account for some clusters, while situational factors such as functional area, location and shift, account for others (Joyce and Slocum, 1987). In the case of collective (statistical cluster) climate, interactions are postulated to play a substantial role in determining shared perceptions, though their role has not been satisfactorily empirically assessed.

Organizational climate   The distinction current climate research seems to make between what is referred to as organization-level climate as opposed to organizational structure or other such constructs measurable through individual perceptions, is that climate reflects an insider's orientation, as opposed to an outsider's analytic categories. Climate and structure constructs thus respectively appear comparable to the insider and outsider orientations. Many constructs used by researchers to characterize organiza-tions reflect outsider orientations, e.g., structures (such as centralization and hierarchy) or processes (such as problem-solving mechanisms, maintenance, and strain amelioration); originating in theoretical frame-works rather than in the cognitive organization of individuals. However, organizational climate can be construed as a descriptor of organizational attributes expressed in terms characterizing individual experiences with the organization. This distribution means that climate assessment employs less abstracted descriptors of organizations from the informants' perspective. The great advantage of climate assessments over more discrete topical measures (e.g., leadership, rewards) is their summary quality. The summary quality does not mean that descriptions become more abstract, but rather that they are representations of how organizations feel to the people within them, or to those who must deal with them as vendors or customers.

THE CAUSES AND CONSEQUENCES OF CLIMATE

The antecedents of climate can, in principle, be specified, measured, and delineated. Indeed, various 'models' (discussed later) have been developed to explain which and how various factors interact to 'produce' climate.

There are many ways to categorize these factors:

- External forces: economic, market, political, social, technological.
- Organizational history: the culture, values, and behaviour patterns of the organization.
- Management: the organizational structure and leadership pattern.

Two kinds of influence of climate on individuals may be distinguished. First, there is *direct* influence, that affects all or almost all members of the company, or some sub-unit of it. The second kind of effect is termed *interactive* influence, which exists when a climate has a certain effect upon the behaviour of some people, a different effect on others, and possibly no effect at all on still others.

Certain behaviours never occur in some organizations, because the stimuli that would elicit them are never presented. Organizations themselves place constraints on people through rules and regulations, routine practices, instructions, taboos and explicit injunctions. It is not uncommon for the ambitious person to find him/herself in a climate that puts restraints upon freedom, thus narrowing alternatives of action. Out of it develop ways of behaving, ways of working, ways of loafing, ways of co-operating, and ways of resisting. Newcomers to an established subculture may rebuke the current job-holders as being cynical about the system, apparently unaware that there is good reason to be cynical. They may find to their embarrassment that hasty evaluation of people and established practices can backfire.

How do management programmes affect organizational climate? Moxnes and Eilertsen (1991) have pointed out that few researchers have examined the influence of training on organizational variables such as climate. They argue that just as climate variables facilitate and disrupt various training initiatives, so programmes can affect overall climate. Using a fifty-one-item questionnaire, they measured ten dimensions of climate, including enthusiasm and communication about personal problems. First they examined all employees who had or had not taken part in the training programme, but found few significant differences. Second, looking at two different years' results, it seemed management training had a small but specific effect on organizational climate. Curiously, participants in training programmes had a more negative perception of their work climate than non-participants on seven or eight of the ten climate indices. The authors offer three different explanations for these findings: the data reflect real changes in the working environment; the managers become more aware that the climate is bad – the scores thus reflect changes in participants' perceptions of organizational environment without any 'real' change; and participants use words ('conflict', 'trouble', 'criticism') in new and positive ways, having reconceptualized their environment: 'By giving supervisors a sense of dissatisfaction with their own performance and opening their eyes to the prevailing conflicts in their divisions, they should, according to change theory, become more motivated to perform well' (p. 409).

This paradoxical case has important implications for studies on climate because it points to three things:

1   Training programmes can and do affect organizational climate, which no doubt affects enthusiasm for training programmes.
2   Programmes which emphasize increased awareness may increase dissatisfaction and negative perceptions which may, or may not, have strong motivating effects.
3   Climate is relatively sensitive to training programmes.

Various researchers in the human resources and organizational psychology field have attempted to describe the effect or consequences of organizational climate. For instance, Gordon and Cummins (1979) argued that considerable research has showed that various 'climate' issues were clearly related to company profit. They listed thirteen:

1   The organization has clear goals.
2   The organization has defined plans to meet its goals.
3   The planning system is formal.
4   Planning is comprehensive.
5   Information for decision-making is available.
6   Information for decision-making is used.
7   Good lateral communications exist.
8   Overall communications are good.
9   Units understand each other's objectives.
10   Clear measures of managerial performance exist.
11   Managers are clear about the results expected of them.
12   Benefits are competitive.
13   Compensation is related to performance.

Thus they assert, with some supporting evidence, that if these structural and climatic features occur in an organization it is likely to be profitable. There is no shortage of models or theories explaining, or at least describing, how climate is both the cause and consequence of critical organizational factors. As we shall see there is little agreement between these models, and even less empirical evidence to support them. Campbell *et al.* (1970) describe the relationship the organizational climate has on an organization through the use of the diagram shown in Figure 4.2.

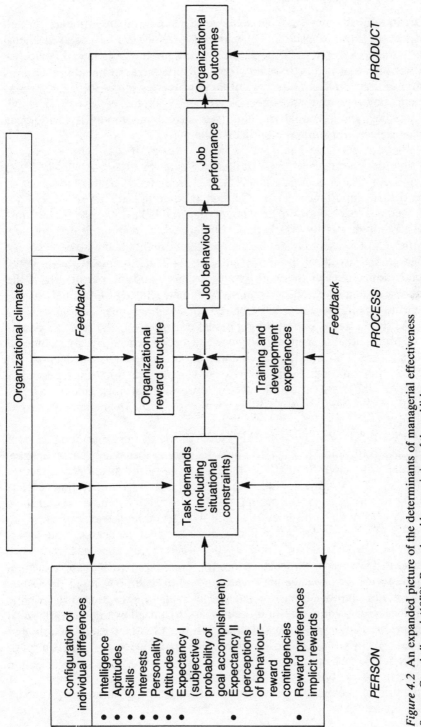

Figure 4.2 An expanded picture of the determinants of managerial effectiveness
Source: Campbell *et al.* (1970). Reproduced by permission of the publisher.

Organizational climate is depicted here as having an influence on *all* aspects of the organization. The manager is involved in all stages in Figure 4.2, from the person, through the process to the outcome. Managerial effectiveness, which is the ability to manage the organizational climate, will have a direct effect on all stages of these processes within the organization. Note, however, that the direction of nearly all the errors is 'one-way', suggesting unidirectional causality. Also, from this model it is not clear what causes or maintains a particular climate.

Researchers have been particularly interested in the behavioural and attitudinal correlates of organizational climate. Field and Abelson (1982) provide a clear model (see Figure 4.3). Three aspects of this model are of particular importance. First, there is the multiplicity of influences on individuals' perceptions of climate. Managerial behaviour may be the most significant means by which these influences are communicated to individual employees, but it is still only one determinant of climate perceptions. The second aspect of the model in Figure 4.3 that merits attention is the moderating effect of the work group, the task, and the personality of the individual employee on perceptions of climate. Finally, individual characteristics modify responses to perceived climate in a similar fashion.

As shown at the bottom of the model in Figure 4.3, the three responses to a work situation generally believed to be influenced by organizational climate are motivation, performance, and reported job satisfaction. Of these three, the relationship between climate and job satisfaction has received the most attention. Note, however, that this model has few feedback loops nor does it explain whether organizational climate is shared or stable.

Bonoma and Zaltman's (1981) model shows that organizational climate has a strong and direct effect on managerial behaviour, as managers interact with subordinates. This interaction, in turn, has a direct effect on peer leadership, affecting such group processes as co-operation, enthusiasm for doing a good job, and sharing information. These relationships are shown by the solid lines in Figure 4.4. The dotted lines represent the indirect effects of organizational climate on peer leadership and group processes, that is, effects that do not operate through managerial behaviour. Having developed their model, Bonoma and Zaltman discuss its implications for investigating organizational problem solving. This discussion is not empirically based, but it does help to strengthen the case for further research into the influence of an organization's climate on work behaviour as well as on job satisfaction. It represents a path model, though precisely why certain facets or dimensions are included and others are not is not fully explained.

Perhaps the best-known and most influential model of the role of organizational climate in business performance is the Burke-Litwin model (see Figure 4.5).

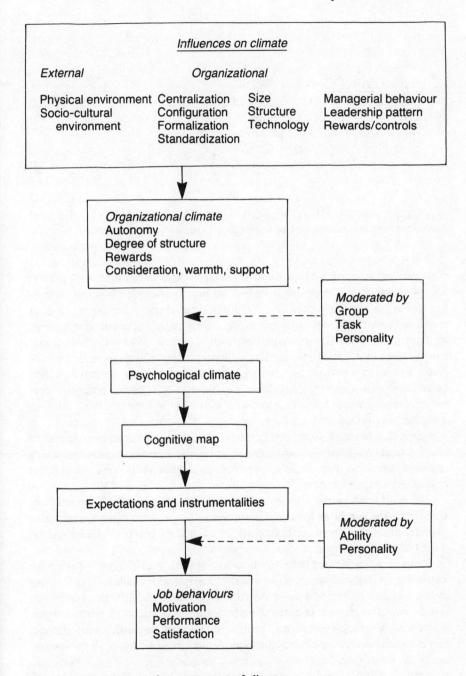

Figure 4.3 The causes and consequences of climate
Source: Field and Abelson (1982). Reproduced by permission of the publisher.

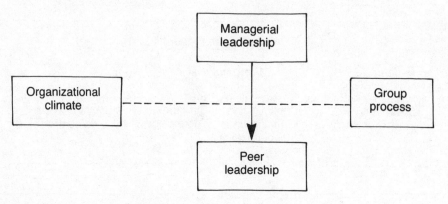

Figure 4.4 The indirect effects of climate
Source: Bonoma and Zaltman (1981). Reproduced by permission of the publisher.

This model suggests that external social, political, economic, and market forces shape or determine not only who becomes leader but the style of leadership in any organization. As well as developing the organization's mission and strategy, and influencing its culture, leaders sanction, promote, and prescribe a host of management practices that determine how things are done in the organization. These management practices relate to the structures and systems in the organization which are formal, explicit structures that support particular practices. It is these practices that determine the work unit climate. Note here that it is 'work unit' climate, and not organizational climate, which is the focus of attention. It is assumed that because some management practices might not be inherent or consistent throughout the organization, it will be work unit climates, which are dependent on them, that are influenced, rather than some managerial organization-wide climate.

The work unit climate, in turn, affects the motivation of all members of that unit, which relates logically to its output, be it personal motivation or production. Thus, through its operations at different levels, climate can be a central facet of organizational functioning.

Though it is not clear precisely how one would test this model (although Lisrel or standard path analysis offer analytical possibilities), it does indicate clearly what one needs to change, to alter the climate. And from the model it is not clear how climate leads to changes in performance. Certainly the research that has been done to date suggests that the most direct path is down the centre of the model, yet note that not all the 'boxes' are connected (and therefore presumably do not influence each other), and that the direction of influence is uni- rather than bi-directional.

Despite the appeal of many of these models, they have certain drawbacks. First, they cannot all be correct, or even useful, because they do not concur with one another. Some scholars see climate as a moderating

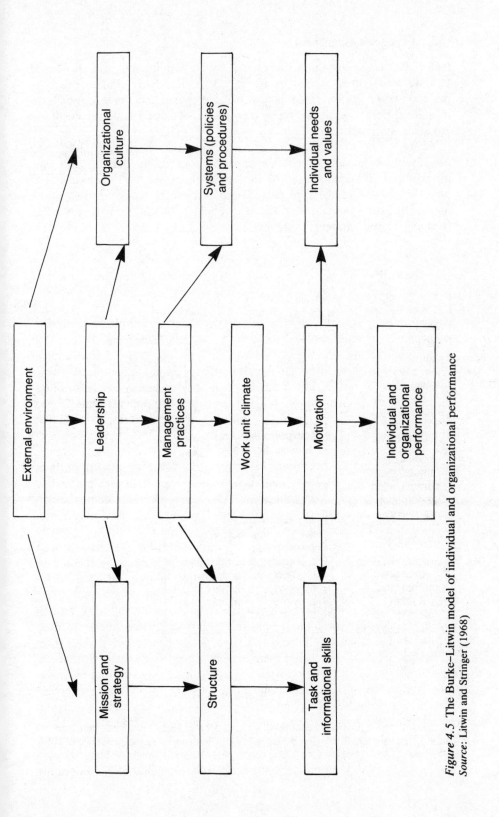

Figure 4.5 The Burke–Litwin model of individual and organizational performance
Source: Litwin and Stringer (1968)

factor which is strongly determined by environmental and structural factors, while others see it as all-pervasive. Rarely is climate precisely defined and explained, and it is possible that researchers are using the term in quite different ways. Secondly, few of these models have received any empirical support.

Perhaps rather than berate previous research, it is more useful to describe how models of climate can be theoretically derived and empirically tested. Dastmalchian, Blyton and Adamson (1991) demonstrated how the climate of work-place relations affects the outcomes of union/management relations. First on theoretical grounds they described a relatively simple model (Figure 4.6).

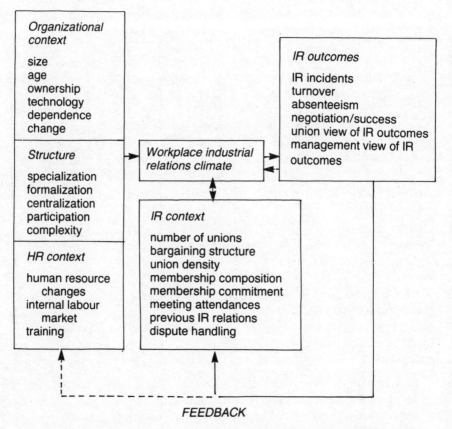

Figure 4.6 The industrial relations climate model and summary of relevant factors
Source: Dastmalchian, Blyton and Adamson (1991). Reproduced by permission of the publisher.

They then set about devising specific research questions to test the model:

- Do some aspects of structure relate more strongly to climate than others? In particular, what are the configurations of input variables which tend to be associated with more co-operative/consensual/positive industrial relations climates, and what are the configurations which tend to be associated with more conflictual/negative climates? Are similar configurations identifiable across markedly different types of work organization (e.g. manufacturing and service organizations)?

- Within these overall configurations of input variables, what is the strength and direction of specific factors (which other studies would suggest might be particularly important)? Do the organizations with positive industrial relations climates have a noticeably stronger commitment to participative management, for example? Are they the more flexibly designed organizations? Does the presence of strong unionism tend to be associated with a more co-operative or more hostile industrial relations climate?

- Does the climate variable strengthen our understanding of the relation between industrial relations/organizational inputs and industrial relations outcomes? That is, are the patterns of association stronger if we take a mediating role of climate into account – does the placing of the climate variable between input and output information improve the explanatory power of the model?

- Does the model appear to work in the directions suggested? For example, is it more appropriate to conceptualize climate as an intervening variable in the model rather than as a subjective part of the outcome variables?

(Dastmalchian, Blyton and Adamson, 1991, pp. 47–8)

In any empirical attempt to test the model it is necessary to define climate and provide a robust, psychometrically valid measure of it. This is set out below in Table 4.2.

They then tested the model through four systematic steps . First they correlated all the variables, then they regressed (using step-wise multiple regression) the input variables on to climate and then climate variables on to the outcome variables. The results were very promising, and they concluded:

In summary, a strong similarity with the main findings is evidenced: structural flexibility and industrial relations context are the most important factors for explaining climate; also, climate and training are most significant for determining the outcomes of industrial relations. The only exception was the strong negative impact of organizational size on outcomes. This indicates that, controlling for other variables in the

Table 4.2 Preliminary IR climate scales, their sample items, and reliability estimates (*N*=161)

Climate scales	Number of items	Sample items	a	Mean-corrected item-total correlation
1. Union–management co-operation	6	Union and management work together to make this organization a better place to work	0.765	0.575
2. Mutual regard	3	Union and management have respect for each other's goals	0.808	0.652
3. Apathy	4	Employees here rarely express interest in the outcomes of negotiations	0.722	0.501
4. Joint participation	3	In this organization joint union–management committees achieve definite results	0.867	0.663
5. Trust/fairness	5	The parties in this organization keep their word	0.810	0.602
6. Hostility/aggression	5	The parties regularly quibble over minor issues	0.861	0.679
Total items	26			

Source: Dastmalchian, Blyton and Adamson (1991). Reproduced by permission of publisher.
Note: *a* = alpha.

equation, smaller organizations tend to have more positive industrial relations outcomes than larger ones.

(Dastmalchian, Blyton and Adamson, 1991, p. 104)

Next they tested the overall model by looking at climate as an intervening variable to determine whether the input variables *on their own* explain more of the outcomes' variance, compared with the situation where climate is included in 'the model'. The results do indeed show that the inclusion of climate increases substantially the explanatory power of the equations. By including work-place relations climate in the model, they were able to increase the percentage of explained variance of industrial relations outcomes by 20 to 33 per cent. They conclude:

One important conclusion from this analysis is that the indirect paths of variables such as context (both IR and organizational) and organizational structure to outcomes are much stronger than their respective direct paths. That is, organizational context and structural variables impact more strongly on outcomes through their effects on perceived climate than by any direct effects on those outcomes. Similarly, it can be argued that the contexts within which the interactions between union and management take place have their greatest influence on results through their potential impacts on employees' perceptions of the climate, rather than directly in the form of industrial actions, turnover, and the like.

Similarly, it is evident in this sample that a more positive IR context has a much stronger impact on the outcomes of industrial relations when one considers its effects through the creation of a more favourable work-place relations climate, rather than directly to outcomes. In other words, a facilitative background, a positive history, and policies and practices that encourage problem solving and informal handling of disputes, do affect people's perceptions of the quality of union–management relationships. It is through the creation and development of such perceptions that the results or outcomes of industrial relations are more positive.

(Dastmalchian, Blyton and Adamson, 1991, pp. 112–13)

This work is impressive because it represents a clear test of a simple model which puts climate at its centre. It demonstrates, as others have argued, that consensually experienced organizational climate does significantly moderate between structural variables and outcome variables.

MEASURING CLIMATE

There are numerous ways of measuring organizational climate. The first is *categorical*, which attempts to classify organizations into pre-existing theoretical types. The second is *dimensional*, which attempts to classify organizations on a set of pre-established dimensions which are thought to capture or fully describe the organizational climate. A third, less well used method is to obtain archival data or other objective evidence to get an aggregate index of an organizational climate. Miceli and Near (1985) used this method to look at organizational climate factors associated with 'whistle-blowing'.

The categorical approach has not been very popular or successful. Examples of this approach can be seen in the work of Ginsberg (1978), who described three basic climates (inception, post-entrepreneurial, and bureaucratic) and Halpin and Croft (1962) who felt climates could be categorized as either open autonomous, controlled, familiar, paternal, or closed. Although this approach has attracted a certain amount of research (Hall, 1971), its limitations are those of all typologies – lack of fine discriminability, inappropriate categories, and most importantly, the idea that organizational climates are multidimensional and should be measured on various salient, albeit related, dimensions.

Early attempts to measure organizational climate tried perceptually to generate taxonomies of climate, usually through factor-analytic methods. Campbell *et al.* (1970) reviewed four investigations of the structure of managerial climate (Litwin and Stringer, 1968; Schneider and Bartlett, 1968; Taguiri, 1968; Kahn *et al.* 1964), and found four dimensions common to these studies. These were individual autonomy, degree of structure imposed on the position, reward orientation, and consideration, warmth, and support. While other dimensions were found in these studies, Campbell *et al.* were somewhat concerned about the relatively few dimensions uncovered. They stated:

> Even though the sets required of the respondents werc different, perhaps the content of the stimuli (items) were very similar across the four studies. Also, the relatively small number of factors which were found implies that a great deal of environmental variation remains to be uncovered.

(p. 394)

A number of dimensional organizational climate measures exist. Litwin and Stringer's (1968) fifty-item organizational climate questionnaire (Form B), is designed to measure nine characteristics reflecting the degree of organizational emphasis on structure, responsibility, reward, risk, warmth, support, standards, conflict, and identity.

House and Rizzo (1972) developed the organization description questionnaire, also referred to as the organization practice questionnaire. The scales have the following labels: conflict and inconsistency, decision timeliness, emphasis on analytic method, emphasis on personal development, formalization, goal consensus and clarity, communication adequacy, information distortion and suppression, job pressure, adequacy of planning, smoothness of horizontal communication, selection on ability and performance, tolerance of error, top management receptiveness, upward information requirements, violation in chain of command, work flow co-ordination, adaptability, and adequacy of authority.

Taylor and Bowers (1972) 'Survey of Organizations' includes twenty-two items designed to measure organizational climate. Smallest space analysis revealed five principal clusters, subsuming thirteen items. These are labelled: technological readiness, human resources primacy, communication flow, motivational conditions, and decision-making practices.

Payne and Pheysey (1971) described a business organization climate index. Three hundred items from Stern's (1967) organizational climate index were reduced through content and factor analysis to 192 items which compromised the measure. These are distributed across 245 scales, labelled as follows: leader's psychological distance, questioning authority, egalitarianism, management concern for employee involvement, open mindedness, emotional control, physical caution, practical orientation, future orientation, scientific and technical orientation, intellectual orientation, job challenge, task orientation, industriousness, altruism, sociability, interpersonal aggression, homogeneity, rules orientation, administrative efficiency, conventionality, readiness to innovate, variety in physical environment, and orientation to wider community. Payne and Mansfield (1973) describe a 157-item revision of this measure, covering twenty of the original scales.

Jones and James (1979) describe a 145-item psychological climate questionnaire (James and Jones, 1974). This has a very broad focus, covering perceptions of jobs and work roles, as well as organizational properties, aspects of leadership style, and trust. Developed and worded for use with navy personnel, its thirty-five scales fall into four sets. The first group is concerned with perceived job and role characteristics; the second set of scales reflects leadership style; the third set of scales is focused on the work group; the final scales are concerned with the sub-system or organization as a whole.

A sixty-four-item organizational climate description questionnaire was introduced by Halpin and Croft (1963). It contains eight scales, namely disagreement, hindrance, esprit, intimacy, aloofness, production emphasis, trust, and consideration. The instrument was developed for educational organizations and the item content reflects this; the first four scales refer to teachers' behaviour and experience, the last four to the principal's behaviour. Lawler, Hall, and Oldham (1974) describe a fifteen-item organizational climate questionnaire. Each item is in the form of a seven-point semantic differential scale, and factor analysis suggested a five-dimensional solution. The five scales are labelled as competent, responsible, practical, risk-oriented, and impulsive. A three-factor solution apparently based on the same data is described by Hall and Mansfield (1975).

Pritchard and Karasick (1973) provide the first published source for an organizational climate measure developed earlier. Eleven dimensions are described: autonomy, conflict versus co-operation, social relations, structure, level of rewards, performance–reward dependency, motivation to achieve, status polarization, flexibility and innovation, decision centralization, and supportiveness. Downey, Hellriegel and Slocum (1975) report the use of a six-dimensional measure of organization climate. Based on factor analysis, its scales are decision-making, warmth, risk, openness, rewards, and structure. Dieterly and Schneider (1974) offer a measure of perceived organizational climate, which has twenty-eight items equally divided across scales of individual autonomy, position structure, reward orientation, and consideration. Items are given in full, as are scale reliabilities and intercorrelations obtained in a laboratory study of 120 undergraduate students.

Some multidimensional climate surveys are nevertheless quite specific in what they cover. Hence Zohar (1980) offered a forty-nine-item, eight-dimensional questionnaire which, he argued, was both characteristic of industrial organizations but also related to actual safety behaviour in organizations. A major problem with many of these earlier measures was their poor psychometric properties – poor internal reliability and little or no validity. This study set out specifically to devise a psychometrically sound employee perception questionnaire (useful in corporate audits) that had six basic criteria:

1 The questionnaire should be parsimonious yet comprehensive, in that all the salient dimensions of climate are measured, but the questionnaire is not over-long and redundant.
2 It was planned that the questionnaire should be reliable, showing most importantly internal reliability.
3 The questionnaire should be valid (in the sense that it measured what it said it measured), able to discriminate between different parts of an organization, and able to reveal important and sensitive differences.
4 The questionnaire should travel well, in that it could be used in different organizations and different cultures, or in the same organization in different countries, so that comparisons could be made, in order to audit similar and/or different companies in different countries.
5 Most climate or employee perception questionnaires require respondents to rate the extent to which they agree or disagree that such a 'climate' situation exists, but not to point out the salience of that situation or dimension to the organization. It was the aim of this questionnaire to get respondents to rate both the truthfulness and *salience* of each dimension to the individual. Having a rating of importance or salience, as well as agreement, offers one way of assessing the validity of the questionnaire for the organization, although it should be pointed out that there is limited evidence of variation on measures of importance.
6 The questionnaire should produce a measure that could be used to highlight international differences within and between multinationals where it was appropriate.

THE DIMENSIONS OF CLIMATE

A major debate in climate research concerns not so much *how* to measure climate, but rather *what* to measure. There are numerous measures of climate that disagree fundamentally over what organizational dimensions should be measured. For instance, Litwin and Stringer (1968, pp. 200–2) developed a measure to assess seven dimensions. The items* in the original climate questionnaire (Form A), listed by scale were as follows:

*The items in the first six scales formed Part I of the questionnaire, and the subject could respond 'definitely agree', 'inclined to agree', 'inclined to disagree', or 'definitely disagree'. The items in the seventh scale, 'expect approval', formed Part II of the questionnaire, and the subject rated the degree of approval or disapproval he would most likely receive for this action in his organization, on a six-point scale.

Structure

- The jobs in this organization are clearly defined and logically structured.
- In this organization it is sometimes unclear who has the formal authority to make a decision.
- The policies and organization structure of the organization have been clearly explained.
- Red tape is kept to a minimum in this organization.
- Excessive rules, administrative details, and red tape make it difficult for new and original ideas to receive consideration.
- Our productivity sometimes suffers from lack of organization and planning.
- Our management isn't so concerned about formal organization and authority, but concentrates instead on getting the right people together to do the job.
- In some of the projects I've been on, I haven't been sure exactly who my boss was.

Responsibility

- We don't rely too heavily on individual judgment in this organization; almost everything is double-checked.
- Around here management resents your checking everything with them; if you think you've got the right approach you just go ahead.
- Supervision in this organization is mainly a matter of setting guidelines for your subordinates; you let them take responsibility for the job.
- There is not enough reward and recognition given in this organization for doing good work.
- You won't get ahead in this organization unless you stick your neck out and take a chance now and again.
- Our philosophy would emphasize that people should solve their problems by themselves.

Risk

- The philosophy of our management is that in the long run we get ahead fastest by playing it slow, safe, and sure.
- Decision-making in this organization is too cautious for maximum effectiveness.
- You won't get ahead in this organization unless you stick your neck out and take a chance now and again.
- We have to take some pretty big risks occasionally to keep ahead of the competition in the business we're in.

Reward

- You won't get much sympathy from higher-ups in this organization if you make a mistake.
- Mistakes in this organization just aren't tolerated.
- We have a promotion system here that helps the best man to rise to the top.
- In this organization the rewards and encouragements you get usually outweigh the threats and criticism.
- You get quite a lot of support and encouragement for trying something new in this organization.
- In this organization people are rewarded in proportion to the excellence of their job performance.
- There is a great deal of criticism in this organization.
- There is not enough reward and recognition given in this organization for doing good work.
- A person doesn't get the credit he deserves for his accomplishments in this organization.

Warmth and support

- A very friendly atmosphere prevails among the people in this organization.
- You wouldn't get much sympathy from higher-ups in this organization if you made a mistake.
- This organization is characterized by a relaxed, easy-going working climate.
- You get quite a lot of support and encouragement for trying something new in this organization.
- There is a good deal of disagreement, even some fighting among various people in this organization.
- There is a great deal of criticism in this organization.
- The philosophy of our management emphasizes the human factor, how people feel, etc.

Conflict

- A very friendly atmosphere prevails among the people in this organization.
- The attitude of our management is that conflict between competing units and individuals can be very healthy.
- There is a good deal of disagreement, even some fighting , between various people in this organization.
- In this organization co-operation and getting along well is very important.

Expect approval (see explanation above)

- Showing routine and imaginative thinking.
- Avoiding responsibility.
- Coming up with excellent ideas or making improvements or solving problems.
- Making a risky decision which turns out to be a wrong decision.
- Achieving the goals of your component by taking advantage of others in the section.
- Keeping costs down to the minimum and striving to reduce all expenses.
- Encouraging others to come up with new ideas or recommendations for changes.
- Failing to follow through on a commitment.
- Having an inquisitive mind and constantly questioning the *hows* and *whys* of things.

Gordon and Cummins (1979) advocated the following eight-dimensional scale:

Organizational clarity

- To what extent do goals provide a useful context for the every-day functioning of this organization?
- To what extent does this organization have clear goals?
- Planning for the achievement of goals in this organization tends to be formal.
- Planning for the achievement of goals in this organization tends to be complete.
- Planning for the achievement of goals in this organization tends to be oriented toward the long term.
- Decision-making in this organization tends to be based on a long-range view.
- To what extent does this organization have defined plans to meet its goals?

Decision-making structure

- To what extent does the current reporting structure facilitate or hinder implementation of the organization's strategies?
- To what extent does the current reporting structure facilitate or hinder the achievement of the organization's goals?
- To what extent do the systems in this organization provide a manager with the information he needs for decision-making?
- To what extent are decisions in this organization based on adequate information?

- To what extent does the current reporting structure facilitate or hinder co-ordination of efforts?

Organizational integration

- To what extent do the various units in this organization understand each other's problem and difficulties?
- Communications laterally to you from others at the same organizational levels tend to be extremely good.
- Everything considered, communications in this organization tend to be extremely good.
- How clear are managers concerning the interrelationships of their own jobs with those of others?
- To what extent do the various units in this organization understand each other's objectives and goals?
- To what extent do various units in this organization truly co-operate with one another?
- To what extent do you feel that you are sufficiently aware of things that are happening in other areas of the organization which might have an effect on how you do your job?

Management style

- To what extent are people in this organization free to take independent actions that are necessary to carry out their job responsibilities?
- To what extent are managers encouraged to take reasonable risks in their efforts to increase the effectiveness of this organization?
- To what extent is open discussion of conflicts encouraged?
- To what extent are managers encouraged to innovate in their jobs?
- To what extent is constructive criticism encouraged within this organization?
- Communications downward to you from above tend to be extremely good.
- To what extent do managers receive the support they need from higher levels of management to successfully carry through their job responsibilities?

Performance orientation

- To what extent are managers held personally accountable for the end results they produce or fail to produce?
- The measures or yardsticks used to judge managerial performance in this organization tend to be very clear.
- To what extent are managers within this organization expected to meet demands for high levels of performance?

- To what extent are the goals in this organization truly challenging?
- How clear are managers about the end results that are expected of them in their jobs?

Organizational vitality

- To what extent is this organization responsive to changes in its business environment?
- Goals in this organization tend to be venturesome.
- Decision-making in this organization tends to be innovative.
- Decision-making in this organization tends to be timely.
- Relative to its competition, this organization is a pacesetter.
- What is your estimate of the overall vitality of this organization as reflected by such things as a sense of urgency and a rapid pace of activities?

Compensation

- To what extent are managers in this organization offered benefits which are competitive with similar organizations?
- Considering the work you do, how satisfactory is your present compensation?
- To what extent is your pay high compared to others in this organization with similar responsibilities?
- To what extent is your pay high compared to people in other organizations with similar responsibilities?
- The relationship in this organization between compensation and individual performance tends to be very strong.

Human resource development

- Overall, how would you rate the opportunities for promotion within the organization?
- When a management vacancy exists, the search within the organization to fill the vacancy tends to be very broad.
- How successful is this organization in developing people from within for bigger jobs?
- To what extent does this organization provide opportunities for individual growth and development?
- To what extent does your job present a significant challenge to you?
- To what extent are the talents of managers appropriately matched to the demands of their job?

Bluen and Donald (1991) devised the following six dimensional measure to evaluate the industrial relations climate of an organization.

Supervision

- How easy to approach is your supervisor?
- To what extent is your supervisor willing to discuss problems?
- How much does your supervisor help you with your problems?
- To what extent is your supervisor capable of solving your problems?
- To what extent does your supervisor treat all workers fairly and equitably?

Worker representation

- To what extent are representatives truly representative of the workforce?
- To what extent are workers able to approach their representative?
- How much do representatives help workers with their problems?
- To what extent do representatives take worker problems to management?
- To what extent do representatives report back on what has been discussed with management?

Grievance procedure

- How thoroughly are grievances looked at?
- To what extent are grievances handled fairly?
- To what extent are grievances responded to in a satisfactory amount of time?
- To what extent are grievances solved?
- How much does the grievance procedure help solve worker complaints?

Company IR policy

- To what extent is the company IR policy acceptable to workers?
- To what extent are the views and opinions of workers considered when management decisions are made?
- To what extent is this company a fair and just employer?
- To what extent is the company's approach to worker/management relations the right one?
- To what extent has the company succeeded in establishing a good relationship with its workers?

Disciplinary procedure

- To what extent are workers made aware of what disciplinary action can be taken against them if they commit an offence?

- To what extent are worker offences properly investigated before disciplinary action is taken?
- To what extent is evidence shown of what the worker has done wrong?
- To what extent are workers given the correct discipline for what they do wrong?
- To what extent is discipline applied in the same way to all workers?

Communication

- How up to date are workers kept on matters that affect their job (e.g. pensions, pay)?
- To what extent are the reasons for changes in the company explained to the workers?
- To what extent does the company inform workers of what they want to know?
- To what extent is it possible to obtain relevant information when you need it?
- To what extent is the information given by management to workers accurate?

More recently Furnham (1992) has devised an adaptable 108-item, fourteen-dimension climate questionnaire:

Role clarity

- I have clear goals and objectives for my job.
- I am clear about my priorities at work.
- I know what my responsibilities are.
- I know exactly what is expected of me.
- I know what most people in the company do.
- Work in the company makes best use of people's experience.
- I know what most people locally do.
- I know what most departments do.
- The company has good-quality staff.

Respect

- I feel valued by my colleagues in the department.
- I value my colleagues in my department.
- I feel valued by my colleagues in the company as a whole.
- I value my colleagues in the company as a whole.
- My department respects the other departments.
- My department is respected by the other departments.

Communication

- I receive all the information I need to carry out my work.

- I believe that too much time is spent on inessentials.
- I am kept adequately informed about significant issues in the company as a whole.
- The grapevine keeps me appropriately informed.
- My department works well with other departments.
- The department receives all the information it needs to carry out its function well.
- The department is kept adequately informed about significant issues in the company as a whole.
- I understand clearly how I can contribute to the general goals of the company.
- I have adequate opportunities to express my views in my department.
- My colleagues are generally keen to discuss work matters with me.
- In general, communication is effective in the company.
- I could work more effectively if other employees communicated better with me.

Reward system

- Good work is appropriately recognized.
- I think X is too tolerant of poor performers.
- Work which is not of the highest order is dealt with appropriately.
- In general, people are adequately rewarded in the company.
- In my opinion X pay is competitive.
- I receive an appropriate salary.
- I receive appropriate benefits.
- There is an appropriate difference between the pay awarded to good and bad performers.
- I feel a strong sense of job satisfaction.
- Virtually everyone in the company receives an appropriate salary.

Career development

- My work is regularly reviewed with my development in mind.
- I understand how the appraisal system works.
- There is an adequate means of appraising my performance.
- I will not have to leave the company in order to develop my career.
- I believe that I should see my appraisal report and discuss it with my superior.
- In general there is an adequate system for career development in the company.
- I would like to work for this company till retirement age.
- People are fairly promoted in this company.
- My current job makes full use of my talents.
- Career development is taken seriously by the company.

Planning and decision-making

- The work of departments is well co-ordinated.
- People here rarely start new projects without deciding in advance how they will proceed.
- In general, planning is carried out appropriately in the company.
- I am allowed to participate sufficiently in significant decisions which affect my work.
- I am delegated work and authority appropriate to my expertise.
- I am only made responsible for those things I can influence.
- My superior likes me to consult him/her before I take any action.
- I have confidence in the process by which important decisions are made in the company.
- I'm kept well enough informed for me to make decisions well.
- I sometimes feel that I do not have the right amount of authority over my subordinates.
- In general, delegation, responsibility and decision-making are all well handled in the company.

Innovation

- I am encouraged to be innovative in my work.
- My department is encouraged to innovate.
- The company plans adequately for the future.
- The company responds promptly to new commercial and technical innovations.
- Work methods here are quickly changed to meet new conditions.

Relationships

- X's needs are well met by this company.
- X's needs are greatly respected here.
- Virtually everyone in X is aware of X's needs.
- This company is willing to be flexible in order to meet a X's needs.
- The way in which X's needs are handled in this company is likely to attract others.

Teamwork and support

- My department collaborates well with other departments.
- By and large, people pull their weight in X.
- I am rarely put under undue work pressure by my colleagues.
- People here generally support each other well.
- I have to put in long hours to complete my work.
- I often feel that the pressure of work is excessive.

- Work rarely piles up faster than I can complete it.
- There is rarely too much work and too little time.
- In general this is a caring and co-operative organization.

Quality of service

- When it comes to the provisions of our services, only the best will do.
- We are proud of the quality of service in X.
- We are proud of the quality of service in our department.
- This company has quality standards which are higher than those of its competitors.

Conflict management

- Conflicts are constructively/positively resolved in this company.
- We are generally encouraged to resolve our conflicts quickly, rather than let them simmer.
- There are helpful ways of preventing conflicts in the company.
- There is little conflict between departments.
- In general, conflict is managed well here.

Commitment and morale

- Motivation is kept at high levels in the company.
- Morale is high in most departments.
- Morale is high in my department.
- My personal morale is high.
- The commitment of the staff is an important asset to any company.
- The company will solve the vast majority of its important problems.
- I am proud to be part of this company.
- I feel that I am a valued member of X
- In general, people are strongly committed to the company.

Learning and training

- Most departments review their work on a regular basis.
- There are appropriate induction procedures in this company.
- I have received the training I need to do a good job.
- Most of us in this company are committed to help each other learn from our work.
- In general, this company learns as much as is practically possible from its activities.
- The training I receive is of high quality.
- I would like more training.

Direction

- The future of this company has been well communicated to us all.
- We all feel part of the company.
- I am clear about the part I can play in helping this company to achieve its goals.
- The future objectives of the company are consistent with my personal objectives.
- The future of this company will be much brighter than its past.
- The vast majority of the company shares a clear understanding of where this company is going and what it is trying to achieve.

However, to prevent the situation arising where there were as many climate questionnaires as there were climate surveys conducted, Koys and De Cotiis (1991) did a content analysis of dozens of studies (Table 4.3). This provided them with the evidence and material to construct their own eight dimensional scale.

Keys and De Cotiis (1991) reviewed the literature and categorized various dimension labels under eight headings. Their content analysis is itself interesting reading (see Table 4.4):

Finally, Furnham (1992) has proposed that all climate questions could be responded to on *two* dimensions: A simple agreement/disagreement rating on performance in the organization, but also a measure of importance. This acts both as a validity check and also as a means to help the organization diagnose how it wishes to proceed, though it can have limitations.

This 2 × 2 analysis yields the following pattern:

		Importance	
		Low	*High*
Performance	*High*	Consider	Celebrate
	Low	Ignore	Fix

This leaves four different courses of action, given the results:

1 **Ignore** Those questions with low agreement on performance and importance can be ignored because although performance was low, so was importance.
2 **Consider** Where performance is high (i.e. good) but the importance is low, it suggests that employees see certain things done well which are really not very important. Those need to be considered, as they may represent misguided effort.
3 **Celebrate** Where performance is high and importance is high, one can celebrate the fact that important issues are being perceived as being done well.

4   **Fix it** The major cause for action occurs where the issues are
    considered high in importance but performance is low. It is these items
    that most warrant attention, particularly the very low performance,
    high importance scores.

Table 4.3 Psychological climate dimensions

Summary dimension	Dimension label as found in the literature	Summary dimension	Dimension label as found in the literature
Autonomy	Autonomy Closeness of supervision (reversed) Individual responsibility Leader's initiation of structure (reversed)	Support	Support Leader's consideration Leader work facilitation Leader's psychological distance Hierarchical influence Management awareness
Cohesion	Cohesiveness Conflict (reversed) Esprit Peer relations Status polarization (reversed) Universalism Work group co-operation, friendliness, and warmth Sociability	Recognition	Recognition and feedback Opportunities for growth and advancement Reward–punishment relationship Rewards
Trust	Intimacy vs. aloofness Leader trust Management insensitivity (reversed) Managerial trust Openness	Fairness	Fairness and objectivity of the reward system Promotion clarity Policy clarity Policy clarity and efficiency of structure Altruism Egalitarianism
Pressure	Job pressure Role overload, role conflict, role ambiguity Time-span orientation Achievement emphasis Job standards Measuring of results Production emphasis	Innovation	Innovation Organizational flexibility Impulsive Security vs. risk Challenge and risk Future orientation

Source: Koys and De Cotiis (1991). Reproduced by permission of the publisher.

Table 4.4 Definition of each of the eight dimensions of the universe of psychological climate perceptions

Dimension name	Definition
Autonomy	The perception of self-determination with respect to work procedures, goals, and priorities.
Cohesion	The perception of togetherness or sharing within the organization setting, including the willingness of members to provide material aid.
Trust	The perception of freedom to communicate openly with members at higher organizational levels about sensitive or personal issues with the expectation that the integrity of such communications will not be violated.
Pressure	The perception of time demands with respect to task completion and performance standards.
Support	The perception of tolerance of member behaviour by superiors, including the willingness to let members learn from their mistakes without fear of reprisal.
Recognition	The perception that members' contributions to the organization are acknowledged.
Fairness	The perception that organizational practices are equitable and non-arbitrary or capricious.
Innovation	The perception that change and creativity are encouraged, including risk-taking into new areas or areas where the member has little or no prior experience.

Autonomy
1   I make most of the decisions that affect the way my job is performed.
2   I determine my own work procedure.
3   I schedule my own work activities.
4   I set the performance standards for my job.
4   I organize my work as I see best.

Cohesion
6   (Company name) people pitch in to help each other out.
7   (Company name) people tend to get along with each other.
8   (Company name) people take a personal interest in one another.
9   There is a lot of 'team spirit' among (company name) people.
10 I feel I do have a lot in common with the (company name) people I know.

Trust
11 I can count on my boss to keep the things I tell him confidential.
12 My boss has a lot of personal integrity.
13 My boss is the kind of person I can level with.
14 My boss follows through on his commitments to me.
15 My boss is not likely to give me bad advice.

Table 4.4 continued

Pressure
16   I have too much work and too little time to do it in.
17   (Company name) is a relaxed place to work (reversed).
18   At home, I sometimes dread hearing the telephone ring because it might be someone calling about a job-related problem.
19   I feel like I never get a day off.
20   Too many (company name) employees at my level get 'burned out' by the demands of their jobs.

Support
21   I can count on my boss to help me when I need it.
22   My boss is interested in me getting ahead in the company.
23   My boss is behind me 100 per cent.
24   My boss is easy to talk to about job-related problems.
25   My boss backs me up and lets me learn from my mistakes.

Recognition
26   I can count on a pat on the back when I perform well.
27   The only time I hear about my performance is when I screw up (reversed).
28   My boss knows what my strengths are and lets me know it.
29   My boss is quick to recognize good performance.
30   My boss uses me as an example of what to do.

Fairness
31   I can count on a fair shake from my boss.
32   The objectives my boss sets for my job are reasonable.
33   My boss is not likely to give me a 'greasy meal'.
34   My boss does not play favourites.
35   If my boss terminates someone, the person probably deserved it.

Innovation
36   My boss encourages me to develop my ideas.
37   My boss likes me to try new ways of doing my job.
38   My boss encourages me to improve on his methods.
39   My boss encourages me to find new ways around old problems.
40   My boss 'talks up' new ways of doing things.

Source: Koys and De Cotiis (1991). Reproduced by permission of the publisher.

Few questionnaires use this twofold response method, which does increase the time it takes to fill out and analyse the questionnaire, but yields invaluable data.

PRACTICAL ISSUES

There are a number of all-important practical issues when conducting a survey.

Confidentiality

The importance of complete confidentiality cannot be over-stressed. Respondents are asked to give their feelings on certain contentious issues that they would otherwise not give in so direct a manner, and if accurate and honest results are expected, complete confidentiality must be assured. This is normally achieved most successfully by giving respondents anonymity and by involving a third party whose credibility is acceptable to both parties. An example might be an academic institution or psychological consultancy. The third party should be responsible for the collection and collation of all data and only after it has been suitably reprocessed, so that no one person can be identified, should it be released to the company.

Confidentiality must again be considered when designing the subdivisions of the respondents into groups. The balance here must be drawn between designing the demographics (sex, age, rank) such that very small cells are generated in the search for improving the accuracy of the data, within which it would be relatively easy to pinpoint an individual, and having the cells so large that the quality of the data is diluted to an ineffective level. Should the cells become too small, individuals will be apprehensive of completing the survey, thus negating the value of the exercise.

It is an assumption that all staff are normally surveyed, so that the sense of participation is as widespread as possible, and in order to avoid the possible bias involved in making choices.

Confidence

The staff must feel confident that the management are genuinely interested in obtaining their feelings, and that the whole exercise is not a placebo. Management commitment is essential, as is the prompt reply to all staff on the results of the survey, followed by immediate action for improvement in the deficient areas discovered. Here it is well worth considering restricting the initial survey (whilst confidence is being built up) to areas where prompt remedial action is possible, rather than attempting to cover all areas where deficiencies are thought to exist, knowing that a remedy for some of these deficient areas is beyond the immediate resources of the organization.

The climate survey is really only applicable to large organizations, where it should prove to be the cheapest and most effective way of obtaining the required data. In small organizations (under fifty people), or if the cell size is very small within a large organization, two problems arise. First we lose the ability to ensure confidentiality, as mentioned above, and second we face the reality of having a group which is too small to be representative of the population it purports to represent. Also when looking at subgroups, small samples fail to yield reliable response bases.

Evidence from previous surveys has shown a response rate of 40 per cent to be achievable, and above 50 per cent overall to be exceptional. The pattern will vary between departments, however.

Planning the survey

The undertaking by an organization to conduct a climate survey must be considered an important management decision. Success is most important. It is a serious public relations exercise with the staff, in which the impact may well be negated if the confidence and confidentiality are lost or suspected. If possible, take as broad a view as is practicable in deciding the question areas, in order to bring out problems which may or may not have been predicted. However, addressing problems whose solutions will undoubtedly be beyond the immediate resources of the organization is not recommended. The follow-up action designed to remedy the areas found to be deficient should be swift, as this will reinforce the perceived view of management commitment to the exercise and do much to enhance the flow of positive communications.

The temptation always exists to attempt to find out precisely what is deficient in any perceived problem area. This temptation must be avoided, or the balance of the survey will be lost as one particular area may become dominant. It is essential to identify the problem areas themselves, and to leave the further research, almost certainly using another form of diagnosis, to discover the exact details of a particular problem and its remedial action.

In determining the question areas, it is important to try to identify the processes that exist between the organization (structure) and the people. Previous experience has identified the following areas as those where tensions commonly arise: communications – written/verbal, horizontal/ vertical; leadership style; identity with the organization; clarity of control; career development; subgroups – separate identity; conflict, openness and resolution; reward pattern.

Having decided on the areas for the questions, it remains to write the questions themselves. There are, of course, many ways of probing staff perceptions. A method used in some surveys is to ask for each factor: (a) whether it is important or not, and (b) how strongly people feel about it, independently of its importance. This is to avoid the problem of being deceived by strong feelings about unimportant matters. This adds complexity to the analysis, and is perhaps better retained for later probes into greater detail. Constant reference to the theory will ensure that the thrust of the question is kept under control and that there is a high probability of obtaining meaningful data. The area of leadership may be used as an example here of the link between theory and practice in the formation of the questions.

Research by Bowers and Seashore (1966) led to their identifying a model for use when attempting to measure the effectiveness of leadership. Known as the Four-Factor Model, it highlights the following dimensions of effectiveness:

1 **Support** Behaviour that enhances someone else's feeling of worth and importance.
2 **Interaction facilitation** Behaviour that encourages members of a group to develop close, mutually satisfying relationships.
3 **Goal emphasis** Behaviour that stimulates an enthusiasm for meeting the group's goal or achieving excellent performance.
4 **Work facilitation** Behaviour that helps achieve goal attainment by such activities as scheduling, co-ordinating, planning, and by providing resources such as tools, materials, and technical knowledge.

Support and interaction facilitation are obviously 'people' concerns. Emphasizing these dimensions recognizes the need to encourage continued support of individuals in the organizational endeavour and the need to maintain and improve interpersonal relationships and group processes such as teamwork. Goal emphasis and work facilitation relate to task concerns and to the path-goal theory of leadership. Good leaders are typically seen as helpful in both setting goals and in structuring or designing means of achieving them. This approach builds on the concept of achievement motivation, and if goals are achieved there is an increase in satisfaction. Performance leads to satisfaction and increased motivation in the future.

Details about the respondent are as important as the questions themselves. Here the population of the organization is broken down into manageable and meaningful groups. Too definitive a breakdown will allow individuals to be pinpointed, and this will affect their attitude to completing the survey. Great care is needed in this area in drawing the balance between pinpointing individuals on one extreme and collecting data that is too loose and undefined on the other. The cells chosen should be large enough such that, even with a response rate of as high as 40 per cent, the total number of respondents within that cell would generate a figure that could be considered significant in statistical terms. This tends to mean leaving the analysis at the level of larger units of organization rather than smaller.

Implications and options for managerial action

The feedback to staff of the results plays a major part in the confidence-gaining aspects of the survey. They should be given as much information as possible, and as soon as is practicable. Senior management should be privy to all the data, presented in a digestible form. In addition it is important to decide at an early stage what form, if any, the remedial action may take. Where the follow-up action has been slow and weak (especially in areas where a deficiency has already been identified and the company knows it should do something) then there is the danger of a drop in morale.

An important value of feedback sessions is to allow subordinates to work with managers in solving company problems. For this, it is useful where feasible to use an outsider (perhaps the third party doing the data processing) to present the key results to each department and to compare them with the company average. This often delicate process may then lead to a fertile interchange on the meaning of the data, its underlying explanation, and what might be done about it. Depending on the size of the department, this might begin with the supervisory group, but should be dispersed to all with some urgency.

NEW DIRECTIONS AND EMERGING TRENDS

The field of organizational climate continues to attract research. What are the current questions and issues emerging? Reviews of this topic tend to list similar questions (Rousseau, 1988; Schneider and Reichers, 1983).

*   How do employees, confronted with a quite different, complex, and varying set of organizational experiences, share a common experience of the objective reality of organizational climate?
*   To what extent do organizational selection and socialization procedures lead to climate homogeneity?
*   Do organizations have sub-climates, and how can they be measured?

Evans (1968), over twenty years ago proposed a 'system' model for organizational climate, which allowed him to formulate some interesting, and testable, hypotheses. He lists six:

1   The climate of an organization tends to be perpetuated from one generation of members to another unless the structure of the inputs and outputs and intra-organizational processes are changed along with the feedback effects. This hypothesis, if true, in effect cautions against the inclination to solve an organizational climate problem by recruiting a new executive. He is not likely to succeed unless he is sufficiently knowledgeable, powerful, and charismatic as to alter the inputs, the intra-organizational processes, the outputs, and the feedback effects.

2   Inertial forces maintaining organizational climate tend to increase with the size of an organization. As the size of an organization increases, differentiation increases both as regards number and type of statuses and number and type of subunits. Accompanying an increase in status and functional differentiation is an increase in the scope of problems of role socialization, role performance, and inter-subunit co-ordination. In the face of mounting problems associated with an increase in size, the difficulties of deliberately modifying the internal organizational climate are correspondingly greater.

3   If the organizational climate as perceived by members of the focal organization is more favourable than the climate as perceived by members or organizations comprising the organization-set, there will be a lower rate of innovation because of a reduced motivation to change. Conversely, if the climate as perceived by members of the focal organization is less favourable than the climate as perceived by members of organizations comprising the organization-set, there will be a higher rate of innovation.
4   Organizational climate is more susceptible to deliberate efforts to modify it when there is a low degree of consensus regarding it. As between *internal* and *external* organizational climate, it is probably easier to alter the former than the latter because of the greater control that the focal organization can exercise over its members than over the members of organizations comprising its organization-set.
5   As differences in subunit climates of an organization increase, there is a tendency for a greater conflict to arise concerning proposals for innovation and for a discrepancy to occur in the rate of technical and administrative innovations, viz., for the degree of 'organizational lag' to increase.
6   Technical innovations, because they are manifested in the products or services of an organization, are more likely to generate faster changes in the external organizational climate than administrative innovation.

(pp. 120–1)

In summary, future research should take the following into account:

1   Theoretical and conceptual issues should serve to guide measurement, and not the other way around.
2   Organizational climate should be differentiated from psychological climate. Organizational climate refers to organizational attributes, while psychological climate refers to individual attributes, namely the intervening psychological process whereby the individual translates the interaction between perceived organizational attributes and individual characteristics into a set of expectancies, attitudes, behaviours, etc.
3   With respect to organizational climate, the following appear necessary: (a) to determine the conceptual bounds, variables, and dimensions relevant to the organizational climate domain; (b) to investigate the relationships between multiple sources of measurement of organizational climate variables, both objective and subjective; (c) to determine the accuracy of perceptual organizational climate measurements with respect to objective organizational climate variables; (d) to ascertain the role of consensus versus diversity or perception as a situational influence; (e) to develop

realistic organizational models for organizational analysis and to determine the position of organizational climate in such models; (f) to ascertain appropriate levels of explanation for each level of analysis for the data (e.g., can perceptual measures be accumulated to represent group, subsystem, or organizational levels of explanation); (g) to investigate relationships between measures of organizational climate and both individual behaviour and attitudes and organizational performance.

4   With respect to psychological climate, the following appear needed: (a) to determine the conceptual boundaries, variables, and dimensions relevant to the psychological climate domain; (b) to investigate the relationships between psychological climate and organizational climate, particularly perceptually measured organizational climate; (c) to investigate more fully the relationships between psychological climate and job attitude variables where differences in situational contexts are taken into account; (d) to ascertain whether the concept of an intervening psychological process is meaningful in more sophisticated organizational models; (e) to investigate the role of psychological climate as both a predictor of individual behaviours and attitudes and a moderator of the relationship between the situation and individual behaviours and attitudes.

CONCLUSION

The concept and many measures of corporate climate predate the concept of corporate culture. Indeed corporate climate, possibly because it is a more obvious concept, and one borrowed from meteorology, has attracted far less academic debate and passion, but still much speculation. The idea that employee attitudes and perceptions are influenced by and influence an organization is self-evident. But what is less clear is which attitudes (perceptions about what?), and precisely how the process works. Nevertheless, a climate audit or survey is nearly always found to be a very useful management tool, providing clear, explicit data on employee attitudes, beliefs, and behaviours.

5 Communication audits

INTRODUCTION

Communication, which is influenced by many factors, is a vital process in every organization. When the communication of information flows accurately and effectively, an organization can function smoothly, but when there is failure or breakdown in communication, or when information is distorted, this can have serious repercussions for the performance of any organization.

This chapter will examine the importance of corporate communication – how it can go wrong, and how it can be assessed and audited, so that communications problems can either be reduced, or even better, avoided altogether. Defining communication has been attempted by a number of organizational researchers. One useful definition has been offered by Baron and Greenberg (1990), who describe communication within organizations as 'the process by which a person, group, or organization (the sender) transmits some type of information (the message) to another person, group, or organization (the receiver).'

The process begins when one party has information that it wishes to transmit to another (either party may be an individual, a group, or an entire organization). It is the sender's mission to transform the idea into a form that can be sent to and understood by the intended receiver (see Figure 5.1). This is what happens in the process of *encoding* – translating the idea into a form that may be recognized by the receiver, such as written or spoken language.

After the message is encoded, it is ready to be transmitted over one or more channels of communication to reach the intended receiver. These channels may be the pathways along which encoded information is transmitted. Telephone lines, radio and television signals, fibre-optic cables, postal routes, and even the airwaves that carry the vibrations of our voices all represent potential channels of communication.

The target of the message is the receiver. Once the message is received, the recipient must begin the process of *decoding*. This amounts to converting the message back into ideas. This can involve many different

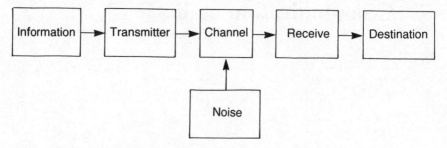

Figure 5.1 The basic communication chain
Source: Fiske (1982). Reproduced by permission of the publisher.

processes, such as comprehending spoken and written words, interpreting facial expressions, and so on. To the extent that the sender's message is accurately decoded by the receiver, the ideas understood will be the ones intended. The ability of receivers to comprehend and interpret the information received from others is never perfect, with unclear messages or weaknesses in the language skills of the receiver being among the factors which can cause communication to break down.

Once a message has been decoded, the process can be reversed such that the receiver transmits a message back to the original sender. This is known as *feedback* – that is, knowledge about the impact of messages on receivers. Receiving feedback allows senders to determine whether or not their messages have been understood and had the desired effects. Further, by giving feedback, the receiver is informing the sender that he or she has taken notice of what the sender has to say (see Figure 5.2).

This model provides a simplistic impression of the way in which interpersonal and organizational communication works. It is rarely the case that this is the way the process turns out in practice. There are many potential barriers to effective communication, as we will see. These factors are often referred to collectively as *noise*. Noise can occur at almost any point in the communication process. For instance, messages may be poorly encoded by senders (e.g., written in an unclear way), inadequately decoded by receivers (e.g., failure to understand what was said), or sent through channels of communication that produce distortions in the message along the way. These factors, and many others which exist within the organizational setting, can contribute to the distortion of information sent by one party to another, or may sometimes prevent it from completing its journey altogether.

A communication audit enables an organization to conduct a thorough assessment of its internal information channels, both formal and information; print and audio-visual; and, if required, its modes of contact with the outside world. This audit can provide a quantifiable measure of the extent to which different forms of communication are utilized with respect to

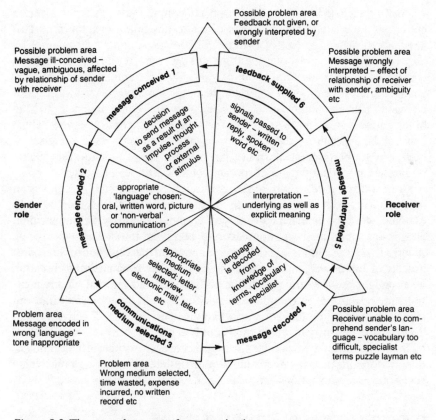

Figure 5.2 Theory and process of communication
Source: Evans (1990). Reproduced by permission of the publisher.

internal and external communications, and an evaluation of the appro-priateness and effectiveness with which communications are employed in different functional contexts. It is only through a systematic and compre-hensive audit of this sort than an organization can find out if it is utilizing the right kinds of communication channels for different tasks and using them to the maximum effectiveness.

Organizational communications are intimately tied up with corporate culture and corporate climate. The strength of the indigenous corporate culture is, as we have seen earlier, strongly tied to the style and charisma of an organization's leadership. However, the extent to which it permeates all levels of the organization is significantly dependent upon internal channels of communication which flow up, down, and across the organization between different hierarchical strata and among sections and departments on the same level. Similarly, corporate climate, which is closely linked to work-force satisfaction and morale, is both shaped by and reflective of the effectiveness of internal corporate communications.

Given the close links between corporate communications and corporate culture and climate, a communications audit may often form an important ancillary to or component of culture/climate assessment. Any attempt by an organization to introduce culture change may require not simply a culture audit, but also an audit of corporate communications. Culture change, after all, cannot be expected to occur purely through a process of changed management vision. It needs to be communicated to the organization's work-force in a carefully planned and controlled way. Thus, culture change, culture rejuvenation, or culture strengthening exercises, if they are to be successful, must be based upon a sound, thoroughly researched understanding of corporate communications processes.

Corporate climate, as a barometer of morale and satisfaction, enables an organization to discover areas of discontent among its staff. A climate audit may uncover a particular problem with communications which might then require a subsequent communications audit to understand it in full. Alternatively, a climate model may uncover a perceived problem with aspects of job clarity, management style, or a key organizational function which might require strategic application of selected internal communications for resolution. A communications audit could be applied to find out which lines of communication are likely to prove most effective and to discover the best way in which they could be used.

In this chapter we examine the significance of corporate communications to organizational effectiveness, and outline different ways in which corporate communications can be audited.

DIFFERENT TYPES OF COMMUNICATION

There are many kinds of communication in organizations. Organizational communications forms can be distinguished in terms of whether they are verbal or non-verbal; spoken or written; vertical (up or down) or lateral; one-way or two-way; and formal or informal. For instance, verbal communication involves the transmission of ideas using words, while non-verbal communication consists of gestures, posture, the way we behave towards others, and the way we dress and present ourselves. Formal methods of communication may include reports, memos, and organized meetings. Informal communication includes the grapevine. Communication takes place between two parties – a sender of a message and a receiver of it. Sometimes the receiver will respond to the sender, thus message traffic flows one-way or two-ways. Table 5.1 provides an illustration of the range of methods which organizational communications can take.

Table 5.1 Methods of communication

Two-way: upwards and downwards	*One-way: downwards*
Briefing groups	Mass meetings
Interviews	Notices, posters and public address systems
Walking the floor	Brief meetings
Employee councils	House journals and newspapers
Consultative committees	Bulletins
Collective bargaining negotiations	Staff handbook
Induction programmes	Annual report to employees
The grapevine	Pay-packet inserts
Response systems	Personal letters
	Exhibitions and films
Two-way horizontal or sideways	*One-way: upwards*
Reports	Suggestion scheme
Memos	Union newsletter
Telephone	Response to surveys
House journals	Industrial action
Quality circles	Labour turnover
	Absenteeism and lateness
	Quality circles

Verbal communication

What types of verbal communication are most effective? Research has shown that supervisors believe communication is most effective when oral messages are followed by written ones (Level, 1972). This combination is especially preferred under several conditions: when immediate action is required, an important policy change is being made, a praiseworthy employee is identified, and a company directive or order is announced. When the information to be communicated is of a general nature, or requires only future action, written forms are judged to be most effective.

Oral messages are perceived to be useful in getting others' immediate attention, and the follow-up written portion helps make the message more permanent, something that can be referred to in the future. Oral messages also have the benefit of allowing for immediate two-way communication between parties, whereas written communiqués are frequently only one-way (or take too long for a response if they are two-way). Not surprisingly, researchers have found that two-way communications (e.g., face-to-face discussions, or telephone conversations) are more commonly used in organizations than one-way communications (e.g., memos). Klauss and Bass (1982) found that approximately 83 per cent of the communication taking place among civilian employees of a US Naval agency used two-way media. In fact, 55 per cent of all communications were individual face-to-face interactions. One-way, written communications tended to be reserved for more formal, official messages that needed to be referred to in the future at the receiver's convenience (e.g., official announcements about position openings).

Written or spoken communication

Do people generally prefer to communicate in writing or speech? The choice of communication channel depends greatly on one very important factor – the degree of clarity or ambiguity of the message being sent. Daft, Lengel and Trevino (1987) reasoned that oral media (e.g., telephone conversations and face-to-face meetings) are preferable to written media (e.g., notes and memos) when messages are ambiguous (requiring a great deal of assistance in interpretation), whereas written media are preferable when messages are clear. The researchers surveyed a sample of managers about the media they preferred using to communicate messages that differed with respect to how clear or ambiguous they were. Daft *et al.*'s data reveal two interesting trends. First, the more ambiguous the message, the more managers preferred using oral media (such as telephones or face-to-face contact). Second, the clearer the message, the more managers preferred using written media (such as letters or memos). Apparently, most managers were sensitive to the need to use communications media that allowed them to take advantage of the rich avenues for two-way oral communications when necessary, and to use the more efficient one-way, written communications when these were adequate.

Thus some managers were what could be termed 'media sensitive', while others were less so. Was there any evidence to show that media-sensitive managers were more effective than media insensitive ones? Comparison of the performance ratings of managers who were sensitive or insensitive to the most appropriate forms of communications under different circumstances showed that most media-sensitive managers (87 per cent) received their company's highest performance ratings, whereas only about half of the media insensitive managers (47 per cent) received equally high evaluations. Apparently the skill of selecting the appropriate communications medium is an important aspect of a manager's performance.

One-way versus two-way communication

Table 5.1 listed a range of methods of organization of communication. Many of these methods were one-way. Such messages are commonplace in many organizations, and can play a significant part in facilitating the flow of information around different parts or across different levels of an organization. One problem from which all kinds of one-way communications suffer, however, at least potentially, is that the sender cannot be completely confident that the message has been received and understood.

If reception and understanding do not take place, then properly effective communication will not occur. One-way methods of communication do not allow the receiver the opportunity to comment upon, check understanding of, or ask questions about the message.

Direction of communication

Communications flow in and around an organization in different directions. Information also flows into and out of the organization. Within the organization, communication takes place up (from lower to higher levels), down (from higher to lower levels), and across (between people at the same level) the organization. Messages which flow around the organization can be differentiated according to content and presentation format or channel (see Figure 5.3).

Downward flow of communication from a superior to subordinate might consist of instructions, directions, and orders, or message which tell subordinates what they should be doing (Hawkins and Preston, 1981). Alternatively, they might comprise requests for information or positive feedback, and praise for work well done.

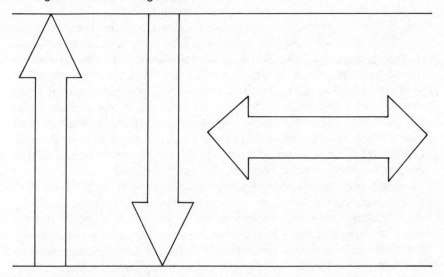

Figure 5.3 Upward, downward and horizontal communication
Source: Baron and Greenberg (1990), p. 344. Reproduced by permission of the publisher.

Downward communication flows from one level to the next lowest one, eventually, in some instances, finding its way to the bottom of the organization. A message can lose some of its original meaning as it flows from one level to the next, becoming less and less accurate. Not surprisingly, research has shown that the most effective downward communication techniques are those in which the information is issued as directly as possible to those at whom it is principally targeted. Thus, small group meetings at which management address subordinates, or written messages sent directly to intended receivers, are recognized as being among the most effective (Szilagyi, 1981).

Upward communication flows from subordinate levels to superordinate levels. It consists of staff requesting information, in the shape of advice, guidance or instruction, from managers and supplying information to managers so that they are aware of how various aspects of work are progressing.

Upward communication is not simply the reverse of downward communication. Because each originates with parties of differing status within the organization, the nature of the communication varies too. Downward communication occurs much more frequently than upward communication (Walker and Guest, 1952). One study has revealed among managers that less than 15 per cent of their total communication was directed at superiors (Luthans and Larsen, 1986). Furthermore, when people do communicate upwards, their conversations tend to be shorter than discussions with their peers (Kirmeyer and Lin, 1987).

One important finding about upward communication is that it often tends to suffer from serious inaccuracies. One aspect of this problem is due to the fact that subordinates frequently feel they must highlight their accomplishments and play down their mistakes if they are to form a favourable impression with their bosses (Read, 1962). Another factor is that some individuals are afraid to speak to their bosses for fear of being rebuked, and especially if they fear that apparent outspokenness might reduce their chances of promotion (Glauser, 1984). As a result of such dynamics, it is not unusual to find that upward communication tends to be quite limited. This can cause serious problems in jobs requiring a high degree of co-ordination between people at different levels.

One important application of upward communications utilized in recent years by some major companies is to have employees rated not simply by their superiors but by their subordinates. In the United Kingdom, British Petroleum, British Airways, and Cathay Pacific Airways have implemented subordinate employee appraisal schemes. Although this approach needs to be handled with sensitivity, and can cause considerable anxiety among managers, companies which have experimented with it have found that its benefits generally outweigh its costs.

The horizontal flow of communications within organizations takes place between people on the same level, either within the same department or across departments. Because there is no status differential between the individuals involved, horizontal communications tend to be more relaxed, easier and friendlier. There are circumstances, however, under which even horizontal communications can be problematic. For instance, people in different departments may feel that they are competing against each other for valued organizational resources and may show resentment toward each other, thereby substituting an antagonistic competitive orientation for the friendlier and co-operative one needed to get things done (Rogers and Rogers, 1976).

The vertical and horizontal flow of communications just discussed represents forms of information distribution internal to the organization. Communications, of course, can also take place between an organization and individuals or groups in the external world. These communications commonly occur between the organization and its suppliers or its customers. Customer-related communications interactions will be focused upon more closely in the next chapter.

Formal communications channels

The patterns determining which organizational units, whether people or groups, communicate to which other units are referred to as communication networks. Such networks can take on a variety of forms. Most organizations have both formal and informal communications networks. Organizational behaviour research has explained how these networks work under controlled conditions (Katz and Kahn, 1966). The important question here is whether the particular arrangement in place in an organization facilitates effective communications or not. Communications networks can play a significant part in how well the organization functions and how much satisfaction its employees derive from working there (Shaw, 1978). It will help, at this stage, if we pause to examine the types of communications configurations which are commonplace among organizations, and which researchers have studied.

The first thing to note about communications networks is their degree of centralization. This refers to the extent that information has to flow via one particular member of the network. Figure 5.4 illustrates diagrammatically, the principal network forms. Networks such as the Y, Wheel, and Chain are centralized. In each case, information must flow through one person in a central position, in order to be distributed around the rest of the network. Networks such as the Circle or Comcon, however, are decentralized, and information can flow freely among members without going through one key individual. People in decentralized networks have equal access to information, whereas those in centralized networks are unequal because some individuals at the centres have access to more information than others.

These communications networks have been shown to affect significantly

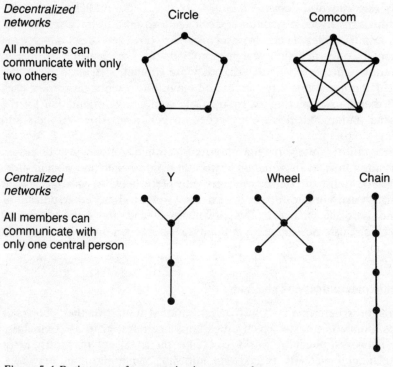

Figure 5.4 Basic types of communications network

how effectively groups perform different jobs. One general finding is that when the tasks being performed arc simple, centralized networks perform better, but when the tasks are more complex, decentralized networks work best (Forsyth, 1983). On comparing these two types of networks Baron and Greenberg (1990) observe: 'Centralized networks are faster and more accurate on simple tasks, whereas decentralized networks are faster and more accurate on complex tasks' (p. 346).

The chief reason for this difference in performance has to do with the pressure placed on the central member of a centralized network. The greater the volume of information with which any single member of a group has to deal, the more likely it is that that person will suffer from information overload and reduced processing efficiency. This has a knock-on effect whereby the performance of the whole group suffers and becomes slower and less accurate. When a problem is a fairly simple one, the central person may easily be able to solve it alone after receiving all the necessary and relevant information. Thus, the more speedily that information reaches this person, the sooner the problem can be resolved. When the latter kind of problem-solving task is spread out over the entire group, though, the process is slowed down.

Research has also shown that centralized and decentralized networks differ in terms of the satisfaction of their members. The greater equality in decision-making which characterizes the decentralized network tends to be preferred by most people. In a centralized network where the key decisions are taken by the person at the centre, the individuals left on the periphery can feel left out of things. These individuals can often feel that their contributions are not fully appreciated.

Formal communications networks represent only one factor which influences organization communications. Lines of communication can influence both the performance and satisfaction of people employed by an organization, but research has indicated that the advantages or limitations of different communications networks often tend to disappear the longer the groups are in operation (Burgess, 1968). With time, group members become more accustomed to dealing with each other and develop ways of overcoming difficulties created by the nature of the network in which they find themselves working.

Informal communications channels

As well as formalized networks of communication, most organizations contain informal networks within which information is shared between individuals, without any formally imposed obligations or restrictions. Employees talk to each other in and outside the organization and pass information around among themselves about both work and non-work-related matters. Informal communications channels can form a very influential conduit through which messages concerning the organization may pass more swiftly than through any formal line of communication. Krackhardt and Porter (1986) showed, for instance, that the informal communications within any organization were significantly related to staff turnover. One person left her job for a better one, and encouraged others to do the same. The message got around by word of mouth that better opportunities were to be had elsewhere.

Informal communication networks are often comprised of individuals at different organizational levels. Members of this network can pass on any information they choose. One researcher found, for example, that jokes and funny stories tended to cross organizational boundaries, and were freely shared by those in both the managerial and non-managerial ranks of organizations (Duncan, 1984). There are limits even within informal networks to what members will communicate with each other. It is unlikely to be acceptable for a lower-level employee to tell a higher-level employee how to do their job. However, many kinds of information do flow around an organization through informal networks and do so very rapidly along what is often termed the organizational 'grapevine'. Indeed, information often flows along the grapevine much more quickly than it does along formal lines of communication (Baskin and Aronoff, 1989).

Another point about the grapevine is that it has been found to be an accurate source of information. Walton (1961) found that 82 per cent of the information communicated along a particular company's organizational grapevine was accurate. Baron and Greenberg (1990) observe, however, that there may be a problem with interpreting this figure, in that the inaccurate portions of some messages may be likely to alter their overall meaning. They give an example of what they mean:

> If, for example, a story is going around that someone got passed up for promotion over a lower-ranking employee, there may be quite a bit of dissension caused in the work-place. However, if everything is true except the fact that the person turned down the promotion because it involved relocating, then this important fact completely alters the nature of the situation. Only one fact needs to be inaccurate before the accuracy of communication suffers.

(pp. 350–1)

Of course, information can be passed around organizations that has no basis in fact. These messages, or rumours, are often based on speculation, imaginative guesswork, or wishful thinking. Rumours can spread very quickly and permeate even very large organizations so swiftly that practically everyone will have heard the rumour within a matter of hours. It is because everyone seems to know the rumour that it can often be assumed to be true. Rumours can be very damaging to an organization, particularly when they concern some central aspect of an organization's business activities (Thibaut, Calder and Sternthal, 1981). Refuting a rumour can be difficult and may not always help to counter its effects. A better technique can be to distract attention away from the rumour by focusing on other things which are believable and even incompatible with the rumour.

Informal communications networks can have positive as well as negative effects on organizational functioning. The more involved people are in their organization's communications networks, the more powerful and influential they become on the job. Informal connections can help people attain formal power.

THE IMPORTANCE OF ORGANIZATIONAL COMMUNICATION

People at work spend a great deal of their time engaged in communicating with others. Communicating effectively, that is, being able to put a message across in a way that people can understand and accept, is a vitally important skill. One survey of personnel managers in 175 large companies in the USA asked them to name the factors and skills most important in helping graduating students obtain employment. Written and oral communications skills were the two factors named most often (Benson, 1983) (see Table 5.2). In another survey, most chief operating officers in the USA were found to rate employee communication skill as vital (Williams, 1978).

Table 5.2 Factors or skills considered most important by personnel managers in helping business graduates obtain employment

Rank score	Factor skill	Score
1	Oral communication skills	6.29
2	Written communication skills	6.17
3	Work experience	5.70
4	Energy level (enthusiasm)	5.70
5	Technical competence	5.64
6	Persistence/determination	5.52
7	Dress grooming	5.23
8	Personality	5.11
9	Resumé	5.11
10	Appearance	5.00
11	Poise	4.88
12	Specific degree held (finance, marketing, accounting, and so forth)	4.86
13	Grade point average	4.23
14	Letters of recommendation	4.05
15	Interview skills	4.05
16	Accreditation of the school college	3.94
17	Social graces	3.82
18	Physical characteristics	3.64
19	School attended	2.94
20	Age	2.52
21	Marital status	2.00
22	Race	1.58
23	Sex	1.47
24	Religion	1.00

Others reportedly believed there was a direct link between employee communication and profitability (Hersey and Blanchard, 1986).

Kar (1972) estimated that between 40 and 60 per cent of work time in a typical US manufacturing plant involved some phase of communication. Beach (1970) estimated that top and middle-level executives devoted 60 to 80 per cent of their total working lives to activities involving some form of communication with others. The effective transmission and receipt of information is especially important for those parts of an organization involved in key decision-making, whose decisions can affect the future direction and success of their organization. Being aware of market developments, competitor strengths and weaknesses, employee problems, the adequacy of organizational resources and equipment, and factors affecting organizational performance, is essential and depends on the effective communication of information.

Organizational communication never functions perfectly, however. It is often the case that organizations experience problems, often serious ones, with their communications systems. Any failure in communication will impede organizational functioning. If it occurs regularly on a wide scale, such failure can cripple an organization.

Dawson (1989) has identified five characteristics of an ideal communication:

1   **accuracy**: message clearly reflects intention and truth as seen by sender and is received as such;
2   **reliability**: diverse observers would receive message in same way;
3   **validity**: message captures 'reality', is consistent, allows prediction and incorporates 'established knowledge';
4   **adequacy**: message is of sufficient quantity and appropriate timing;
5   **effectiveness**: message achieves the intended result from sender's point of view.

(p. 171)

Communication can often fail in respect of any of these ideals. As Dawson further observes:

A basic problem which faces all participants in organizations is how to get 'appropriate' information to the 'right' place at the 'right' time so that it has the intended effect, particularly when the complexities of life often make it difficult to determine what the 'right place', 'right time', and 'right information' actually are.

(1989, p. 171)

She examines some reasons underlying these communications difficulties in organizations. These are summarized in Table 5.3.

Dawson warns against paying too much attention to information which is quantifiable, to the extent that qualitative information is ignored or discounted. While it may be important to be able to quantify communicative interactions in organizations, the 'quality' of the information they convey may be just as vital to the effective functioning and performance of the organization.

It is important to be sure that information upon which crucial organizational decisions are to be based can be independently verified. Some details, such as future costs in relation to equipment or facilities, or changes to the working environment or employment practices, can be verified against external sources. Other information which comes in the form of 'expert' opinion may be less open to separate verification. It is essential that an organization has confidence in the accuracy and reliability of its information.

Table 5.3 Information and communication in organizations: general issues

Quantification:	(a) Information varies in the extent to which it is quantifiable.
	(b) Quantifiable information is often given precedence over non-quantifiable information in decision-making.
Verification:	Information varies in the extent to which it can be subject to external verification.
Neutrality:	Information is rarely used in a completely neutral way.
Security:	Information is a costly and scarce resource.
Formal and informal communications networks:	Hierarchies often emerge even if they are not imposed on communication networks.
Gatekeepers:	Control access and interpretation of information across physical, social and technical barriers.
Partiality:	Information held and transmitted by people is often partial and reflects their interests and resources.
Suppression:	Some information may be consciously or subconsciously excluded from consideration, if it questions or counters the dominant view.

Source: Dawson (1989). Reprinted by permission of the publisher

ORGANIZATIONAL STRUCTURE AND COMMUNICATIONS

The design of an organization can have a considerable influence over the flow of communications through it. Organizations are often designed in ways that determine who may or may not communicate with whom, as well as how and when. It is important, therefore, to give some consideration to the part played by the structure of an organization in studying the effectiveness of organizational communications.

Organizational structure has been defined as 'the formally prescribed pattern of interrelationships existing between the various units of an organization' (Baron and Greenberg, 1990, p. 342). The structure of an organization can be described using a diagram called an organizational chart or organogram. This can provide a graphic representation of an organization's formal, official structure, revealing the different units or sections into which it can be divided and the formal connections which exist between these. The composite units of an organization tend to be functionally defined, each one providing a different function as part of the business of the organization. The organizational chart can also show the lines of authority which exist between different individuals in the organization. The *organogram* shows the structure of the hierarchical relationship within the organization as perceived by the people at the top. In addition to this, there is the *formalogram*, which shows the vertical and horizontal structure of the formal relationships, as mutually perceived by members of the organization. A further chart, the *informalogram*, is designed to reveal informal relationships among individuals within the organization, independently of their official positions (see Figure 5.5). These charts reveal to whom each individual must answer, as well as the people for whom line managers are responsible. Thus, employees in the organization are differentiated according to their position in the hierarchy.

The formalogram is based on the answers to the following questions:

1   Name the person to whom you report, i.e., the person who supervises your work.
2   Name any other persons to whom you report (in addition to the person you normally report to in Question 1).
3   Name the persons who report to you, i.e., whose work you supervise.
4   Name any other persons who report to the same person as you (the one whom you named in Question 1), i.e., your equals in the hierarchy.

On this chart a line connecting two people (represented by rectangles) indicates mutual agreement. For example, if the first person names the second as the one to whom he reports, and the second person names the

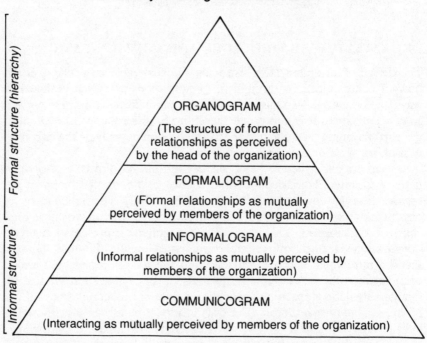

The territory of the organizational structure

ORGANOGRAM

(The structure of formal relationships as perceived by the head of the organization)

FORMALOGRAM

(Formal relationships as mutually perceived by members of the organization)

INFORMALOGRAM

(Informal relationships as mutually perceived by members of the organization)

COMMUNICOGRAM

(Interacting as mutually perceived by members of the organization)

Formal structure (hierarchy)

Informal structure

Figure 5.5 The tools used in measuring managerial relationships and interactions – as they approach the territory of the organizational structure

first as the one who reports to him, they will be connected on the chart by a solid line. Dotted lines are usually employed to indicate mutual agreement with an additional supervisor, and with equals in the hierarchy.

The informalogram chart, showing the system of informal relationships as mutually perceived by members of the organization, is based on the answers to the question: 'Name the person with whom you *generally* work *most closely* regardless of their position in the organization.' When it occurs that two participants (represented in the chart by circles) name each other, they are connected by a solid line.

One of the problems with producing a map of an organization based on answers to the above questions, is that while two people may mutually identify a formal link between them, they may not necessarily perceive, value, or weight that link in the same way. Unless the meaning and character of a communication are perceived in the same way by those participating in the interaction, a break can occur in the communications network. Thus, a different conceptual analysis is required which examines communications links at a deeper level, in order to understand fully the shape of the organizational communication system.

This alternative scheme views the communications networks as including not only the total spoken or written contacts (or interactions) between members of the organization, but also the degree of agreement regarding the communication. In order that the organization shall continue to exist and survive, it is not enough that a proportion of these interactions should be mutually perceived by participants as having occurred; it is equally essential that those transmitting the communication should agree, in a proportion of instances, as to its character and spirit.

The conceptual tool which has been developed to assess communications at this level has been called the communications chart, or *communicogram*. The communicogram is a chart representing the communication system in an organization. The chart shows the interactions that take place within the organization as reported by its members, with the emphasis being put on mutually perceived interactions, that is, on those cases where there was mutual agreement between the two sides that the interaction had occurred, and at the stated time.

The data for this chart can be obtained from a questionnaire or a diary which the participant is required to fill in daily, noting the interactions both face-to-face and by telephone in which he/she took part, as far as he/she remembers them. Participants are required to record the topic of each interaction, its nature, their impressions of it, and to state who was the active party. Typical response categories include:

- With whom the communication took place.
- The topic of the communication.
- Whether the communication was by telephone, or face-to-face.
- The initiator of the communication.

- The type of communication.
- Identification of the main role player.
- Rating of the importance of the communication.
- Rating of the success of the communication.
- Whether a decision was required or not.
- Whether a decision was made or not.
- Identification of the decision-maker.
- Rating of preference for the decision that was made.
- Rating of satisfaction with the decision that was made.

An analysis of these data will show the method of communication which is most generally used in the organization (telephone or facc-to-face), as well as the amount of mutual agreement between the participants regarding the interaction itself, and the amount of mutual agreement on its topic, nature, impressions of it, of who was the active party, and so on.

The method of communication generally refers only to telephone or face-to-face communication. It is generally accepted that for many purposes written communication is less effective than oral, because it employs neither the voice nor the expression of the eyes. But the main reason that written communication is not included in the communicogram is that it makes for difficulties in estimating mutual perception, since approach and response are not simultaneous.

The interactions are recorded from memory by the participant twice a day, and not immediately after they have taken place. This is based on the belief that those interactions which impressed themselves on the participant's memory are the most important. Even when the record takes the form of a diary, not all the interactions are recorded. Placing a limit on the requirement continuously to be filling out a record of interactions also reduces the load for the participant.

The communicogram facilitates learning about the organization in its entirety, as well as about specific groups of people within it; it also facilitates an examination of each participant individually and in relation to the average for the whole group.

The data yielded by this technique comprise reports from each individual participant of all work-related interactions during an n-day period. The most important feature of these data is that in the case of interactions with other respondents (in-group communications), an independent report of each interaction is obtained from each party to the interaction. Thus, by means of a matching procedure, discrepancies in the two reports can be identified; further, differences between the participants in the extent to which they see themselves as achieving desired outcomes can be identified. These matchings are achieved via a computer program developed to complete the task.

Communications research using a communicogram tends to be carried out over a period of ten working days (two weeks). Respondents may vary in respect of the number of days on which they provide daily logs of their communications interactions. The aim must always be to get them to produce comprehensive catalogues of interactions on as many of the days as possible.

'Daily interactions forms' are filled out twice a day, usually just before lunchtime and then again before the end of the day. These forms are then collected by the researchers/consultants within twenty-four hours. Participants are instructed to record all conversations which take place while they are at work. Face-to-face and telephone conversations are distinguished. Each form allows for the provision of a variety of different types of information. Each day, participants fill out a 'morning' form and an 'afternoon' form. A computer program is used to process the data from these forms. Data are produced by feedback to the client and for the detailed analysis usage of the researcher.

For the participants, data can be fed back concerning the participant himself alongside summary statistics for his department, his salary bracket, and totals for all participants, e.g.:

- Average number of interactions per person, per day, per day of participation in the research.
- The proportion of all potentially mutual interactions which were mutually perceived.
- The characteristics of the interaction (initiator, type, etc.), with separate figures for mutual, non-mutual, and total interactions.
- The extent of consensus as to the characteristics of mutual interactions.

All data fed back to participants can be aggregated in order to compare the results for different departments/divisions within the organization, as well as between salary brackets.

For the purpose of drawing up a communicogram, a matrix is produced showing the extent of mutual perception between each pair of participants. In order to identify any systematic differences in the results at different times of the day, and different stages of the research, hourly data are obtained for each participant showing the number of mutual, non-mutual, and total interactions for each day.

A communicogram technique can produce a picture of the shape of communications networking within an organization, based on information obtained from employees themselves about whom they communicate with, and how often. Questions can also be asked about the amount, content, or importance of the communications. Doing this with appropriate groups within the organization enables 'maps' indicating communication routeways to be produced. In addition to questions dealing with the frequency of communications, valuable additional information can be obtained by asking employees to rate the importance of different communications to their work.

The following types of individual or groups may be identified in this way:

- The 'communication star': individuals who do a large amount of communicating compared with the organizational or departmental average.
- The 'clique': a group of individuals who communicate mainly with each other.
- The 'bridge': a person who is a member of one communications clique and links it via a communication dyad with another clique. (A dyad is a group of two people only.)
- The 'liaison': a person who interpersonally connects two or more cliques in a system without himself/herself belong to any clique.
- The 'isolate': an individual who has relatively few communication contacts with the rest of the system.

The information is most easily classified in a matrix chart form and is then transferred to some type of diagrammatic form (see Figure 5.6). The network may then be compared with the formal organizational chart to see how official lines of management are reflected in actual communication behaviour. This stage may explain many problems (and prevent future ones prior to reorganization).

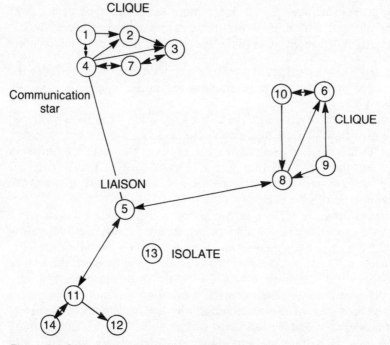

Figure 5.6 Sociometric chart mapping internal organizational communications
Note: Each circle represents a member of the organization.

The answers to the second question provide information about the informal network, or 'grapevine'. Studies of organizational grapevines have shown them to be sometimes inaccurate, but very much faster than formal means of communication (as they tap people's need for affiliation at work). We turn now to examine formal and informal communications networks within organizations in more detail.

Measures of power and salience

A great deal of the communications and interactions that take place within organizations are concerned with taking decisions or obtaining information which will guide decision-making processes. Decisions are geared to facilitate courses of action which lead to, and produce desired outcomes. Issuing instructions from a position of authority, or negotiating a preferred outcome through persuasive arguments, both involve power plays among the participants. By inviting participants in a communications audit to provide opinions about the nature of any outcome deriving from an interaction, the communicogram can reveal a power profile of the organization. One rating scale that is used for this purpose takes the following form:

1 The decision was one that I wanted.
2 The decision was close to what I wanted.
3 The decision was a compromise.
4 The decision was close to what the other person wanted.
5 The decision was not what I wanted.
0 No preference.

This scale can be used as a basis for two different measures of power. The first is a measure of each individual's ability to obtain his preferred outcomes as perceived by the other parties in the interactions. This measure of individual power is derived from the average of all other organization members' ratings of their interactions with any given individual. Since this measure is an average of the reports of a possible $(n-1)$ factors about their interactions with one other person, the influence of personal bias is minimized in the measure. This measure has been referred to as the *collective power index* of a given individual. The second measure is based on each individual's ability to obtain his preferred outcomes as perceived by himself. This is averaged over all decisions and, therefore, removes any effect of relationship with particular individuals. This measure has been referred to as the *self-perceived power index* of a given individual.

These measures permit power relationships to be estimated between pairs or groups of individuals, between levels of the hierarchy, between departments or any other groupings. The discrepancy between them, i.e. between the way in which the individual sees his own power position and the way in which others see it, may provide measures of individual social adaptation and of organizational climate.

Subjective salience

The subjective salience of each decision can be measured by an appropriate rating scale of the importance of that decision to the particular individual concerned. One scale that has been used here is: not very important; fairly important; very important; crucially important.

Participants are carefully briefed on how they should use the salience rating scale. Rather than ask for ratings of the salience of interactions in terms of attaining organizational goals, participants tend to be asked to rate the communication in terms of its salience to them in carrying out their job. The latter approach has been found to be more meaningful for the recording of ongoing events, rather than the importance of the interaction for the organization as a whole. The formulation given is: 'Please indicate your evaluation of the importance of the interaction to you in carrying out your job.'

Thus the communicogram represents a method for describing the pattern, frequency, and accuracy of communications within an organization. Two of the most important problems confronting leaders of organizations are how to describe the structure of their organization to themselves and others, and how to decide when, where, and how to introduce changes in their organizational structures and systems.

The most prevalent method of describing organizational structures is the organization chart, which represents the formal relationships in the organization as perceived by people at the top of the hierarchy pyramid of the organization. It is a mixture of what they believe to be the formal relationships and of what, in their opinion, such relationships should preferably be. Other types of chart present the relationships as perceived by all members of the organization entered in the chart. After each member has indicated how he himself perceives his own formal or informal relationship, the overall structure is then drafted. One such chart confined to formal relationships has been referred to as a 'formalogram'. Another better-known chart relates to informal relationships; it is known to social scientists as the 'Sociogram' and has also been called an 'informalogram'.

The basic difference between the organization chart, on the one hand, and the formalogram and informalogram, on the other, lies in the depth of insight they allow into the organizational structure. The organization chart is a sort of map, an aerial photograph if you like, in which all linkages between the individuals listed are complete and no disagreements or omissions occur. In the formalogram and informalogram, disagreements or omissions between people as to their roles relative to each other always appear; they thus tend to pinpoint people who are 'strongly situated' in the organizational structure, on the one hand, and people who are organizationally 'deviant' or 'isolated', on the other. Nevertheless, the formalo-gram and the informalogram both have shortcomings, especially in as much as they are normally incapable of dealing with communication dynamics in the time dimension.

Thus, in view of the 'single-shot' character of the charts, a person who was missing from work for several days is likely to be overlooked by his colleagues when describing their organizational relationships. It is the events immediately preceding the moment when the respondent is reporting his relationships that would most probably affect his choice of individuals and his perception of their organizational positions the most. Again, an unpleasant or, alternatively, a very pleasing, recent interaction with somebody would impress the memory in such a way that the particular person in question would undoubtedly be organizationally perceived, while others might be omitted.

Furthermore, the fact that two people mutually perceive each other as formal or informal colleagues does not really mean that all goes well between them in the organizational sense. The relationship might exist in their minds, but the communications, or perhaps even the rapport between them, are far from conducive to the maintenance of a healthy organiz-ational climate.

The volume of information flow

Another important feature of organizational communications is the assess-ment of how much information flows along different channels. Different individuals or channels of communication may vary in their capacity to carry and process information. If an individual, group, department, or the organization as a whole becomes bogged down with more information than it can handle, a condition of overload develops. Under this condition, the functioning of the organization can become seriously impeded. Information can become distorted or even omitted from decision-making processes, with the result that the organization may make bad or incorrect decisions about its business. Such problems can be overcome through the use of *gatekeepers*, who are individuals whose job is to regulate and control the flow of information so that overload does not occur. Another solution lies in the general management of information through processing systems which themselves regulate the way in which incoming information is handled (see Figure 5.7).

As well as easing the flow of information to prevent overload, gate-keepers may sometimes deliberately restrict access to information under their control as a power ploy. Thus, senior management may withhold information from staff down the line. Staff can also prevent information from flowing up to their managers. Specialists may control the flow into and around the organization of special, technical information which is important to an organization's performance. Individuals with different

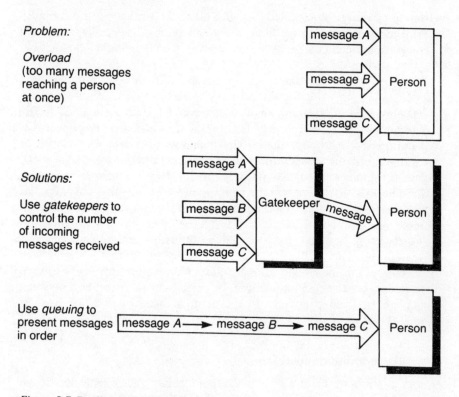

Problem:

Overload
(too many messages
reaching a person
at once)

Solutions:

Use *gatekeepers* to
control the number
of incoming
messages received

Use *queuing* to
present messages
in order

Figure 5.7 Dealing with information overload
Source: Baron and Greenberg (1990), p. 359

vested interests and who have unique control over the flow of certain essential information within the organization may use their position to gain personal benefits.

There are dangers inherent in control over information and decision-making residing in the power of just a few individuals in an organization. The information held by individuals is usually partial and reflects their own interests and objective. It is rare that an individual or even a management team will hold all the information on a subject. Information breakdown or inadequacy may then occur because individuals whose responsibility it is to feed a particular category of information to the organization are insufficiently aware, skilled or motivated to do so.

Information which questions or runs counter to accepted wisdom may be selectively ignored or discounted. Individuals in organizations may have their own solutions to problems and be unwilling to consider alternatives. This 'groupthink' mentality (Janis, 1972), in which members of the organization suppress doubts and mutually reinforce a plan of action, even though it may be misguided, can lead to disastrous results. It is essential not simply to verify facts, but also to doubt them by questioning 'established' evidence with contrasting views, until all counter arguments have been comprehensively dispelled.

Overcoming barriers to communication

It is important that communication is controlled and systematic in order to be effective. The worst communication method management can allow is the grapevine. Although facts can be communicated accurately and swiftly via this route, the reasons for a particular decision may be less charitable than if the news had been spread more formally. The grapevine will say that someone is being promoted because she is marrying the boss's son, and not because she is good at her job, with the result that other people who are not promoted may feel resentful. Clearly this is a situation to be avoided. It is essential then, for the smooth running of the organization, that staff learn about happenings and decisions in a systematic manner.

There are a number of ways in which news within the organization can be communicated down the line:

- Through face-to-face communication between managers and their staff.
- Through written memoranda.
- Through discussing matters with staff representatives.
- Through mass methods, such as a house journal or notice boards.

Managers must decide which method to use, and be clear about what can be communicated through each of these channels, and what limitations each method has. All too often, communication breaks down because managers use the wrong methods, or because they try to communicate the wrong type of information through a particular system.

Many attempts to improve communication fail because executives and senior managers have not considered communication as a highly complex and dynamic human process. Too often, the *substance* of communication (information) is mistaken for its *form* (a complex, interpersonal process of people relating to other people). Ineffective communications tend to emphasize techniques and devices for sending and regulating the flow, and content of information throughout an organization.

The pseudo-information approach assumes that communication is primarily the responsibility of the sender and is an influence process through which people can be changed, controlled, guided, or influenced. Much attention is paid to media devices, refinement of the message, timing of presentation, public relations, visual aids, and so on. Emphasis is placed on getting the 'facts' to the right people, informing subordinates about the goals of the company, motivating people to work, seeing that people understand what it is that management is trying to do, and getting the message across. This approach tends to assume that information will change attitudes and behaviour, and that information can be reliably transmitted through formal channels.

The reality is, that information approaches to organizational communication usually accomplish considerably less than management would hope. Organizational information alone does not necessarily change attitudes, value systems or perceptions. People tend to perceive information or to reinterpret data in the directions of their motivation and wishes: they hear what they want to hear, and forget what they want to forget. In short, people select from available information, overreact, or underreact, and add their own distortions, to the information received.

Adding this 'one-way' or 'unilateral' information approach to communication assumes a completely active sender and a completely passive receiver; it assumes that the sender knows what the receiver hears, and how the receiver feels about and interprets what he or she hears. Rarely are receivers of communications passive; rarely do they hear all that was communicated; rarely do they perceive the facts as intended. Rather, the receivers of such communications interpret the information in the light of their own needs, values, viewpoints, and motivations. Communication not only involves the message, but it also involves mutual perceptions, feelings, attitudes, and values. In short, communication is a highly competitive relationship between sender and receiver which involves emotion and feeling, as well as topic or task. The manager or executive who concentrates on the task level of communication in a work operation, and neglects the emotional level, often fails in human relationships.

There are many barriers to successful communication which a sensitive communicator must strive to overcome. In addition to those pointed out above, there may be the normal differences in culture, education, age, race, religion, social status, nationality, value systems, and language. Finally, there are obstacles to communication which may arise from lack of intelligence, impaired vision or auditory skills, inadequate time, illness, and fatigue. It is more than worth the effort to cope with the challenges inherent in ordinary human communication. Improper communication can inhibit personal growth for both sender and receiver; ideas of value may remain unshared, or at least not fully appreciated.

Enhancing the flow of communication

Efforts directed towards improving communications can have considerable benefits for the organization and the people who work for it. Improvements to communications can be addressed at two levels: the individual level and the organizational level. Hints for individuals who wish to improve either their spoken or written communications include keeping the language used as simple as possible, whilst minimizing jargon; and paying more attention to listening carefully to (and trying harder to understand) others' communications. These are simple rules of thumb to state, and seem quite obvious. However, it is surprising how often they underlie communications failure between individuals within organizations.

Removal of the barriers to communications needs to be addressed if communication is to be improved. This entails examining many aspects of the organization. How does the structure of the organization inhibit effective communication? Are there certain role positions within the organization which help or hinder communication? It is necessary, therefore, to know what the barriers to effective communication are before they can be removed, and a communications audit has an important part to play in answering such questions. Steers (1977) has provided the following general advice about improving organizational communication effectiveness:

Downward communications

- Job instructions can be presented clearly to employees, so they understand more precisely what is expected.
- Efforts can be made to explain the rationale behind the required tasks to employees, so they understand why they are being asked to do something.
- Management can provide greater feedback concerning the nature and quality of performance, thereby keeping employees 'on target'.
- Multiple communication channels can be used to increase the chances that the message will be properly received.
- Important messages can be repeated to ensure penetration.
- In some cases, it is desirable to bypass formal communication channels and go directly to the intended receiver with the message.

Upward communications

- Upward messages can be screened so only the more relevant aspects are received by top management.
- Managers can attempt to change the organizational climate so subordinates feel freer to transmit negative as well as positive messages, without fear of retribution.
- Managers can sensitize themselves so they are better able to detect bias and distorted messages from their subordinates.
- Sometimes it is possible to use 'distortion-proof' means of communicating messages, such as providing subordinates with report forms requiring quantified or standardized data.
- Social distance and status barriers between employees on various levels can be reduced so messages will be more spontaneous.

Horizontal communications

- Efforts can be made to develop interpersonal skills between group members and departments, so greater openness and trust exist.
- Reward systems can be utilized which reward interdepartmental co-operation and minimize 'zero-sum game' situations.
- Interdepartmental meetings can be used to share information concerning what other departments are involved in.
- In some cases, the actual design of the organization itself can be changed to provide greater opportunities for interdepartmental contacts (e.g., shifting from a tradition to a matrix organizational design).

At the organizational level, it is important for organizations to examine their internal communications systems in two areas. First, communication with those whom organizations employ is essential. In particular, obtaining effective feedback from employees can be a crucial aspect of monitoring organizational performance, and causes underlying good and poor performance.

The role of feedback in maintaining and improving performance has been researched over many years (Arys, 1917) and in many different contexts (e.g., education, industry). Usually, studies have consisted of a demonstration that providing performance-related information is far better than withholding such information. Very often, though, these studies have failed to take into account the full range and complexity of feedback information derived from different sources, which the individual may take into account in judging his or her own performance.

Studies which have taken place in contrived, laboratory settings, for instance, frequently provide an oversimplified 'reality' which underplays or fails to account comprehensively for the complexity of an actual job setting. It is known that performance-related information can derive from a variety of sources (Greller and Harold, 1975; Hamser and Muchinsky, 1978; Ilgen, Fisher and Taylor, 1979). Many variables influence whether or not these sources of information and the information they supply are given any significance (Ilgen *et al.*, 1979). Also, feedback information is generated by many factors other than simply objective measures of performance (Fisher, 1979).

In a theoretical assessment of the nature of feedback, Ilgen *et al.* (1979) classified sources of feedback into three types: (a) other individuals who have knowledge of the recipient's performance; (b) the task environment itself (through inherent properties of the task, or feedback mechanisms built into the task), and (c) the recipient judging his or her own performance. Greller and Harold (1975), on the other hand, postulated five sources (the formal organization, immediate supervisor, co-workers, the task, and self) and found that people did report getting feedback information from each of these and that generally the informativeness of these sources increased as they moved from psychologically distant (i.e., the formal organization) to psychologically closer (i.e., one's own feelings and ideas) sources. Hamser and Muchinsky (1978) replicated these findings and went on to show that people were able to distinguish between work information received from these sources, and other constructs such as satisfaction with the sources.

In addition to the question of where the feedback comes from, it is important to address the issue of the nature of the content of the feedback message itself. Perceptions of the source as a ready and reliable provider of feedback does not reveal much about the nature of that feedback information.

One important aspect of feedback is its sign – that is, whether it is positive or negative. Positive feedback is recalled more readily than negative feedback (Feather, 1968; Ilgen and Hamstra, 1972). Sources can vary in the extent to which they give positive or negative feedback (Fisher, 1979; Herold and Greller, 1977). Going beyond the good–bad dimension of the feedback, what other information does it convey? Research has shown that a wide array of information can be contained in feedback messages (Herold and Greller, 1977). Indeed, it is possible to develop a taxonomy of messages based on type of source, information quality and valence. Herold and Parsons (1985) set out to develop a means for assessing the amount and type of performance feedback available to individuals in work settings. Their findings indicated support for fifteen identifiable dimensions (or source and type combinations) for measuring 'how much' of 'what' is 'out there'. These dimensions shed light on the content or nature of the message being received by the employee. The findings also showed that:

1 Some source distinctions are not as important as is the nature of the content of the message.
2 Negative feedback is not only important, but needs to be assessed independently of positive feedback.
3 Some feedback concepts commonly used, such as self-generated feedback, are really multidimensional and need to be explored as such.
4 Relatively stable measures of feedback available in work environments can be developed.
5 These measures have the potential to differentially describe objectively different environments, rather than just reflecting socially desirable responses or other problems associated with paper-and-pencil measures.

The last point is very important given, the many contexts in which the concept of feedback is supposedly central. Yet it does not automatically follow that we know what kinds of feedback are relevant – how much, from whom, and so on. For example, if job redesign calls for more feedback, should it consist of more feedback from the organization, from a line manager, or from a task that the employee has to carry out? Or should employees be taught how to self-monitor more effectively? To what extent does the type of feedback need to fit the nature of the work being monitored? How important is the value employees themselves attach to different forms of feedback mechanism in judging its probable effectiveness in a given work situation? All of these are important questions that need to be borne in mind when assessing or implementing any changes of organizational feedback processes.

There are a number of techniques for obtaining feedback from employees. These most popularly include *employee surveys, suggestion systems, quality circles,* and *corporate hotlines.* Surveys can be used to measure employees' attitudes towards different aspects of the work environment, management effectiveness, and organizational communications. Previous chapters have explored how survey techniques can play a part in measuring organizational culture and climate.

Suggestion systems are a way of tapping into the creativity of those who work for the organization. Employees at all levels are a potential source of ideas concerning how different parts of the organization could operate more effectively. In so many organizations, however, the voice of the individual employee is never heard. Few, if any, opportunities are provided enabling employees to put their views and ideas forward and to ensure that they reach the people who have the authority to implement them. Suggestion boxes represent one technique that is designed to overcome this problem. American research has shown that within companies who supply suggestion boxes, about 15 per cent of employees tend to use them and that about 25 per cent of the suggestions made are implemented (Vernyi, 1987).

Another technique is corporate hotlines and telephone lines which are staffed by corporate personnel who are assigned to listen to employees' comments and opinions. This technique can provide a very quick and efficient channel through which senior management can learn about the issues and concerns which are high on the agenda of the people they employ.

AUDITING CORPORATE COMMUNICATION

Communication, or the failure to communicate, is often cited as a cause of problems within an organization. Communication problems, however, are often the symptoms of deeper-seated difficulties which exist within companies. Communication, other than the most formal kinds, generally flows along friendship channels. When trust exists, content is more freely communicated and more accurately perceived by the recipient. When individuals have different goals and value systems, it is important to create understanding about needs and motives. Often, the free flow of ideas and information is restricted by the feeling that one may not receive credit for the contribution or, by fear, that one's idea(s) will be stolen.

The organization as a communication system can be defined in terms of four elements:

1 There are characteristics of the information taken into the organization from the outside in a wide variety of ways, ranging from sales orders, reports about competitors, or the state of the market place, through to family problems told by one employee to his/her manager.
2 There are the organization's rules for doing something about the information. What happens to the sales order? What will be done in response to information about a competitor? How are an employee's personal/family problems to be dealt with?
3 There are rules about handling information generated from inside the organization. What parts of the organization make decisions, or issue orders? How does information move through the organization?
4 There are the characteristics of information leaving the organization, through orders to suppliers, deliveries to customers, and public relations releases. It makes a difference who gathers the information, who filters it and for what purpose, and how various people perceive and interpret the information.

Getting accurate information upward through the organization is a particularly difficult problem. The supervisor may sense the feelings of a group of workers, filter out that which makes him or her look at fault, and pass the information to the boss, who in turn follows a similar screening procedure. The use of the problem-solving approach not only stimulates less-filtered upward communication, but also helps to create a climate more favourable to decision-making and helps to remove sources of resistance to change. When people near the bottom of the pyramid feel their views are getting to the top unfiltered, they are more receptive to orders coming down through channels.

An important question to ask about the best way of communication is 'Communication for what?' One experimenter set up a laboratory situation in which A talked to B without return talk, which was termed one-way communication. Two-way communication was set up similarly: this time there was conversation, that is, communication from A to B and from B back to A. Later the same format was followed involving more people. Several practical findings emerged showing that the one-way communication was much *faster*, but two-way communication was more *accurate*, and the receivers felt more sure of themselves in the two-way system. The sender was more vulnerable in the two-way condition because the receiver picked up mistakes and oversights, and told the sender about them. Thus, if speed alone is of primary importance, the one-way system is best. But if accuracy is essential, a two-way system is more advantageous.

Effective communication within an organization matters:

1   Communication failures are costly. Many organizations have suffered poor productivity, and industrial problems which could have been prevented, had internal lines of communications worked more effectively.

2   During times of change within an organization, the full benefits of change can be achieved only where there is an adequate communication system for explaining directly to the employees – preferably face-to-face – what is required of them and why.

3   Adequate communications results in greater productivity, because employees direct their work more effectively and co-operate more with their leaders. Some companies have found, for example, that regular management briefings can produce a significant upsurge in work activity.

4   Poor communication may lead to good executives leaving the organization because they are not aware of their prospects. Finding and training a successor from outside the organization can be a costly matter, and it lowers morale among colleagues. In order to avoid such situations, it is important for top management to communicate to staff down the line about their progress and what their futures will be within the organization.

5   There is no monopoly of wisdom at the top of organizations. Staff can have useful ideas, which if put into action would benefit the organization. It is wasteful to ignore and fail to put to good use the inventiveness and initiatives of subordinates. Thus, organizations need to have a communication system in which good ideas generated from below are given every opportunity to reach the highest level for full consideration.

6   People will give of their best to their work if they fully understand the decisions that affect them, and the reasons behind those decisions. Employees need to understand what they have to do and why, how they are performing against budgets and targets they have been set, and what their conditions of employment are. Given this understanding, employees can become more involved in what they are doing, giving rise to higher staff morale, greater co-operation, efficiency and productivity.

The scope of a communications audit

Different authors use the term 'communications audit' to cover a number of different meanings, some very limited and some too wide-ranging.

One definition (Booth, 1988, p. 8) runs as follows: 'The process whereby the communications within an organization are analysed by an internal or external consultant, with a view to increasing organizational efficiency.' This meaning is primarily concerned with communication within the organization and so does not include any measurement of the organization's advertising or PR capability. However, some communications with the outside environment do need to be included, such as for example, the systems used to communicate with clients/customers, or the ordering system used when purchasing from raw material suppliers.

A key factor in effective leadership and management is the extent to which managers pay serious attention to communication, both upward and downward. The more trouble organizations take over communication, the better its employees are likely to work for it. Taking action to improve communication can have many positive benefits, in terms of improved staff morale and efficiency, and better productivity. Checking the effectiveness of organizational communication, like the communication process itself, needs to be taken seriously and carried out in a systematic fashion. One technique, which has been referred to as 'management by walking about' involves the manager in walking around the work-place, chatting with staff about their work and other matters, and above all, listening to what they have to say. Management by walking about may not always provide an effective procedure to obtain communications feedback, however: it may be insufficiently systematic and influenced by personality factors among both managers and staff.

A more formal means of checking things out is through the use of a communications audit. This process involves a survey of employee communications behaviours and of their attitudes towards communications systems within the organization. There are a variety of different instruments available for conducting communications audits; some may be 'off-the-shelf' items which have been used elsewhere, while others are custom-built for the organization in question. Instruments, as we will see, include diaries and a range of questionnaires on which staff supply information about the forms of communication they themselves use, how often they use each one, and how effective they perceive it to be, or a parallel range of questions concerning the communications they receive from others, above, below, or on the same level as themselves.

Reasons for a communication audit

We have already established the significance of effective communication systems for organizational functioning. There may, however, be specific reasons why communications in general or in certain parts of the organization are failing to work as effectively as they might.

Organizations may need to audit their communications for a number of reasons:

- To establish communications effectiveness and efficiency – questioning information underload or overload, potential communications opportunities or inhibiting factors.
- To evaluate the quality of communications within the organization or between the organization and external parties.

- To assess the quality of communications management to assist in planning the development of an improved communications structure.
- To identify operational communications networks, their effectiveness and the impact of new technology.
- To determine communications bottlenecks and gaps.
- To learn from communications failures and incidents.
- To define communications, as a part of management behaviours and styles.
- To establish the cost effectiveness of presently used channels of communication.

Other writers have provided further lists of reasons for doing a corporate communications audit and have identified the occasions when conducting such an audit would be positively appropriate. Emanuel (1985) listed nine important functions of a communications audit:

1 To find out how well communications programmes are working.
2 To diagnose current or potential communication problems or missed opportunities.
3 To evaluate new communications policy or practice.
4 To assess the relationship of communications to other organizational operations on corporate and local levels.
5 To develop communications budgets.
6 To develop benchmarks against which the impact of future changes to communications would be compared.
7 To measure progress against previously established benchmarks.
8 To develop or restructure the communications function within an organization.
9 To provide background for developing formal communications policies and plans.

According to Emanuel, communications audits could prove to be positively useful to organizations at times of major reorganization; during mergers or acquisitions; when a new management team is being introduced; during business turndown; when external events cause concern; and when facing important negotiations with unions.

In Britain, Booth (1988) found the following typical reasons for carrying out such audits, according to consultants working in this area:

- Prior to a large-scale company restructuring or to a rationalization exercise.
- After a large-scale company restructuring or rationalization exercise.
- When there is a need to increase the motivation of employees.
- When telephone or fax bills are increasing rapidly, or are perceived to be too high.
- When customers have difficulty making contact with the sales department.

- When long-term plans and strategies are being developed.
- When there is a need to check that managers and their subordinates see things in the same light (e.g. when a strike is threatened that will, with hindsight, be blamed upon poor management/union communications).
- Before any decision is taken on the purchase of telecommunications hardware.
- When there are too many memos and not enough relevant information.
- When labour turnover is too high.
- When there is an obvious communications problem.
- When a routine check of organizational effectiveness is required.

THE COMMUNICATIONS AUDIT PROCESS

Of necessity, this starts with a review. Such a review often begins with preliminary research into internal communications within the organization, comprising open discussions or a workshop with senior management about their approaches to employee communication. This exercise can have a number of benefits:

- It can begin to identify problems with communications which need to be pursued further in later stages of the audit.
- It can increase senior management awareness of the importance of good internal communications.
- It can encourage the commitment of senior management to a communications audit.
- It can reduce any feelings of threat of an audit and promote understanding of what it can and cannot achieve.

It is very important with a communication audit, as with the other corporate audits we have discussed, to obtain full senior management backing and co-operation. Initial stages of auditing communication therefore should concentrate on consensus-building with senior managers in the hope of gaining their support right from the start.

While individual interviews can provide useful insights, a group gathering of senior executives can add extra cohesion to top management commitment to the project. It also has a number of specific benefits.

- It provides an opportunity for senior managers to exchange views on employee communications and associated topics.
- It affords an opportunity for consultants to input relevant background information about communications audit benefits.
- It allows for a full discussion of how communications audit findings should be used.

- It identifies the areas to be measured in communications effectiveness instruments.
- It defines the employee sample to be monitored.

Some consultants recommend a staged approach to communication auditing. This allows for proper control over the amount of data being produced. Too much research data all at one time can lead to reporting overload, which can impede gaining the full benefits from the exercise.

Communications auditing can take a number of forms with different foci of attention. One perspective is to examine communications *effectiveness*, in which consideration is given to the key communications performance areas for all employees. Another approach is to assess communications *efficiency*, which concentrates on the use of particular channels of information flow in the management chain.

The audit process is not a stand-alone exercise. If it is regarded as such, its benefits will be limited or non-existent. It is necessary to consider the results of the audit in a broader context and to derive recommendations which involve far-reaching changes within the organization management system. Among the latter it is not simply a willingness in principle to implement changes, but a clearly worked set of action points. Among these should be a programme of long-term training and development.

The techniques of communications auditing

On conducting interviews with a number of leading communications-oriented consultancies, Booth (1988) reported that the following eight techniques are the most widely used in auditing communications in the United Kingdom. In order of descending frequency of usage, they are:

- structured interviews;
- unstructured interviews;
- questionnaires;
- group discussions;
- network analysis, or sociograms;
- communications diaries;
- telephone call logging/monitoring;
- in-tray/out-tray analysis;

Other techniques used by consultants include:

- checking and analysis of telephone bills;
- looking at house newspaper, videos, and training films, etc.;
- reviewing all printed matter;
- carrying out a structured systems analysis;
- drawing a picture of the principal information flows;
- running computer simulation models of proposed networks to evaluate traffic flow, etc.;

- use of the Delphi forecasting technique;
- monitoring telex usage;
- mail tagging;

The choice of technique is very much dependent upon the objectives of the audit and some techniques are applicable in many cases, whilst others are specifically oriented to individual aspects of the communications process.

The very first step in deciding upon a communications audit is to define the nature of the problems. Sometimes this can be done relatively simply and speedily, but on other occasions it may be a complex and lengthy procedure.

Communications questionnaires

The audit instrument usually takes the form of a questionnaire. This will include questions which will obtain a number of background details about each respondent, such as their sex, age, length of service, location within the company, and so on. In each case, however, assurances will be given to respondents that they will not be identifiable through their answers to these questions, and that all questionnaires will be completed anonymously. In addition to these matters, the questionnaire would probe the communications issues identified by senior managers during earlier individual and group discussions within them.

Any such questionnaire would generally be piloted first on a small number of employees and among senior managers in order to iron out any ambiguities, inaccuracies, or other problems there may be with it. Once tested and refined in this way, it is then ready to be distributed throughout the organization to all employees. It would generally be accompanied by a covering letter explaining its purpose and a reply pre-paid envelope for return.

The advantages of this methodology are that:

- Information can easily be gathered from staff who may be widely dispersed.
- The questionnaire can be given to all staff, thus it involves everyone in the organization.
- It can form the basis of future audits which may be used to follow trends in communications effectiveness over many years.
- It affords an upward communication channel, promoting the transfer of employee views and suggestions which will reach the highest levels of the organization.
- Information from the questionnaire is quantifiable and will give statistically analysable data.
- Where normative data are available from similar surveys conducted elsewhere, the company can draw comparisons between itself and other organizations.

The earliest reference to the term 'communication audit' involved the use of a questionnaire technique (Odiorne, 1954). This instrument, which was used in a survey carried out with a US electronics research and development corporation, comprised a list of sixteen questions which asked employees for their opinions about various aspects and type of organizational communications (see Table 5.4). The questionnaire was given to a sample of managers and engineers. The managers, however, were asked not for their own opinions about corporate communications but were invited to predict what answers they thought would be given by the engineers. These managerial predictions were then compared with engineers' actual responses.

Network analysis

Network analysis is a technique that combines information provided by a 'map' of information flow within the organization, or selected parts of it. It allows the auditor to identify both key communicators and those who communicate very little. It is one way of gaining an organizational overview of communication behaviours that can highlight present and potential problems.

Network analysis obtains from individuals information about whom they communicate with and how frequently they do so. Questions may also be included about the volume or importance of the communication. Thus, communications routeways within the organization can be mapped, much as we have seen illustrated earlier in this chapter. The information is provided on a specially prepared form which enables employees to categorize the types of communications they use, the times of day when communications take place, whether they are the senders or receivers of information, who the communications were with, and how important these communications were thought to be. A more elaborate, lengthier instrument can be used to collect this same information, such as a communications diary.

Communication diaries

A communication diary may be kept by an individual for at least two purposes: to provide information on the communications behaviour of the individual, and to provide information on an individual who is picked as being representative of a group. In the former case the information will be used by the individual and/or his or her supervisor to change communication procedures or behaviour. In the second case the same sort of outcomes are applicable to the group of which the individual is taken to be representative. Communication diaries are particularly useful prior to large-scale restructuring or problem-solving, and may be a logical follow-up to a network analysis, typically to be kept by those who emerge as

Table 5.4 The 'original' communications audit

Question	Summary of answers				
	Management's prediction		Engineers' answers		
	Yes	No	Yes	No	Other
1 Do you feel that you are a part of management?	20	10	24	3	3
2 Do you feel that you have a part in management planning?	2	28	12	15	3
3 Do you feel that you are adequately informed on management aims and long-range planning?	26	4	5	25	0
4 What management information would you like to receive?	DATA OMITTED				
5 Do you feel that present information channels are adequate?	29	1	5	23	2
6 What suggestions do you have to improve present meetings?	DATA OMITTED				
7 Is there enough management participation in departmental meetings?	26	4	8	14	8
8 Would you like to participate more in company planning?	2	27	27	3	1
9 Is your authority commensurate with your responsibility?	26	4	20	9	1
10 Do you feel free to seek counsel on special problems related to but not part of your job?	30	0	25	5	0
11 Do you feel closer to the people you supervise than to the people who supervise you?	9	21	12	5	13
12 Are promotions given generally to proper and deserving individuals?	28	2	18	8	4
13 Do you receive proper tools, information, and incentives to function as part of management?	2	28	8	17	5
14 Is co-operation and contact with other departments satisfactory?	15	15	19	7	4
15 Does management inform you adequately about the industry, the company, products, financial standing, and proposed changes?	29	1	6	23	1
16 How could your work be made more effective?	DATA OMITTED				

Source: Booth (1988), p. 65. Reproduced by permission of the publisher.

'communication stars' and for those who are seen to be isolates.

The amount of organization or structure required when using a communication diary as a research tool will depend upon the uses to be made of the information collected by this method. With some jobs, the keeping of such a diary is somewhat of a nuisance, but for most white-collar jobs a diary may be kept at a 'cost' of a little more than one hour of working time per week. In a small organization it may be worth while to ask all employees to keep such a diary. In the larger organization, various types of sampling processes are available. Communication diaries are kept for specified periods of time which are determined by the project objectives and the type of volume of information they provide. A typical period might be a week. Figures 5.8 and 5.9 present examples of the types of form used.

This type of diary can yield the following information for each individual:

- number of interactions during period surveyed;
- number (and percentage) of face-to-face interactions;
- number (and percentage) of telephone calls;
- number (and percentage) of written communications;
- number (and percentage) of electronic communications;
- number (and percentage) of interactions less than three minutes in duration;
- number (and percentage) of interactions over one hour in duration;
- percentage interaction classified as important;
- percentage interaction classified as satisfactory.

Averages may be obtained from all the diaries of individuals. Diaries are useful in providing evidence on how much communications is internal or external to chosen boundaries, e.g., department, office, or total organization.

Diaries, however, are not without their problems. Although they can yield a great deal of information about the day-to-day (or even hour-to-hour) flow of communications, written and spoken, face-to-face and telephonic, within an organization, they depend for their accuracy on the diligence of the individuals who complete them. The greater the amount of communications-related information they require the diarist to supply, the more problematic diaries can become, if placed with a single individual for any length of time. The accuracy of the diary method can often depend critically upon how it is handled by diarists. Filling out a diary as communications occur can provide an individual record of communications received or sent, but can also be a bothersome task for someone who is kept very busy anyway just dealing with a regular flow of information. The extra workload of diary completion may not always be very welcome. If, however, the diarist completes his/her record of communications activities only periodically, say at the end of each day, the audit information may be much less accurate as memory failure disturbs the record of what really

Name: Steve ID#1			Date: 15 July 1975								Sheet#	1					

	Communication		1	2	3	4	5	6	7	8	9	10	11	12	13	14	15
	ID#	*Name*															
	1	Steve															
	2	Helen	X														
	3	Nash		X													
	4	Boss			X												
	5	Bill				X											
	6	Dennis					X										
	7	Kiwanis Club						X	X								
	8	Friend								X							
	9																
	10																
	11																
	12																
	13																
	14																
OTHER PARTY	15																
	16																
	17																
	18																
	19																
	20																
	21																
	22																
	23																
	24																
	25																
	26																
	27																
	28																
	29																
	30																
	31																
	32																
	Other																

INITIATOR		1	2	3	4	5	6	7	8	9	10	11	12	13	14	15
Self			X		X	X		X	X							
Other		X		X			X									

CHANNEL		1	2	3	4	5	6	7	8	9	10	11	12	13	14	15
Face-to-face		X		X		X			X							
Telephone			X		X											
Written							X	X								

KIND		1	2	3	4	5	6	7	8	9	10	11	12	13	14	15
Job Related		X		X			X	X	X							
Incidental informal, nonjob related			X			X			X							
Organizational rumours					X											

LENGTH		1	2	3	4	5	6	7	8	9	10	11	12	13	14	15
Less than 3 minutes					X	X		X								
3 to 15 minutes		X	X				X									
15 min. to 1 hour																
Over 1 hour				X					X							

QUALITIES		1	2	3	4	5	6	7	8	9	10	11	12	13	14	15
Useful		X		X			X	X								
Extremely or very important		X		X			X	X	X							
Fairly or very satisfactory		X			X	X			X							
Timely																
Accurate																

Figure 5.8 The ICA communication diary
Source: Booth (1988), p. 51. Reproduced by permission of the publisher.

DAILY INTERACTIONS FORM: Morning

Name:................. Date ....

Confidential

Time	1 With whom	2 Topic (see list)	3 How T or F	4 Initiator Self Other	5 Type (see list)	6 Main role player Self Other(s) Equal	7 Importance 1–4	8 Success 1–5	9 Decision(s) required Yes/No	10 Decisions made Yes/No	11 Decision taken Self Other Equal	12 Decision preference 1–5	13 Feeling about decision 1–5	Decisions Contact lasted approximately ...... minutes (round off to –, 5, 10, 15, 20 etc
01														
8 to 9														
02														
9 to 10														

Time: One-hourly time periods throughout the day. One line for each interaction

Column 3: T = Telephone F = Face-to-face

Figure 5.9 Daily self-recording interaction form

happened. The best advice, therefore, is to keep diaries as simple as possible, and place them for relatively short periods of time, during which diarists are asked to keep a complete and ongoing record of communications events as they happen.

Telephone call logging and monitoring

The telephone system within an organization can be examined in its own right and audited separately from other forms of corporate communications. An organization may wish, for example, to stem rising telephone costs. Continuous logging of telephone calls both within the organization and going outside can provide accurate quantifiable evidence of the volume of usage in the organization as a whole, within different sections or departments, and also from particular extensions.

A call-logger attached to an organization's internal telephonic system can record 'the time, date and duration of each call; dialled numbers; the extension from which the call has been made; the cost of each call; the time that incoming callers have to wait before their call is answered; and the number of incoming callers who do not wait until the call is answered' (Booth, 1988, p. 57). The data can reveal peak usage time and ineffective use or abuse of the telephone system, thus providing valuable financial and functional information to the organization.

In-tray, out-tray analysis

This technique can be used to audit the flow of written documentary communications received and sent by individuals. It may form a component of a communications diary or it can be used as a stand-alone measure of communications. The in-tray, out-tray analysis provides an audit of the volume and flow of paper communications (see Figures 5.10 and 5.11).

As with most other communications auditing techniques, the data are gathered on paper through the use of a specially designed form. The respondent provides a catalogue of all written (paper) communications received and sent; how much time is spent processing (reading and writing) documents, as a proportion of the working day; and with which individuals or departments communications take place. This paper communications audit can also include questions about the degree of satisfaction with different communications their form, content, or the way in which they are used. The individuals may be invited to provide some kind of self-classification as a generator or hoarder of paper communications, with some accompanying evaluation of the personal effectiveness of such communications.

In-tray analysis

Name and organization/department of sender:

....

Document title and/or brief description:

....

Length of document (pages): ....

Time taken to deal with document (i.e. reading and actions required as a consequence of its receipt)

....

Was the document: Useful?   ☐
(please tick any relevant box)
                                            Important?   ☐

                                            Inappropriate?   ☐

After reading the document did you?   Pass it on?   ☐

                                            Retain it?   ☐

                                            Take a copy of it? ☐

Please specify any actions you had to take as a consequence of receipt of the document (other than the above).

....

....

....

Comments ....

Figure 5.10 In-tray analysis form
Source: Booth (1988), p. 60. Reproduced by permission of the publisher.

Out-tray analysis

Destination(s) of document (Name and organization/department):

....

Document title and/or brief description: ....

....

Length of document (pages): ....

Time taken to prepare document ....

Comments: ....

....

....

Figure 5.11 Out-tray analysis form
Source: Booth (1988), p. 61. Reproduced by permission of the publisher.

Critical incident technique

This technique is useful for obtaining from employees of an organization evidence concerning the most common or most memorable communications problems in the organization. The initial incident technique is well established and has been successfully used to examine a wide range of organizational problems. It can be usefully applied to an assessment of corporate communications.

The technique invites employees to describe critical communications episodes which they feel are representative of typically successful or unsuccessful incidents. From these descriptive accounts it is possible to diagnose and understand why communications problems occur. In using this technique, care needs to be taken to ensure that the replies do not all point in a particular direction. For instance, there is often a tendency for respondents to recall ineffective communications episodes more often than effective ones.

(Booth, 1988)

Benefits of communications audits

A communications audit is a positive and motivating exercise, being in itself an internal consultation process through which:

- senior management can come to understand better the role of employee communications;
- employees are given what they often regard as a very satisfactory opportunity to have their opinions sought and listened to, and perhaps in consequence, to have their suggestions and ideas acted upon;
- both management and other staff can begin to identify and comprehend the problems of a communication gulf, if one exists between them.

Conducting a communications audit can also herald a change in emphasis in internal communications practice if employees are made aware of the exercise and its objectives before it starts, are informed about progress during the exercise, and are well briefed on the results of the eventual findings.

Top-down feedback, throughout all staff levels who are participating, of the findings and action points after an audit, is essential to satisfy the expectations which may be created by the audit procedure. Regular progress reports will further reinforce the commitment to improving three-way internal communications – up, down, across. Other advantages of a communications audit include:

- It can allow a company to place internal communications more firmly on the agenda of management issues to be monitored and periodically assessed.
- It can help to address the evolving communications needs of both management and staff generally in an environment of rapid change.
- It permits a far-reaching 'health-check' to be made of the organization and its management systems and procedures.
- It causes relatively little disruption to the operation of the company concerned.
- Expectations from the audit exercise can be managed and tested through ongoing implementation of feedback loops from testers to tested, and vice versa.

CONCLUSION

Goldhaber and Rogers (1979) illustrate the need for the use of a communication audit by using two analogies. They believe that companies need financial audits and individuals need physical check-ups. Both these types of check-up provide clients with information necessary to ensure the 'health' of the system, be it individual or organizational. In the same way, communication audits provide an organization with advance information which may prevent serious breakdowns affecting overall performance. In this sense, communication audits are both preventative and restorative. Goldhaber and Rogers argue that communication audits fulfil at least eight functions, making it possible to:

1 determine the amount of the information underload or overload associated with the major topics, sources, and channels of communication;
2 evaluate the quality of information communicated from and/or to these sources;
3 assess the quality of communication relationships, specifically measuring the extent of interpersonal trust, supportiveness, sociability and overall job satisfaction;
4 identify the operational communications networks (for rumours, social and job-related messages), comparing them with planned or formal networks (prescribed by organizational charts);
5 determine potential bottlenecks and gatekeepers of information by comparing actual communication roles of key personnel (isolates, liaisons, group members, etc.) with expected roles (provided by job descriptions, etc.);
6 identify categories and examples of commonly occurring positive and negative communication experiences and incidents;
7 describe individual, group and organizational patterns of actual communication behaviours related to sources, channels, topics, length and quality of interactions;
8 provide general recommendations derived from the audit, which call for changes or improvements in attitudes, behaviours, practices, and skills.

6 Customer audits

INTRODUCTION

As the preceding chapters have shown, corporate audits designed to assess an organization's culture, climate or communications can provide valuable insights into how effectively it is performing. A strong sense of identification with the corporate culture, a positive climate which breeds high morale, and an effective system of internal communications represent essential ingredients of efficient organizational functioning and high competitive performance. Employees who feel that they 'belong', and know what they belong to, are healthier, more committed and more productive. In increasingly competitive business environments, ineffective operations internally will lead to loss of market share and profitability, and may eventually lead to the collapse of the business altogether.

The current chapter brings us to the last of the four major categories of corporate audit, that which is concerned with customers. Although we have chosen to treat customer audits as a separate conceptual category from culture, climate and communications, in practice, customer audits might be used in parallel with any of the others, or may form a component of a multi-faceted corporate audit package.

Many organizations survive by their customers patronizing them regularly. The all-round nature of the service given to customers has always been important, but in recent years the concept of customer care has captured the corporate imagination like at no other time before. Handling customers properly can give the organization or department (if your customers are other departments or sections within the same organization) a competitive edge. When the economic climate takes a downturn, the quality of service it supplies to its customers can be vital to the health and even the survival of an organization.

Organizations are, of course, not all driven by the same objectives or targets. The main drive of an organization defines the reason for its existence and can underpin the culture which permeates every part of its structure, activities and staff perceptions of its business. Peel (1987) has distinguished between organizations that are product-driven, profit-driven and employee-driven. The first type of organization is focused on the product it makes. Its primary mission is to make what it regards as a 'good' product. The second type of organization takes no special pride in the product, but is concerned principally with retaining those activities which make the most money, and dropping or selling off those which are either loss-making or whose margins are too narrow. The third type is concerned with providing security of employment for its work-force. Peel argues that an important aspect of organizational success in the future will be the degree of attention that is paid to the treatment of customers.

This last point seems to have been well-taken by many corporations. Serving the customer better is an objective which, with steadily increasing prevalence, has been elevated to the top of the corporate agenda for the 1990s (Holberton, 1991).

There is, however, precious little management theory on the subject of customer care. Organizations are therefore largely learning for themselves what it means, how it can be operationally defined, and what implications it has for management policy and practice. A major purpose of a business is to create and keep a customer. In those businesses where competition is toughest (good examples being retailing, air travel and increasingly banking/financial services), organizations find themselves searching hard for that one distinguishing feature which sets them apart from and, they hope, ahead of their main rivals. It is in this context that customer care can come into its own. If customers perceive that one supplier of a product or service provides enhanced value for money, this will be the one to whom they will choose to take most of their trade.

THE CONCEPT OF QUALITY

Concern for customers has been underlined by increased attention to the notion of quality. Whether an organization manufactures a product or provides a service, there is a general belief that it should be of the highest standard. A survey by ODI (1987) showed that top British management considered quality as a vital issue for their organizations which could affect their survival. Chief executives interviewed in this survey nearly all believed that their company's future performance would be significantly influenced by gaining a reputation for providing quality products or services. There was a realization among many of these top managers that they must do more to create environments in which quality could flourish. There was, in addition, a recognition that quality was important to customers' buying decisions. Quality was also essential if a company was to perform successfully against its major competitors.

Quality is intimately tied up with customers. In organizations of all kinds, whether product or service-oriented, quality can be regarded as a means to an end – customer satisfaction with the products or services provided. Linked to quality of product or service is the concept of quality in the way an organization is managed. Quality management is a systematic way of doing things, which guarantees that the organization will work more effectively and ensure that its products or services are provided to the highest standards at the first attempt. Controls are implemented to check that things are being done the right way, and management systems are so designed as to minimize problems which might impede high quality performance.

Companies are turning to quality to help them cope with and survive the competitive challenges facing industry. Deregulation, the onward march of globalization, and the advance of technology have redefined industrial success. Only those companies which are able to develop new products quickly, which can supply them at a consistent level of high quality, and on time, will command positions of leadership in the 1990s.

In order to compete at this level, European and American companies are seeking to improve their business performance by changing organizational structures and work practices. Management layers are being cut out to save costs and to bring top management closer to the shop floor, and responsibility for product quality is being diffused throughout the company.

Change is the *leitmotif* of this trend, and the desire of companies to achieve change is forcing them to confront the most fundamental managerial task: that of striking a new balance between control on the one hand, and consent on the other. If 'control' was the dominant mode of management in the past, 'consent' or at least a more consensual approach is beginning to supersede it and might even become the dominant mode in the 1990s.

Total quality management

The origin of total quality management (TQM) is American and is associated largely with a handful of statisticians who, in the 1920s and 1930s, worked for the quality control section of Western Electric, the manufacturing arm of ITT. The problem with which Western Electric was trying to grapple was variation. Variation is the enemy of, but inherent in, any manufacturing process, because mechanical processes tend to produce products which are subtly different. The statisticians of the Western Electric's Hawthorne plant sought to analyse this variation, measure it, and where possible, modify the process to reduce variation. The techniques pioneered there today go under the name of statistical process control (SPC).

Pre-eminent among these men are W. Edwards Deming and Joseph Juran, both of whom worked at Western Electric's Hawthorne plant, Philip Crosby, also a former executive with ITT, Armand Feigenbaum, the man who coined the term 'total quality control' and was head of quality at General Electric of the USA, and the late Kaoru Ishikawa, a member of the Japanese Union of Scientists and Engineers. These men comprise the list of quality initiators.

Until the 1980s, it was the Japanese who had most consistently applied the principles of quality management. At the end of the Second World War, it was Deming, Juran and Feigenbaum who had educated Japanese industrialists in the tools and techniques of quality management, as part of the Occupying Power's attempt to breathe life into Japanese industry. The view in the West after the Second World War, however, was that improving quality probably added unnecessarily to costs. While this approach might have certain advantages in the short term, these would not be felt in the longer term. Deming, who some regard as the founding father of the quality revolution, challenged this approach and persuaded the Japanese to take up his new approach of getting things right first time by bringing the customer into the organization, and by creating a close link between worker and supplier to work for continuous improvement.

Juran argued that from the early 1950s at least 85 per cent of the failures in any organization were the fault of systems controlled by management. Fewer than 15 per cent of the problems were actually work-related. The key to success was overcoming negative attitudes among the work-force. There must be a belief that change is desirable and feasible in all aspects of operations within an organization in the long term. Quality is not just about achieving short term results.

Later work by Crosby led to the development of a scheme for managing quality and integrating it into the organization's general management processes. Crosby's quality management maturity grid outlined a number of stages through which quality management in an organization can normally be expected to develop. Crosby identified five factors which he considered the absolutes of quality management:

- Quality means conformance not elegance.
- There is no such thing as a quality problem.
- There is no such thing as the economics of quality – it is always cheaper to do the job right first time.
- The only performance measurement is the cost of quality.
- The only performance standard is zero defects.

Crosby also identified the following five stages of quality management maturity:

- **Uncertainty** When management has no knowledge of quality as a positive management tool.
- **Awakening** When management is beginning to recognize that quality management can help, but will not commit resources to it.
- **Enlightenment** When management decide to introduce a formal quality programme.
- **Wisdom** When management and organization reach the stage when permanent changes can be made.
- **Certainty** When quality management is a vital part of organizational management.

Deming's quality-centred model, meanwhile, outlined the following stages in the process of developing quality management:

- improve quality;
- productivity up;
- costs down;
- prices down;
- market increased;
- stay in business;
- more jobs and better return for investment.

Much later it was the Japanese excellence in manufacturing – which derived partly from their adoption of quality-oriented tools and techniques – that spurred western manufacturers to seek out Deming, Juran, Feigenbaum and Crosby, and relearn what they had apparently forgotten. Today, TQM is a term which embraces much of current best practices in manufacturing. Its scope has broadened from its early concentration on statistical monitoring of manufacturing processes, and it can include just-in-time inventory control – a change in the way people work which focuses on teamwork, training, and greater employee responsibility and involvement in the work process. It also places a major emphasis on customer service, with attention being paid to both external and internal customers.

These are all related devices aimed at reorienting the production process so that it delivers products or services of consistent quality, in a timely fashion, which at least meet customer requirements. Indeed, focus on the customer – as a direct result of competition – is one of the main areas into which TQM has developed over the past few years.

WHAT IS CUSTOMER CARE?

Efforts in defining and measuring the quality of service given to customers have come largely from the goods manufacturing sector. According to the prevailing Japanese philosophy, quality is 'zero defects – doing it right first time'. Crosby (1979) defined quality as 'conforming to requirements'. Garvin (1983) measured quality by counting the incidence of 'internal' failures (those observed before a product leaves the factory) and 'external' failures (those incurred in the field after a unit has been installed).

Knowledge about goods quality, however, is insufficient to understand service quality. Parasuraman, Zeithaml and Berry (1985) underlined three particularly important characteristics of service – intangibility, hetero-geneity, and inseparability – which must be acknowledged for a full understanding of service quality. Services are intangible because they are about performance rather than about products, thus precise manufacturing specifications concerning uniform quality can rarely be set. Most services cannot be counted, measured, inventoried, tested, and verified in advance of sale to ensure quality – services do not work like that (Bateson, 1977;

Berry, 1980; Lovelock, 1981; Shostak, 1977). Thus, it may be difficult for an organization to understand how consumers perceive its services and evaluate service quality (Zeithaml, 1987).

Services, especially those with a high labour content, are heterogeneous: their performance often varies from supplier to supplier, from customer to customer and from day to day. Consistency of behaviour among service personnel may be difficult to assure because what the organization intends to deliver may be different from what the customer actually receives.

Finally, production and consumption of many services are inseparable (Carmen and Langeard, 1980; Gronroos, 1978; Regan, 1963; Upah, 1980). Quality in services is not engineered at the manufacturing plant, then delivered intact to the consumer. Very often, quality occurs during the service delivery, usually in an interaction between the customer and the contact person from the service delivery organization (Lehtinen and Lehtinen, 1982).

Sasser, Olsen and Wyckoff (1978) have discussed three different dimensions of service performance: levels of material, facilities and personnel. Implied in this trichotomy is the notion that service quality involves more than outcome; it also includes the manner in which the service is delivered. This notion surfaces in other research on quality as well. Gronroos (1982), for example, postulated that two types of service quality exist: technical quality, which involves what the customer is actually receiving from the service, and functional quality, which involves the manner in which the service is delivered. In a schema which emphasizes the interaction between customer and service supplier, Lehtinen and Lehtinen (1982) propose three quality dimensions: physical quality, which includes the physical aspects of the service (e.g., equipment, buildings); corporate quality, which involves the company's image or profile; and interactive quality, which derives from the interaction between contact personnel and customers as well as between some customers and other customers. They further differentiate between the quality associated with the process of service delivery and the quality associated with the outcome of the service.

Conceptualizing service quality

One approach to operationalizing service quality has been to devise a mechanism through which customers can themselves provide feedback regarding their degree of satisfaction with any service they receive. In this context, perceived quality is the consumer's judgement about an entity's overall excellence or superiority (Zeithaml, 1987). It is to be distinguished from objective quality (e.g., Garvin, 1983; Hjorth-Anderson, 1984), in that it is a form of attitude, related but not equivalent to satisfaction, and results from a comparison of expectations with perceptions of perform-ance.

Various researchers (Garvin, 1983; Dodds and Monroe, 1984; Holbrook and Corfman, 1985; Jacoby and Olson, 1985; Zeithaml, 1987) have emphasized the difference between the objective and perceived quality. Holbrook and Corfman (1985), for example, noted that customers do not use the term 'quality' in the same way as researchers and managers, who define it conceptually. The conceptual meaning distinguishes between mechanistic and humanistic quality: 'mechanistic [quality] involves an objective aspect or feature of a thing or event; humanistic [quality] involves the subjective response of people to objects and is therefore a highly relativistic phenomenon that differs between judges' (Holbrook and Corfman, 1985, p. 33). Garvin (1983) discussed five approaches to defining quality, including two (product-based and manufacturing-based) that refer to objective quality and one (user-based) that parallels perceived quality.

Quality has been regarded in attitudinal terms by some researchers. Olshavsky (1985) viewed quality as a form of overall evaluation of a product, similar in many ways to attitude. Holbrook concurred, suggesting that quality acts as a relatively global value judgement. Exploratory research by Parasuraman, Zeithaml and Berry (1985) supported the notion that service quality is an overall evaluation similar to attitude. These researchers conducted a total of twelve focus group interviews with current and recent consumers of four different services – retail banking, credit cards, securities brokerage, and product repair and maintenance. The discussion centred on such issues as the meaning of quality in the context of the service in question, the characteristics the service and its provider should possess in order to project a high-quality image, and the criteria customers use in evaluating service quality. Comparison and findings from the focus groups revealed that, regardless of the type of service, customers used basically the same general criteria in arriving at an evaluating judgement about service quality.

A distinction has been made by some writers between quality and satisfaction with a service. According to Oliver (1981), 'satisfaction is a summary psychological state resulting when the emotion surrounding disconfirmed expectations is coupled with the consumer's prior feelings about the consumption experience' (p. 27). This and other definitions (e.g., Howard and Sheth, 1969; Hunt, 1979) and almost all measures of satisfaction relate to a specific transaction.

Oliver (1981) summarizes the transaction-specific nature of satisfaction, differentiating it from attitude as follows:

Attitude is the consumer's relatively enduring affective orientation for a product, store, or process (e.g., customer service) while satisfaction is the emotional reaction following a disconfirmation experience which acts on the base attitude level and is consumption-specific. Attitude is therefore measured in terms more general to product or store and is less situationally oriented.

(p. 42)

Consistent with the distinction between attitude and satisfaction is a distinction between service quality and satisfaction: perceived service quality is a global judgement, or attitude, relating to the superiority of the service, whereas satisfaction is related to a specific transaction. Indeed, in the twelve focus groups included in the exploratory research conducted by Parasuraman, Zeithaml and Berry (1985), respondents gave several illustrations of instances when they were satisfied with a specific service but did not feel the service organization was of high quality. In this way, the two constructs are related, in that incidents of satisfaction over time result in perceptions of service quality.

Expectations are important in relation to customer satisfaction and ratings of quality. A number of writers have offered support for the notion that service quality, as perceived by customers, stems from a comparison between what they feel services should offer (i.e., from their expectations) with their perceptions of performance of organizations providing the services (see Sasser, Olsen and Wyckoff, 1978; Gronroos, 1983; Lehtinen and Lehtinen, 1982).

Parasuraman and his co-workers identified ten determinants of service quality.

1 **Reliability** Consistency of performance and dependability.
2 **Responsiveness** The willingness or readiness to provide service.
3 **Competence** Having the required skills and knowledge to perform the service.
4 **Access** Approachability and ease of contact.
5 **Courtesy** Politeness, respect, consideration and friendliness of contact personnel.
6 **Communication** Keeping the customers informed in language they can understand and listening to them.
7 **Credibility** Trustworthiness, believability, honesty.
8 **Security** Freedom from danger, risk, or doubt.
9 **Understanding/knowing the customer** Making the effort to understand the customer's needs.
10 **Tangibles** The physical evidence of service.

Most of these dimensions of service quality are 'experience properties' that can be known only as the customer is purchasing or consuming (experiencing) the service: access, courtesy, reliability, responsiveness, understanding/knowing the customer, and communication:

- Reliability involves consistency of performance and dependability. It means that the firm performs the service right the first time. It also

means that the firm honours its promises. Specifically, it involves:
— accuracy in billing;
— keeping records correctly;
— performing the service at the designated time.

- Responsiveness concerns the willingness or readiness of employees to provide service. It involves timeliness of service:
  — mailing a transaction slip immediately;
  — calling a customer back quickly;
  — giving prompt service (e.g., setting up appointments quickly).
- Competence means possession of the required skills and knowledge to perform the service. It involves:
  — knowledge and skill of the contact personnel;
  — knowledge and skill of operational support personnel;
  — research capability of the organization, e.g., securities brokerage firm.
- Access involves approachability, and ease of contact means:
  — the service is easily accessible by telephone (lines are not busy and they don't put you on hold);
  — waiting time to receive service (e.g., at a bank) is not extensive;
  — convenient hours of operation;
  — convenient location of service facility.
- Courtesy involves politeness, respect, consideration, and friendliness of contact personnel including receptionists, telephone operators (etc.). It includes:
  — consideration for the consumer's property (e.g., no muddy shoes on the carpet);
  — clean and neat appearance of public contact personnel.
- Communication means keeping customers informed in language they can understand, and listening to them. It may mean that the company has to adjust its language for different consumers – increasing the level of sophistication with a well-educated customer and speaking simply and plainly with a novice. It involves:
  — explaining the service itself;
  — explaining how much the service will cost;
  — explaining the trade-offs between service and cost;
  — assuring the consumer that a problem will be dealt with.
- Credibility involves trustworthiness, believability, honesty. It involves having the customer's best interests at heart. Contributing to credibility are:
  — company name;
  — company reputation;
  — personal characteristics of the contact personnel;
  — the degree of hard sell involved in interactions with the customer.
- Security is the freedom from danger, risk, or doubt. It involves:

- physical safety (Will I get mugged at the automatic teller machine?);
- financial security (Does the company know where my stock certificate is?);
- confidentiality (Are my dealings with the company private?).
- Understanding/knowing the customer involves making the effort to understand the customer's needs. It involves:
  - learning the customer's specific requirements;
  - providing individualized attention;
  - recognizing the regular customer.
- Tangibles including the physical evidence of the service:
  - physical facilities;
  - appearance of personnel;
  - tools or equipment used to provide the service;
  - physical representations of the service, such as a plastic credit card or a bank statement;
  - other customers in the service facility.

A twenty-six-item measurement scale, Servqual, has been developed to assess the service quality provided by organizations in a wide range of service categories (see Figure 6.1); it has been found to have good reliability and validity (Parasuraman, Zeithaml and Berry, 1988). This empirical research was grounded in the theoretical work of Solomon and his colleagues (Solomon, Surprenant, Czepiel and Gutman, 1985). Drawing from sociology and social psychology (e.g., Abelson, 1976; Goffman, 1961; Merton, 1957; Sarbin and Allen, 1968; Schank,1980) and from marketing (Lutz and Kakkar, 1976; Sheth, 1975; Webster, 1968; Weitz, 1981), Solomon and his co-workers build on the service script concept in marketing suggested by Smith and Houston (1983). A script is a coherent sequence of events expected by the individual, who is involved either as a participant or as an observer (Abelson, 1976). A service script contains information about the role set – one's own expected behaviour – and the expected complementary behaviour of others, and reflects a customer's learned (or imagined) conception of the prototypical service experience.

Each service encounter can be analysed to identify several individual but related scenes and acts. For example, a 'dentist script' (Schank, 1980) may include the following first scene in the first act: the patient enters the office, moves to the receptionist desk, and begins to speak to the receptionist. The first act ends and the second act begins with the patient moving to the dental chair and meeting a dental hygienist. The first scene in the service encounter occurs when the patient leaves the office. To measure service quality and customer satisfaction, the key scenes, acts, and sequences of acts that occur in the service encounter must be mapped out in detail. Customer service quality judgements must be measured for each act

DIRECTIONS: This survey deals with your opinions of —— services. Please show the extent to which you think firms offering —— services should possess the features described by each statement. Do this by picking one of the seven numbers next to each statement. If you strongly agree that these firms should possess a feature, circle the number 7. If you strongly disagree that these firms should possess a feature, circle 1. If your feelings are not strong, circle one of the numbers in the middle. There are no right or wrong answers – all we are interested in is a number that best shows your expectations about firms offering —— services.

E1.   They should use up-to-date equipment.
E2.   Their physical facilities should be visually appealing.
E3.   Their employees should be well dressed and appear neat.
E4.   The appearance of the physical facilities of these firms should be in keeping with the type of services provided.
E5.   When these firms promise to do something by a certain time, they should do so.
E6.   When customers have problems, these firms should be sympathetic and reassuring.
E7.   These firms should be dependable.
E8.   They should provide their services at the time they promise to do so.
E9.   They should keep their records accurately.
E10. They shouldn't be expected to tell customers exactly when services will be performed. (–)[b]
E11. It is not realistic for customers to expect prompt service from employees of these firms. (–)
E12. Their employees don't always have to be willing to help customers. (–)
E13. It is okay if they are too busy to respond to customer requests promptly. (–)
E14. Customers should be able to trust employees of these firms.
E15. Customers should be able to feel safe in their transactions with these firms' employees.
E16. These employees should be polite.
E17. Their employees should get adequate support from these firms to do their job well.
E18. These firms should not be expected to give customers individual attention. (–)
E19. Employees of these firms cannot be expected to give customers personal attention. (–)
E20. It is unrealistic to expect employees to know what the needs of their customers are. (–)
E21. It is unrealistic to expect these firms to have their customers' best interests at heart. (–)
E22. They shouldn't be expected to have operating hours convenient to all their customers. (–)

DIRECTIONS: The following set of statements relate to your feelings about XYZ. For each statement, please show the extent to which you believe XYZ has the feature described by the statement. Once again, circling a 7 means that you strongly agree that XYZ has that feature, and circling a 1 means that you strongly disagree. You may circle any of the numbers in the middle that show how strong your feelings are. There are no right or wrong answers – all we are interested in is a number that best shows your perceptions about XYZ.

P1. XYZ has up-to-date equipment.
P2. XYZ's physical facilities are visually appealing.
P3. XYZ's employees are well dressed and appear neat.
P4. The appearance of the physical facilities of XYZ is in keeping with the type of services provided.
P5. When XYZ promises to do something by a certain time, it does so.
P6. When you have problems, XYZ is sympathetic and reassuring.
P7. XYZ is dependable.
P8. XYZ provides its services at the time it promises to do so.
P9. XYZ keeps its records accurately.
P10. XYZ does not tell customers exactly when services will be performed. (−)
P11. You do not receive prompt service from XYZ's employees. (−)
P12. Employees of XYZ are not always willing to help customers. (−)
P13. Employees of XYZ are too busy to respond to customer requests promptly. (−)
P14. You can trust employees of XYZ.
P15. You feel safe in your transactions with XYZ's employees.
P16. Employees of XYZ are polite.
P17. Employees get adequate support from XYZ to do their jobs well.
P18. XYZ does not give you individual attention. (−)
P19. Employees of XYZ do not give you personal attention. (−)
P20. Employees of XYZ do not know what your needs are. (−)
P21. XYZ does not have your best interests at heart. (−)
P22. XYZ does not have operating hours convenient to all their customers. (−)

Notes:
[a] A seven-point scale ranging from 'Strongly Agree' (7) to 'Strongly Disagree' (1), with no verbal labels for the intermediate scale points (i.e., 2 to 6), accompanied each statement. Also, the statements were in random order in the questionnaire.
[b] Ratings on these statements were reverse-scored prior data analysis.

Figure 6.1 The Servqual instrument
Source: Parasuraman, Zeithaml and Berry (1985). Reproduced by permission of the publisher.

occurring in the service encounter, as well as for the entire service encounter experience.

Woodside, Frey and Daly (1989) offer a general framework for the assessment of the customer scenario (see Figure 6.2). Here, a service encounter is shown to include several acts (A, B, and C). Several specific events are shown to be included in each act (e.g., A, to A). An experience-based service quality judgement based on the events of the act is made by the customer for each major act. Customer satisfaction/dissatisfaction with major acts in the service encounter is a function of the service quality judgement of the act. The overall service quality perceived by the customer for the encounter is a function of the satisfaction with, and service quality of, the service acts. Overall customer satisfaction with the service is a function of overall service quality. Behavioural intention is affected by customer satisfaction.

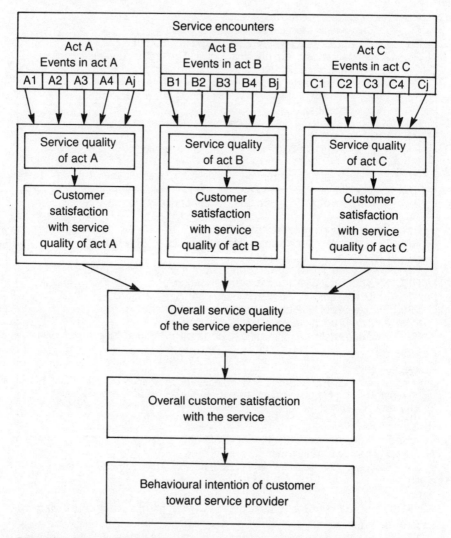

Figure 6.2 General framework of customer evaluation, satisfaction, and behavioural intention of service events, encounters, and providers
Source: Woodside, Fry and Daly (1989). Reproduced by permission of the publisher.

Research among former patients of two hospitals provided some support of the general framework that customers' judgement of specific service events within service acts influences their overall satisfaction with the service acts, and that satisfaction with service acts influences overall customer satisfaction within the service encounter. Overall customer satisfaction with the service encounter does appear to be in moderating variables between service quality and behavioural intention (to use the service again) (Woodside, Fry and Daly, 1989).

The need to take into account 'service script' variations between different service contexts and types of organization was highlighted in research by Carmen (1990). He found that the Servqual instrument provided a useful 'basic skeleton' for use across a broad spectrum of services, with its key dimensions exhibiting an important level of stability. However, the original dimensions identified by Parasuraman, Zeithaml and Berry (1985, 1988) are not completely generic. Thus, new dimensions may need to be investigated in some service contexts other than those used in the initial study. Carmen further recommended that when it is obvious to customers that multiple service functions are performed, the Servqual instrument, or any derivative, should be administered separately for each function.

THE IMPACT OF CUSTOMER CARE

In some countries, such as Japan and, to a lesser degree, the United States, caring consistently for your customers is a way of life. For many years in Britain, service was confused with servility. This notion, however, is totally wrong, and indeed failure to break out of it could spell disaster for many companies. As one business writer has succinctly put it: 'Customer service is the hard-headed pursuit of market share by winning the loyalty of customers' (Holberton, 1991, p. 14). Peel (1987) has offered five different meanings for the phrase 'customer service':

1   The activities involved in ensuring that a product or service is delivered to the customer on time, in the correct quantities.
2   The interpersonal working relationships between the staff of a supplier and a customer.
3   The provision of after-sales repair and maintenance.
4   The department of an organization which handles customer complaints.
5   The order-taking department of an organization.

(pp. 21–2)

It is clear from the above list that customer care is not simply an abstract concept which pays lip-service to the need of customers to be treated properly and have their requirements dealt with efffectively. In fact it comprises a complex set of processes which exist throughout many different parts of an organization. As such, customer care, although dealt with as a distinct chapter in this book, cannot in practice be realistically separated from corporate culture, climate or systems of communication. Installing an effective customer-care outlook means inculcating a corporate culture which places a high value on the customer.

One of the best-known recent illustrations of enhancing customer care through culture change was the British Airways' 'Putting the Customer First' campaign, instigated by Colin Marshall when he became chief executive of the company in 1983. He appointed a four-man team, called the marketing policy group, to identify the broad areas where change was needed and certain plans were put in place. The following corporate objectives were identified (Walker, 1990):

1 To provide the highest levels of service to all customers, passengers, shippers, travel agents, and freight agents.
2 To preserve high professional and technical standards in order to achieve the highest levels of safety.
3 To provide a uniform image world-wide, and to maintain a specific set of standards for each clearly defined market segment.
4 To respond quickly and sensitively to the changing needs of our present and potential customers.
5 To maintain and, where opportunity occurs, expand our present route structure.
6 To manage, operate, and market the airline in the most efficient manner.
7 To create a service and people-oriented work environment, assuring all employees of fair pay and working conditions, and continuing concern for their careers.

This project set out to establish a comprehensive data base on customers' needs and requirements which determined the service standards the company should attempt to achieve. Staff at all levels were made fully aware of these targets and how they were to be attained, and training and performance-linked assessment programmes were introduced to equip and motivate staff to reach these targets.

This programme of change wrought a shift in corporate culture from a bureaucracy which took little account of customer needs in taking decisions how to serve the market place, to one which placed customers' perceptions and requirements at the centre of its concerns. It was recognized that there was a need to change BA's external image, to place its customer orientation as an integral part of the company's character, to change internal attitudes to ensure they supported the new customer orientation, and to implement necessary structural changes to provide a corporate framework in which this new philosophy could flourish. The entire programme embodied a combination of customer surveys, staff surveys, communication initialization, and various other customer service-related audits.

Another good example of a successful customer care programme is the one developed by Southern Electric. When it was privatized in December 1990, Southern inherited a huge business franchise covering 16,500 square kilometres with more than 2.5 million customers, 8,200 employees, and an annual turnover of about £1.6 billion. The prospect of privatization had already provided a crucial catalyst for change even before it happened. The company had been embarked on a quality programme which brought the needs of customers to the forefront over a five-year period prior to going private. The organization was reorganized on a structural plane, while steps were taken to overcome corporate image and staff attitude problems.

This programme of change involved adopting a much stronger and more clearly defined internal and external customer orientation. A quality manager was appointed and a quality improvement programme adopted, with the company aiming for registration with Marketing Quality Assurance, the independent UK body which assesses and designates compliance with BS 5750-type quality standards for marketing, sales, and customer services activities.

The company produced a forty-eight-page quality manual embodying the 'mission' or 'ultimate quality goal'. The aim was to ensure that all Southern Electric employees worked together to provide a quality service which:

- was profitable;
- satisfied customers;
- the company was proud to present.

Wall posters and 'Quest for Quality' leaflets introducing the programme carried the mission message, while employees were encouraged to join or set up odd-sounding committees, like Quigs – quality improvement groups – to tackle problems affecting quality. To ensure the message got through, there were presentations to all managers and employees on quality, a corporate quality video, and articles in the staff newspaper which was sent to each employee's home. Meanwhile the quality management department produced a set of customer service guidelines.

A number of measures were adopted to ensure that customers were made aware of Southern Electric's quality drive. Among the measures adopted to improve the quality of customer service, telephone bureau operators answering customer calls began to give their names and, on a sampling basis, customers were called back afterwards to find out if they were satisfied with the results. Service engineers began to use their mobile telephones to tell customers if they would be late for an appointment. At the same time, Southern successfully managed to exceed the nine guaranteed service standards which Offer, the official industry regulator, imposes on the privatized regional electricity companies. For instance, the regulator requires that customers be given two days' notice of disconnection for maintenance, but Southern extended this to a full week.

The company monitors and scrutinizes its compliance with the externally imposed standards and with its own thirty-nine business indicators. The company also draws up a comparative league table for its six divisions. Each month a performance report is presented to the management meeting. Throughout, emphasis is placed on providing a service which satisfies what the customer wants.

WHY CUSTOMER CARE?

Customer satisfaction is important to organizations, because it is generally assumed to be a significant determinant of repeat sales, positive word of mouth, and consumer loyalty (Beardon and Teel, 1983). The concept of caring for your customers is further reinforced by the view that profits are generated through the satisfaction of customers' needs and wants (Churchill and Surprenant, 1983).

Of course the idea that the customer is always right is far from new. For any business which provides a product or service which it expects people to buy, it should go without saying that customer service ought to be a central consideration at all times. Despite what should be an obvious fact of life, the need for customer care is constantly repeated these days, almost as if it represents a brand new concept of business procedure.

One reason has been linked to the tunnel vision of many companies. Preoccupation with their own internal problems and with the substance of their business can lead employees at all levels to forget that without its customers, their organization would have no business. Indeed, without customers the purpose of their activities and efforts would disappear. In typical, everyday working reality, employees' own problems in the doing of their jobs intrude, and are the primary focus of attention. There are personal targets to meet, budgets to control, company policies and procedures to comply with, and internal priorities to be conscious of. The higher up the corporate ladder employees climb, the more these responsibilities weigh upon them. Moreover, the higher up a company employees climb, the more remote they can become from any direct dealings with customers. Internal matters come to overwhelm customer considerations. An audit of the allocation of staff time to internal and external matters would probably show that in most organizations, customer-directed effort is disproportionately handled by employees in relatively junior positions.

This is not a criticism of procedures inherent in most companies. There are sound reasons why this pattern of behaviour occurs. The complexity of many organizations today means that considerable internal management effort is needed just to keep basic operations running smoothly. Clearly this effort is important. Current thinking on organizational behaviour, however, advises that internally, direct management should not interfere with marketing and sales efforts, or with other support functions – all of which are vital to the goal of reaching and maintaining customers. The ultimate purpose must always be to satisfy customers. In today's organizations, management should strive to harmonize internally-directed efforts with externally-directed efforts. Customer service should thus comprise a 'total quality' package in which internal concerns about the product and the standards of service and product value for the customer all achieve standards of the highest order in concert with one another.

Servicing customers better in this way, according to academic and professional advocates of total quality management, is virtually guaranteed to improve profitability. Customers who are satisfied return again more often than those who are not. Research has indicated that companies often spend between 25 and 30 per cent of their operating budgets rectifying errors in the production process. Exponents of TQM claim it can save about half of those costs by getting things right first time (Randall, 1992).

An effective service strategy, therefore, will permeate many different aspects of an organization. To work effectively, the customer service strategy must be integrated with a total quality programme. The service itself combines attributes associated with the product (e.g., its reliability, delivery, etc.) and a personal element represented by front-line staff who provide the face of the organization in its interactions with customers. Both the product and human aspects of the service can operate to win or lose customers. The service strategy adopted by an organization must be designed to achieve a high standard in both areas.

The 1980s saw a widening of the customer service concept as proponents of total quality management began to apply it to the internal operations of their organizations as well as dealing with it in relation to its outside face presented to customers, Customer care must run more than skin-deep if it is to be taken seriously. To treat it otherwise incurs the real risk of losing customers. In the sections which follow, we explore the different components and stages of an effective corporate customer service strategy.

IDENTIFYING YOUR CUSTOMERS

Any customer-care programme introduced into an organization must make it one of its earliest priorities to identify who its customers are. In some cases, this is relatively simple: its customers are those people who buy the organization's product(s). In some instances, these customers will be other organizations or their representatives, while in others, they will be members of the public. The term 'customer' can also be used to refer to those who buy services rather than products. Patients buy treatment from health-care professionals, students buy tuition from educational establishments, clients buy legal advice or help from solicitors, and guests buy a variety of services from hotels. Thus, customers can come in a variety of guises – the customer role or supplier role is not always formally stated or recognized. Reaching clear role definitions as such represents a vital step in achieving an effective customer service orientation.

Examining in-depth customer requirements is a major aspect of the strategy development of any total quality programme. Since the funda-mental concept of quality is based on meeting customer requirements, it is essential to be clear on those requirements. Lack of emphasis on this particular stage can undermine a total quality programme, however, well-organized (Collard, 1990).

Internal customers

Customers may be identified within organizations: one department may provide a service to another. Examples include the personnel department, which handles staff recruitment, training and rewards on behalf of the rest of the organization. Another example might be the computer services department, which advises other departments on the acquisition and use of computing/word processing equipment, and deals with hardware/software problems.

Within an organization's quality network, the customer–supplier relationship is the key. In determining a strategy for total quality it is also essential to have a mechanism for monitoring quality standards and quality improvements within the organization. One method of doing this is to ask all departmental managers to review functional responsibilities and ensure that the departmental objectives match the business objectives. This is achieved by first carrying out a detailed analytical review of departmental activities, with the emphasis being placed on specific objectives or targets, and secondly, by structured and objective analysis of the service given by the particular department to an 'internal' customer. Collard (1990) has identified the following specific results which such an audit might yield:

- a statement of departmental purpose in terms of specific objectives
- an opportunity to ensure that these objectives match the company and organizational objectives
- a quantitative analysis of departmental activity measured under the main objective headings and major tasks – this is possible both within service departments and within direct production departments
- an objective assessment of departmental effectiveness as seen by an internal customer
- a set of key performance measures – the outcome of determining the key departmental activities and the internal customer requirements
- the basis for an improvement plan
- a list of non-added value or wasted work performed by the department.

(p. 69)

The actual methodology used to go through this process can vary according to individual organizations and the degree of sophistication required at any point. One procedure is for the departmental manager to meet with all individuals reporting to him or her, probably for an uninterrupted whole day. Collard (1990) has identified the following ways in which this process could be managed:

- The departmental manager outlines his or her individual roles and responsibilities and what he or she sees to be the main objectives of the department.
- The group as a whole then discuss the roles and responsibilities.

clarifying issues and as appropriate making changes of emphasis and achieving consensus.

- Each individual in the group is then required to go through the same process, outlining their roles and responsibilities, with discussions – this enables the team as a whole to clarify areas of overlap and to establish a clear idea of the responsibilities both individually and as a group.
- At the end of this process it is possible to:
  - identify the objectives of the department;
  - check whether the department objectives meet the overall company/organizational objectives;
  - provide a framework for analysis by an internal customer against customer requirements.
- After this stage the departmental manager then outlines in specific quantitative terms the 'outputs' that he or she will be required to deliver as an individual, as well as the 'outputs' of the department as a whole – in other words the quantitative analysis of what is required of the department, and the measures for ensuring such objectives can be monitored at the end of an appropriate period.
- Each individual also carries out the same process, explaining their 'outputs' to the team as a whole.
- At the end of the process, the department has moved from broad definitions of responsibilities, to specific measurable outputs which need to be achieved.
- The documentation arising from this process is then pulled together and produced for discussion with internal customers and for review by top management.

DEFINING A 'SERVICE'

Finding a single, concise definition for customer service is not easy. Different organizations form their own distinct ideas about what service actually means. If anything, customer service probably embodies a range of activities which together establish a relationship between an organization or a section within an organization, and others on the outside with whom business or work-related transactions take place.

Further complications are caused by the perceptions and reactions of customers themselves. Customers can react quite differently to the same service. The same customers may even respond in more ways than one to the same service, depending upon different circumstances (Walker, 1990). The customer's mood and previous experience can significantly affect service perceptions, and moods and experiences are by no means constants in the customer's working or social life.

While there is little point in creating definitions for the sake of it, one useful, practical description of customer service which is concise but avoids diluting its meaning is one suggested by Peel (1987): 'Secondary activities undertaken by an organization to maximize customer satisfaction in its primary activities' (p. 26). Thus, customer service activities include specialized activities related to the primary business of the organization such as distribution of goods, dealing with complaints and after-sales service. In addition, there are non-specialist activities which are not necessarily unique to customer service, but which nevertheless involve the interaction of supplier with customer and can significantly influence the effectiveness of their relationship – providing information to customers about the items being sold or distributed, the way in which orders and invoicing are handled, packaging and presentation, credit, terms of payment, and debt collection (Peel, 1987). All these activities can legitimately be included as part of customer service.

Customer service quality priorities can be established by conducting a customer audit. This was done by the Scandinavian airline, SAS, in a major corporate change programme aimed at improving the company's performance. This change programme identified and targeted a particular brand of customer. The whole company's strategy for revival and quality standards was based on what were identified as the key needs of the business passenger.

Service reputation is an impression which customers form about an organization. It is a key part of an organization's image. The nature of this judgement will crucially affect a customer's decision as to whether or not to bring back repeat business. Customers who are not satisfied with the service they have received *may* complain, but as often as not they will take their business elsewhere next time. It is therefore vitally important for an organization's health that it should devise and implement an effective customer-service strategy.

CUSTOMER SERVICE STRATEGY

Awareness that the customer is all-important is vital, but is not enough on its own. Staying close to customers in order to know how best to satisfy their needs and expectations is just the first step in inculcating a customer-focused culture within an organization. Once customers' wants have been anticipated and understood, a proper service strategy needs to be put in place to ensure that noble words are transformed into effective actions which deliver results.

Close and regular liaison should be established with customers to monitor any changes and to ensure that there is an understanding at the technical level of the requirements. One good example of this kind of customer orientation is that which operates at Jaguar Cars, who regularly ring up customers to establish whether there are any individual difficulties or problems with the product, and to determine whether there is any particular need for certain changes. Other companies in the motor industry have established regular audits of customer requirements. Ford survey company car drivers, who represent an increasingly large part of the new car market. The motor industry in Japan has tried to develop an especially close technical relationship between suppliers and customers. Suppliers provide components which meet customer requirements which are defined by specific quality standards. By paying regular visits to assembly lines they are better able to identify particular problems and difficulties.

Collard (1990) has listed a number of key factors that need to be agreed in establishing a close liaison with customers:

(a) what the customer expects in terms of 'deliverables': the detailed specifications in terms of price, quality, delivery dates and so on, so that there can be no misunderstanding;
(b) the actual quality standards that are required by the customer and how these will be measured – for instance, tolerance levels on components, what is acceptable and not acceptable, packaging for customer goods, the flexibility, if any, in delivery times and dates;
(c) methods that will be used to measure the quality standards – this particularly applies to the quality of network within an organization, but is also important with external customers – the use of statistical techniques and other methods provide a foundation for establishing how measurement will be carried out;
(d) it is also important to establish the current level of performance in specific terms so that there is a clear base from which to build ...
(e) finally clear understanding of reporting methods on quality standards and level of performance with the customer is essential to ensure that there exists a clear method for reviewing performance.

(p. 71)

The customer-oriented organization needs clearly to conceive its own position *vis-à-vis* others with whom it interacts. Conceptually, it can be thought of as occupying a position on what has been called a 'value chain'. On one side are its own suppliers, with respect to whom it occupies the role of 'customer', and on the other side are its own customers. The whole chain constitutes a 'value added partnership'. Organizations, in obtaining the total view, need to show an interest in and exhibit an awareness of not just their immediate suppliers and customers, but also their suppliers' suppliers and their customer's customers.

Under this conceptual model, organizations are linked together in a mutually-supporting partnership. The 'value chain' runs through and across organizations – or at least it should do if the customer service ethos has permeated organizations linked in this way. The chain does not simply link one organizational boundary to another, but should run through the organizations themselves. Any customer-led programme of management change needs to be both outward-looking and inward-looking.

There is another significant element in delivering a customer service strategy. Organizations are advised to study the activities of their competitors.

What customer-care strategies do competitors use? What are the reactions of their customers to the strategies they employ? Why are competitors' customers using their services and products, rather than your own?

KNOWING ABOUT COMPETITORS

An essential part of successful customer service is knowing how competitors behave. It is important to be aware of how effectively competitors deal with their customers. It is therefore recommended to any organization interested in improving its customer care strategy that it should audit competitors' performance.

Before doing this, however, a more fundamental question needs to be addressed. Competitors themselves should be clearly identified. Often the answer to this question may be fairly straightforward. Supermarkets compete with other supermarkets. Airlines compete with other airlines. Sometimes, though, the analysis is not as simple as this. New competitors may enter a market and begin to reduce the market share of others in that business category. In other cases, competitors may not be readily identifiable, or organizations may simply have failed to recognize them.

Customer research needs to compare the organization's own performance with that of others on such aspects as value for money, reliability, courtesy and environment. One useful approach is for the organization to compare itself with a number of others offering the same or a similar service, on a range of service dimensions. This 'benchmarking' approach can provide an effective means of identifying various strategies and weaknesses where an organization is placed against others with which it is in competition.

Benchmarking, as a management technique, came into prominence during the 1980s. It represents a method for improving business performance by learning from other companies how to do things better. Benchmarking is designed to supply management with practices that deliver customer value (Osterhoff, Locander and Bounds, 1991). Companies have found that it is an extremely helpful tool enabling them to find out where they are in terms of the best practice. By making benchmarking a line management responsibility, managers are encouraged to probe the underlying business procedures and practices that characterize their own organization's treatment of its customers.

The power of benchmarking was underlined in the case of Xerox, where it is credited with being one of the main factors behind the company's revival in the 1980s. Xerox embarked on competitive benchmarking with its Japanese subsidiary Fuji Xerox in the early 1980s. One of the main findings of the analysis of Japanese competitors was that Canon could sell a photocopier for less than it cost Xerox in the USA to manufacture one. Since then Xerox has moved from studying competitors to evaluating companies in industries as various as railways, insurance, and electricity generation. This has enabled the company to identify best practice ways of improving aspects of its business, ranging from timeliness to customer satisfaction and retention, and statistical process control.

Competitor performance can be charted through a customer survey which examines customers' perceptions of its own performance, compared with that of competitors in a general sense, or with regard to specific aspects of products or services supplied. In addition to this kind of audit, however, it is advisable to carry out other forms of competitor analysis.

Walker (1990) identified the following key questions:

- Who are your key competitors?
- What are their strategies and weaknesses?
- Where do you have competitive advantage?
- What are they doing which you could do better?
- Why are some customers choosing a competitor in preference to, or as well as, yourselves?

Benchmarking may not be appropriate for every company. It may be best suited to organizations which have embraced corporate change or renewal programmes, such as total quality management.

Given a will to succeed, however, competitor audits can be carried out in most businesses which provide a service to customers. A company should try out the products and services provided by its major competitors, survey customers for their views about competitors, and monitor the business performance and development of competitors. A company can benchmark aspects of its own performance by comparing itself with competitors on common performance criteria. This type of audit procedure can help a company identify where it is placed in the quality league within its market sector.

KNOWING ABOUT CUSTOMERS

Customers can be changeable, fickle, and capricious beings. Their needs and expectations are not constant and unchanging. Thus, an effective customer service strategy must allow for these characteristics and be sufficiently adaptable to cope with changing customer orientations. While it is important to take an initial survey of customers' needs and expectations before embarking on any strategic shift in customer care, it is important to realize that a single snapshot is valid only for that point in time, and may not necessarily represent customers' frames of mind at some later date. Knowing one's customers therefore requires constant vigilance and monitoring.

Obtaining an initial profile of customer types can be undertaken relatively inexpensively by using data the organization may already have at its disposal, or which can fairly readily be collated through sources which should be largely at hand. Customer complaints and compliments can be analysed, although these represent only a self-selected sample of individuals and may not be representative of customers in general. What are customers saying about the organization and its service? Are there any indications in this evidence that customers are not getting what they expect? A review of industry data about customer needs and how other organizations have fared is another source worth exploring. In this way, it may be possible for an organization to rate itself against others in the same line or other lines of business. Staff are another source of information. Management should probe staff perceptions of customers and the latter's apparent satisfaction or dissatisfaction with the service supplied by the organization. As we will see later in this chapter, there are systematic ways in which such perceptions, both from the staff and the customers' points of view, can be assessed.

An eventual service strategy must include a mechanism for measuring customers' reactions and collating such data in a systematic fashion. Data may include unsolicited customer remarks (e.g., complaints) and surveyed opinions.

Unsolicited customer communications will rarely be representative of customer opinion about the products or services provided, although if they occur, in respect of one specific factor, in large enough numbers, they may begin to approach representativeness. However, complaints are a highly important indicator of whether the service being supplied is up to acceptable standards. Even a single complaint may be legitimate. In a fully functioning quality programme it should carry as much weight as 100 complaints about the same problem. The product or service supplier must strive to reduce to an absolute minimum the circumstances under which the same complaint might occur again.

Customer audits which are based on a summary of customer impressions or opinions, can sample more broadly across the customer spectrum, but need to ensure that they are asking the right kinds of questions and thus provide valued, sensitive measures of customers' needs, priorities and expectations.

The organization should find a way of clearly expressing to customers its view about customer service. There should be a statement of customer service, such as 'Your money back if not satisfied'. It must then be seen to honour that undertaking. Promises must be backed up by action and that action must be consistently implemented. Another important feature is the information and instructions given to service staff, who need to know what they are empowered to do to satisfy customers' needs, and perhaps more importantly, how to deal with dissatisfied customers.

WHAT DO CUSTOMERS (EXPECT TO) RECEIVE?

Another important question to address concerns what customers receive from the organization, and what they *expect* to receive. If you buy a product, you generally expect that it will function properly in the way it is supposed to. If customers have to visit the premises of a supplier, it is important that the environment reflects the quality of the organization. Disorganized, untidy premises can lead customers to question the standards of the supplier's work. If the product is delivered to the customer by the supplier, delivery systems must work efficiently; goods should arrive on time, undamaged, and fitting the original specification.

Customer service, as already noted above, depends crucially on the people who work for the organization. Good service stems from an organization's ability, through skilled and knowledgeable staff, to fulfil the obligations it undertakes in its service strategy. The attitude of staff towards customers can either support or undermine the organization's dealings with its customers, and is a key component underlying the image of it which develops among those whom it supplies. Staff must therefore be trained and motivated to support the service strategy. Effective management systems, which always have customer care in mind, can go a long way towards ensuring customer loyalty and satisfaction.

There are a number of different ways in which customer and quality priorities can be established and monitored. Auditing the volume of complaints and cataloguing factors which trigger complaints represent one class of customer service assessment. In the manufacturing industry, Mullard (part of the Phillips group) identified the importance of having some simple measure for quality performance. The company concluded that the worst possible situation was that a complaint about any aspect of their performance was sufficiently serious to warrant a customer writing, telexing, or even having to telephone the company with a problem. As a result, Mullard adopted a measure called 'adverse quality communication' (AQC), which included all methods of communication to the organization about something which was wrong. As part of the company's strategy development, a target could be set based on percentage improvement per annum, against a base. The result could then be carefully monitored. This was a useful management tool for monitoring customer performance in an organization with a mixture of product types.

Alternatively, a customer audit within the company could take the form of a survey of staff attitudes, beliefs about, and expectations and knowledge of customers. This kind of audit would be used, in regard to external customers, among staff throughout the organization. In the development of an internal customer orientation, it is important to differentiate between the notion of supplier and recipient of internal services within an organization, a factor which may not be immediately apparent to company workers.

Preparing for customer service

The commitment to good customer service must permeate the organization, cutting across sections and different levels in the hierarchy. A customer-oriented organization will reflect this orientation clearly in its management objectives and style. Any emphasis on production efficiency will not be at the expense of quality of service for the customer.

In auditing an organization prior to designing a customer care programme, there are various important points which need to be addressed. Is the organization in tune with the needs and moods of the market place? Does the organization reflect the characteristics of the market in internal business activities? The identification of customer types through market segmentation analysis is of crucial importance here. An organization which has a strong customer orientation understands its customers (their needs, preferences, foibles) and designs its products and services to fit the different needs and expectations of customers. Internal systems should be designed with customers in mind. Distribution systems need to be aware of customer geography and demography.

A customer-focused organization is adaptable and sensitive to shifts in the market place. It can respond quickly to changing customer needs. The preparatory audit should assess how quickly an organization can respond to market shifts. Market research is another central function in this context, and should be given due prominence in the organization.

The key to effective customer service, however, lies in the organizational culture. The customer orientation should be embedded in the culture, which in turn inculcates in staff and management alike a set of values which emphasize the need to put the customer first. While we have already examined corporate culture in some detail in Chapter 3, it cannot be divorced from the customer function. Culture and customer care are linked inextricably in any organization which provides effective customer service.

In preparing for a customer service programme, in which the organization is to be changed to become more customer-oriented, it is essential to assess a number of perceptions. The customer's perception must be understood, the attitudes of staff must be assessed, and the views of management must be known. What impressions do customers have of the organization, its staff and its management? What perceptions do staff have of customers and the way in which the organization deals with them? How do management perceive customers, staff attitudes towards customers and their own approach(es) to customer care? These are among the kinds of questions which a customer audit must address.

Achievement of effective lasting improvement to customer service depends, first, upon the organization knowing as much as possible about what its customers want, and second, on assessing where current services fall short of the market. Organizations should not cut corners in building a detailed bank of knowledge about those whom they serve and the effectiveness with which they do so.

AREAS OF KNOWLEDGE

Peel (1987) identified three areas about which organizations must have accurate knowledge.

- What service does the organization give its customers?
- What service do customers (existing and potential) want?
- What service is provided by competitors?

Each of these issues needs to be examined in turn in more detail. First of all, an organization can begin by examining the service it currently gives to customers. Organizations ought to have plentiful information about this. However, this information may be poorly organized, or available only in a form which does not readily lend itself to systematic examination. Another point to note is that there may be more than one kind of evidence about customer service, some of which is less reliable than others. It is thus important to attach weight to evidence that is likely to be reliable.

Defining the current service

Accurate knowledge about customer service derives from balanced, objective and comprehensive information. It is important to avoid attaching too much weight to anecdotal evidence, to the remarks of customers who complain, or to the opinions of small numbers of highly articulate customers, especially ones of high status who may be known to top management. Equally significantly, preconceptions within the organization about customer service may be out of date or misguided and therefore need to be checked out thoroughly.

An accurate audit is built upon objective measures of each specific area of customer service. Data on some aspects of customer service performance may already exist within the organization. Any aspects for which data do not will have to be investigated via various audit procedures.

Walker (1990) has outlined two important components of customer service on which organizations can conduct audits using data they should already have: material service and personal service.

Material service

There are three types of material service: product, environment and delivery systems, each of which should be audited. Under the product heading, the audit is concerned with the quality of the product, rather than with primary marketing or policy issues. The aim is to supply a high-quality product which customers regard as reliable and which fulfils their expectations of it. The standards set for production and the procedures adopted to attain them should all be determined by the customer requirement.

According to Walker, if the product falls in quality below the level expected by customers, there are several possible reasons which need to be investigated by the organization:

- The specification is not clear.
- Equipment or facilities are not right for the job.
- Staff don't have the knowledge or skills to produce the specification.
- Standards for measuring how well the process is doing do not exist or have not been communicated to those carrying out the process

(1990, p. 29)

There are many processes which have to work together in an integrated fashion to enable an organization to provide an effective service to its customers. As we saw at the beginning of this chapter, customer care must penetrate deep into the organization, reaching even those internal departments which may have no direct contact with external customers. A general customer orientation within a company may also involve the identification of internal as well as external customers. Employees will need awareness training to ensure that they recognize their internal customers. A total quality programme must be implemented in which the entire organization is involved. Management have a key role to play in ensuring that this process is set in motion, by raising customer awareness among all staff and regulating the tasks and work processes performed by employees so that the best possible service is supplied.

The environment forms the second focus of a material service audit. For many organizations, the service environment plays a significant part in enhancing customer opinion and loyalty. It is clearly important to restaurants, hotels, shops, banks, airlines and other places where customers enter the premises of the service supplier and remain there for some time, that customers feel comfortable in this environment.

Environment is important, however, even for manufacturing companies. Reception areas, meeting rooms and showrooms all display the supplier to the customer and say something about the quality of product or service the customer can expect to obtain. Once again, Walker (1990) provides a helpful list of things in terms of quality, quantity, and satisfaction that a material audit might examine:

- quality of furniture/furnishings;
- colour combinations;
- lighting;
- space available for customers;
- queuing systems;
- barriers between customers and supplier or supplier's staff/products;
- signage and promotional materials;
- cleanliness and tidiness;
- amount of privacy;
- customer facilities, such as coffee and phones;
- ease of finding way around;

- car parking facilities;
- ease of accessing products and services.

All of these features can affect the image of the organization. An untidy reception area makes a very clear statement to customers about the 'personality' of the organization and the quality of product or service they can expect to obtain from it. The environment can not only shape customer behaviour, it can also influence the attitudes and conduct of staff. The facilities, procedures and arrangement of work all affect the health of the organization. Improvements to the environment can often be made relatively inexpensively, but with substantial benefits for the motivation of staff and customer perceptions of the organization. Finally, under material service, we come to delivery systems. This covers product packaging, warehousing and distribution, transport, ordering, and billing systems. All of these are components of customer-oriented behaviour. All too often, these important features are dictated by internal operational or production demands, and show little concern for the needs of customers

Customers will often tolerate deficiencies in deliveries if the product is something they really want, but continued failure to deliver on time, or at a time that is convenient for the customer, will stretch customer tolerance and encourage them to take their business elsewhere.

Some organizations operate systems which assume that quality will not always be right. They offer customers warranties, compensation or replacement options for goods which fail to offer complete satisfaction. Such policies can have a powerful effect on customers' level of regard for the supplier.

Delivery and related problems can often be highlighted by an analysis of complaints. These problems are not always easy to put right. Customer-oriented organizations must be sure to involve staff who run delivery systems and to use them as a source of solutions. Staff suggestion policies have the double advantage of making staff feel involved, thus enhancing their self-image, and may generate workable solutions which are cheaper than ones obtained via experienced consultants, and to which staff will have greater commitment.

Personal service

Customer satisfaction research has indicated that personal service is extremely important, and may even override material aspects of service. The quality of the service can depend critically on those who implement it on behalf of the supplier. Staff at the front line, who have direct contact with customers, reflect the personality of the organization. Data on personal service can be obtained through unsolicited customer comments or complaints and market research.

According to Walker, personal service can be audited under three main headings:

- skills/knowledge;
- attitudes;
- people systems.

This audit should be applied not simply to customer contact staff, but also to other staff who are part of the overall service process.

There is nothing more off-putting to customers than staff who exhibit a lack of skill or knowledge in their job. Under such circumstances customers will lose confidence in the organization and look elsewhere. Negative feedback from customers will probably undermine the confidence of staff, making their performance even worse. This part of the personal service audit should therefore examine various elements of skill and knowledge:

- technical knowledge;
- product knowledge;
- knowledge about the business and the organization;
- customer-handling skills such as selling, problem-solving, clarifying, summarizing;
- handling complaints;
- being polite and courteous.

These skills can be equally important for staff who are not on the front line. They often have internal customers who should be afforded the same quality of service as those on the outside.

Such skills and knowledge need to be monitored in action. There are a number of techniques which can be used to do this, such as observation by supervisors, customer interviews after a service interaction, peer group monitoring, and self-analysis. Management have, as ever, an important role to play in ensuring that standards are set and performance is monitored. If performance fails to attain a satisfactory level, management must assume responsibility for implementing improvement programmes, staff training, etc. Managers require the same skills and knowledge as staff. It is therefore important that a system of checks and balances is employed up and down the service organization in order to reinforce the personal service ethos. Steps to be taken to rectify problems include training, reassignment of staff, restructuring work, and general policy support.

Staff may have the knowledge and skills to do their job effectively enough, but may lack the desire or will to deliver good customer service. Staff who are rude, apathetic and unhelpful towards customers can do untold damage to an organization's business reputation. Management must set the standards once again and managers must clearly demonstrate through their own conduct that the customer comes first. Employee surveys can be used to ascertain the current state of staff attitudes towards customers. As additional context, it may also be useful to include questions on other issues, some of which we have already discussed in the chapter on corporate climate – staff perceptions of own role, the organization, and management.

Staff morale in general can affect the way customers are treated and responded to. The health of the organization can be assessed by examining data on sickness and absence rates, errors in staff performance, and disputes between staff and management.

Attitudes are not always easy to change. An attitude survey will enable an organization to pinpoint problems in staff disposition towards customers. A customer-awareness programme can then be designed to deal with these problems. Such a programme would cover:

- the vision of the organization;
- customer expectations;
- current performance levels and inhibitors;
- service standards;
- personal presentation;
- assertiveness;
- collective ownership of problems;
- positive attitudes;
- the impact of body language.

Finally, under the personal service audit, it is important to understand *people systems*. Essentially, this heading covers a range of staff-related matters: recruitment and selection in the organization; induction and training; appraisal, promotion, pay and incentives. It also covers staff presentation and image projection to customers, general policies and procedures in respect of the treatment of customers, and facilities and equipment which enable staff to do their job. Table 6.1 provides an outline of the kinds of questions which could be included in a people systems audit.

Finding out what customers want

Having audited the nature of the service currently supplied to customers, the next step is to initiate a process of systematic fact-gathering outside as well as within the organization, in order to ascertain whether the kind of service given equates with the sort of service customers really wish to have.

The primary goods or services provided by an organization can be measured objectively. They can be weighed, measured, their components or materials can be checked against established standards. Customer service can also be measured, but its value to customers is subjective. For example, delivery may be slow and customers may perceive it to be slow. But the important question is *how* slow, and slow compared with what standard or benchmark? Is delivery slower than it used to be? Is it slow compared with that offered by competitors? Or is the feeling of slowness on the part of customers really a projection of some other perceived fault in the service? These are matters which need to be investigated and explained.

Customers' feelings are important. They can be surveyed, even though

Table 6.1 People systems audit

Recruitment	1	Do job and person profiles reflect the importance of service?
	2	Do advertisements stress the importance of service?
	3	Are your procedures applicant-oriented?
Selection	1	Are your selection staff and managers trained to identify service-oriented people?
	2	Are your selection methods aiding the process and are they themselves people-oriented?
	3	Does the process leave a good image of your company even with those who fail to get a job with you?
	4	Are promises kept in terms of letting people know the outcomes of job applications?
	5	Is feedback offered to failed candidates?
Induction	1	Do you have an induction programme for all new recruits; does it start immediately on appointment?
	2	Does it cover vision, the importance of service, who your customers are, or does it just cover pay and ration issues?
	3	Are people introduced properly to new colleagues, their manager and other key people, or are they left to find out for themselves?
Training	1	Is a training programme set up to ensure they acquire the appropriate knowledge and skills?
	2	Does the training cover customer awareness and handling skills as well as technical training?
	3	Is the training style and setting supportive of the aim of high-quality service?
	4	Are managers and supervisors helped with their transition to their new role when promoted?
	5	Are skills periodically refreshed?
	6	Does training take place solely in organization compartments?
Appraisal	1	Does an appraisal system exist which encourages regular discussion on performance targets and achievement?
	2	Does this help to continuously motivate and develop people in the organization, or is it an annual chore?
	3	Are people skilled in making it work?
	4	Do the criteria monitored fully reflect the importance of service and quality?
	5	Do those appraised see differentiated service performance recognized?
Promotion	1	Do promotions reflect success in delivering high quality at service agent, supervisor and manager level?
	2	Are decisions seen to be fair, and are they discussed openly?
	3	Is feedback given to unsuccessful candidates?
Pay and incentives	1	Are jobs evaluated in a way which reflects the importance of service?
	2	Do incentive or bonus schemes reflect quality, or are they productivity/quality oriented?
	3	If there is performance pay, is it given for quality of performance, or quantity?

Uniform issue	1	Are those in contact with customers provided with guidelines and practical help on personal presentation?
	2	Does the uniform support your people-orientation?
	3	Is the issue sufficient for the wearer always to present a clean and tidy image?
Policies and procedures	1	Are your policies and procedures oriented towards the customer or internal administrative consideration?
Facilities and equipment	1	Do staff have the tools to do the job?
	2	Is equipment designed to make their job easy to do or does it create unnecessary difficulties?
	3	Are facilities laid out in a way which enables staff to deal with customers effectively?

Source: Walker (1990), pp. 38–40. Reproduced by permission of the publisher.

they are personal to the individual. This exercise must, however, be carried out in a systematic fashion. It is crucial to establish and define the pattern of the limits of tolerance. Some customers are more patient than others. Customers may be more lenient in respect of certain types of complaint or fault compared with other kinds of service or product problems.

Customers may be unhappy with the service they receive when their expectations of a product or service are not met. It is therefore important to be clear about what is being offered, and to inform customers clearly about such matters. Current and prospective customers can then be surveyed for their perceptions of what kind of product and service they think is on offer, how much they are told about such things by the supplier, and whether or not they would like to know more.

The way organizations treat customers is vital. Customers are often sensitive to the way employees of a supplier behave towards them. Rudeness is a common source of complaint, but can be difficult to prove unless witnesses are present. Even so, an organization which acquires a reputation for being rude to its customers is likely to see its business suffer in consequence.

Customer perceptions and expectations vary over time and according to what the competition might offer. Competitors who introduce new service elements can change customers' standards and values and lead them to expect more from suppliers. It is therefore essential that organizations are aware of these changes, both in the competitor and among customers.

Customers themselves vary. Organizations should know their customers demographic and psychographic make-up, and should monitor any profile changes. Segmentation of customers into different types according to their buying patterns, social background, economic status, and psychographic or lifestyle category can help to pinpoint customers' variations in service response, and help to plan ahead.

Organizations should ask themselves about the service provided by their main competitors. Facts about the service provided by competitors are not always easy to obtain, but it can be worth while making the effort to get them. This can reveal the relative position of one's own organization in the league of customer service. It can also provide helpful information concerning any respects in which service must be improved, and respects in which there is wasted effort. Walker (1990) quotes as an example a change of policy at British Airways, who for many years discouraged their managers from flying on rival airlines. As the market place became more competitive, in-depth studies of competitors, looking at all aspects of their service mix, were included in monthly service performance results and discussed in senior management meetings.

Customer service survey

The way to find out from customers how they perceive an organization's service and that supplied by its competitors is to conduct a customer service survey. This survey can be combined with wider market research which might be concerned with the primary products and services offered by the organization. Care needs to be taken in how this exercise is handled. Combining a customer care audit with other market research questions may lead to a cumbersome project which takes a long time to put together, as different departments argue over their different requirements. It is important also not to allow the customer service angle to become submerged by all the other aspects. Adequate resources need to be made available, including the cost of the customer service audit, sparing staff from their duties, and finding the necessary skills, either in-house or with the help of qualified consultants, to put the whole exercise together.

Peel (1987) offers some useful tips to organizations who decide to conduct their own in-house customer survey. These include obtaining the commitment of top management to the project; clearly defining the objectives of the exercise; choosing an effective leader for the survey team; consulting face-to-face with all those who will be concerned, at all levels in the organization, individually or in groups to explain what the aims of the project are; and finally, arranging the method of reporting back any conclusions of the project. As we have noted in earlier chapters, whenever an organization conducts an employee survey of any kind, it is essential than it has the backing of management at the highest level and that its results are fed back to participants with minimal delay, so that no unnecessary suspicions are aroused as to its purpose. The latter hints are important with regard to any survey of employees designed to ascertain their perceptions of customers, or of customers' perceptions of the organization.

This employee-based customer service audit can be supplemented with an audit conducted among customers themselves. This can be done face-to-face, with the employee survey, or via telephone interviews or self-completion questionnaires. Direct, face-to-face interviews are probably the best way to elicit in-depth information, but this is also the most expensive method. Though cheaper, postal surveys may not give such a good response rate, while telephone surveys are more limited than face-to-face interviews in the kinds of questions it is possible to ask. In making the most of a customer survey, it is important to ensure that the questions which will be asked are carefully thought about and planned beforehand. Information obtained through the customer survey should include factors such as 'the goods or services bought, amount spent over time, size of individual transactions, frequency of transactions, length of business connection with the organization, experience of competitors, geographical location, nationality, sex, age and ethnic or socio-economic grouping' (Peel, 1987, p. 68). There may also be an opportunity to refine still further the customer classification by obtaining psychographic and lifestyle data from respondents.

In designing the questionnaire for the main survey, qualitative preparatory work is often recommended whereby small groups of customers are invited to take part in extended discussions about the service provided in an open-ended fashion in sessions moderated by a trained interviewer. This procedure can serve a number of useful purposes. It can generate ideas for questions to ask in the main survey, and it also enables the researchers to form a better understanding of the language the customers use to describe or respond to the issues being raised. All of this information can prove invaluable in putting together the questionnaire for the main survey. Once a questionnaire has been drafted, it is often wise to run a pilot test first in which it is used among a small selection of respondents who are given an opportunity to say if there is anything they find about it which is difficult to understand.

In the survey itself, customers should be asked about the product(s) or service(s) they buy from the organization, how much they have spent in recent weeks or months, and how long they have been customers. Questions should also probe for comparisons with competitors. The surveys should try to ascertain in some detail what elements of the service customers are happy with or dissatisfied with. The customer should also be asked if there are aspects of the service which fail to live up to expectations or promises made by the supplier. While some open-ended responses can enable customers to provide full detail of their views about the supplier, for ease and economy most questions should use pre-coded response options. This speeds up the interview and data preparation and analysis, all of which can have significant cost benefits. Furthermore, it lends more structure to the interview and makes for ease of comparison across subgroups of respondents.

APPLYING CUSTOMER AUDITS

Using the results of a customer audit to achieve the maximum benefit to customers and to the business of the organization requires careful planning. Input from the customer audit should feature as an integral part of long-term strategic plans. Anything less than that will bring about short-term improvement only, which is unlikely to enhance the organization's business prospects and ability to stay ahead of competitors in the longer term.

Customer audits can reveal not just how satisfied customers are with the service being supplied, but also by identifying areas of dissatisfaction, they can pinpoint aspects of customer service which the organization can work to change and improve. Such changes may involve a product or range of products, or the ways in which those products are delivered to customers, or both. Change in the customer service process, however, almost inevitably involves the conduct of the organization's human resources. This means that staff attitudes and behaviour need to be addressed to ensure that they are consonant with the goal of attaining all-round, effective customer service.

Customer service needs to be acknowledged as a distinct function within the organization, which should be under the control of its own director or senior executive whose own status confirms the organization's commitment to the customer. He may need to be supported by a department or dedicated unit of staff whose major purpose is to ensure that the organization places the customer first. Staff in general need to be trained in appropriate ways, if the necessary customer-oriented values and attitudes are to prevail. The customer service director, if the post exists, should work together with the human resources director to ensure that the best possible training is made available.

Peel (1987) has outlined five steps through which any improvement plan designed to enhance customer service should progress. These are:

1   defining problem areas
2   choosing solutions;
3   setting the improvement plan in action;
4   changing attitudes and behaviour by training;
5   monitoring results.

Defining problem areas involves the internal audits described earlier in this chapter, together with customer and employee surveys. Once this has been done, solutions can be chosen which may include moving to a new market, changing the organization's marketing orientation towards existing customers, improving internal systems and procedures, introducing programmes to train and motivate staff, investing in new equipment, changing the service behaviour, and promotional activities.

All of the operations need to be carefully costed. There will be initial set-up costs for acquiring new equipment, alterations to premises, staff training and public relations exercises. Once the programme is under way, there will be running costs which need to be carefully calculated to ensure that the customer service enhancements are maintained.

Part of the ongoing costs will also cover measurement of the impact of the customer-care programme. Periodic audits among employees and customers should be carried out to ensure that both feel they are receiving proper attention from the organization. The organization will then wish to know what impact the programme is having on revenue. Controlled experiments can be set up to assess the revenue effect. These will need to be skilfully designed, however, to eliminate extraneous variables which might contaminate the results. In other words, the organization needs to have confidence that increased revenue is indeed being generated (or at least significantly contributed towards) by the customer-care programme.

It is important that the organization running a customer-care programme avoids placing an overly narrow mode of assessment of its impact. Short-term financial gains may provide a sign of its positive benefits, but a longer-term perspective needs to be taken as well. The effects which a carefully planned and implemented programme can have on the morale and conduct of staff and the perceptions of customers may not be achieved immediately, but through continued effort, such results will eventually be achieved over time, enhancing the long-term market position of the organization. Continued commitment is required from top management, together with involvement of staff in decision-making. The more fully everyone in the organization is involved, the greater the chances are that decisions will be acted upon.

THE SIGNIFICANCE OF CUSTOMER ORIENTATION

This chapter has underlined the importance of an effective customer-oriented strategy for company performance. The need for organizations to care for their external customers has been recognized for a long time. In the western industrial world, however, where this perspective originated, for many years business forgot or chose to play down the emphasis on quality of source. The main reason for this was a perception that a quality service orientation was costly and held no real long-term benefits. The success of Japanese industry, however, where the concept and practice of total quality took hold in the 1950s, led the business world in the West to return to a quality orientation.

Emphasis upon customer requirements was part of a general corporate strategy designed to improve the overall quality of a company's performance. Caring for customers therefore became part of a broader programme of cultural change. The customer service philosophy was directed not only at the way companies treated and responded to their external customers, but also affected a new approach to internal functioning. An 'internal customer orientation' meant that employees within an organization found themselves in the role of both supplier and customer in

respect of their relationship with co-workers in other sections or departments. Customer service can, thus, represent the driving force behind a
whole new corporate management system.

The involvement of the entire organization is essential if a total quality
programme centring on the improvement of customer service is to be
successful. It is important that everyone in the organization understands the
quality issues and how they are to be implemented. A well-formed strategy
is vital so that top management have a clear view of the quality costs, the
attitudes of management and the work-force, and customer requirements.
The corporate strategy will provide a focus for desired change and will
determine what the mission and objectives of the total quality programme
will be. An essential prerequisite of any total quality programme is a clear
mission statement from top management. This will provide clarification of
organizational values and a commitment to the quality programme. At the
same time, top management are able to articulate the direction of the
organization as defined by implementation of total quality.

Customer requirements represent a central ingredient which feeds into
strategy development. These are weighed alongside quality costs, and the
need for the organization to change. The implementation programme
focuses on how to move the organization from the position it is in at
present, to the one it wishes to attain for the future. Corporate quality
strategy is thus aimed at plugging what has been referred to as the
'development gap' (Collard, 1990).

Strategy development can take two years to complete. Using the Crosby
(1978) model, this period takes the organization from the uncertainty
stage, where there may be no realization that there is even a problem, to
the marketing stage where a strategy begins to emerge. Top management
must lead this stage, because their commitment can only be achieved by a
full understanding of the issues involved.

An example of this kind of customer-oriented total quality strategy

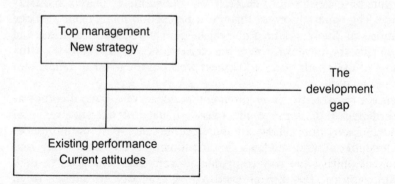

Figure 6.3 The development gap
Source: Collard (1990), p. 73. Reproduced by permission of the publisher.

development is the programme of change implemented in the early 1980s by Rank Xerox. A period of several years spanned the time when difficulties in the market began to emerge and the launch of a total quality programme. Cost reduction was introduced in 1980 and more attention was placed on the products, service, and practices of the competition, which established key criteria for performance. Hence, we have an illustration of a customer audit being led by a competitor audit.

Over the subsequent two or more years, strategy development took shape, new targets were set, and monitoring procedures were set up to ensure that all levels within the organization reported to these new targets. Top management at Xerox then began to pull the strategy together by establishing a focus for change – leadership through quality – and produced a mission statement:

Xerox is a quality company. Quality is a basic business principle for Xerox. Quality means providing our external and internal customers with innovation products and services to fully satisfy their requirement. Quality improvement is the job of every Xerox employee.

The statement provided a means of identifying the development gap, and from there, to preparing a strategy which resulted in a major training programme which ran for a further four years.

EVALUATING A CUSTOMER-SERVICE PROGRAMME

Long-term success of a customer-service programme requires constant effort, including continuous auditing of the results. Establishing a new corporate culture, which places emphasis on quality of performance is dependent upon the routine implementation of procedure to ensure that a climate of continuous improvement is maintained (Collard, 1990). Achieving excellence is not easy and requires the right kind of corporate culture and climate (Peters and Waterman, 1982).

Continuous checks should be run on the costs of quality, on staff attitudes throughout the organization, customer requirements, and the effectiveness of different parts of the organization. Quality costs include the costs of problem prevention, the costs of appraising performance, and the costs of internal and external failure in services supplied. Audits of attitudes need to be conducted with some regularity, but care does need to be taken not to overdo it. A combination of culture, climate, communication, and internal customer audits may be needed, or a selection of appropriate audits from amongst them, depending upon the type of information required. These audits can enable management to target and qualify areas which may be causing difficulty and need resolution.

It is important to conduct regular monitoring of the performance of all groups, sections, and departments within an organization which are involved in a total quality programme. Only through systematic measurement

Table 6.2 Improvement group audit checklist

General
1   List those factors which have helped the introduction of improvement groups.
2   List those factors which have hindered the introduction of improvement groups.
3   Are you satisfied with the progress of improvement groups? Please explain your answer.
4   Do you think the improvement groups have benefited:
    — the company?
    — the employees?
    Please give details
5   What are the main achievements of the improvement group programme?

Detailed evaluation
A *Organization*
1   Are the arrangements for meetings satisfactory in:
    — location?
    — equipment?
    — timing?
2   Are meetings held regularly according to the weekly schedule?
3   Are there any difficulties in attending meetings?
4   Who collects data – leaders, members or both?

B *Leadership*
1   Does the leadership of the improvement group work satisfactorily?
2   Are the opinions of all members taken into account?

C *Management*
1   Does your manager support your improvement group? If so, how?
2   What response have you received to your proposals?
3   Have there been difficulties in implementing your proposals? If so, give details.
4   Do you consider you have top management support?

D *Communication*
1   Was the initial briefing about improvement groups sufficient?
2   Are *all* employees kept briefed about the work of improvement groups?
3   Do you consider there should be any further communication about improvement groups?

E *Facilitator*
1   Is the level of support from the facilitator sufficient?
2   What further support (if any) do you require?
3   Can the facilitator be contacted easily?

F *Training*
1   Was the initial training sufficient?
2   What further training do you think is necessary?

The future
1   What views do you have on the future success of improvement groups?
2   What should be done to further strengthen the improvement of group programmes?
3   Should there be regular review meetings to monitor progress? If so, please give details.

Source: Collard (1990), p. 168. Reproduced by permission of the publisher.

can the progress being made by the programme be properly assessed. Involvement of employees through task groups or quality circles means that the tasks or projects they are required to undertake can provide sets of criteria which can be audited. An internal audit can be carried out using a checklist of key questions. Table 6.2 provides an example.

The checklist is not the sole indicator, however; it should form a basis for discussion about performance among departmental managers, middle managers, supervisory staff and other group leaders, as well as among groups of other employees. Thus, the checklist is not required to be used as a questionnaire. Greater benefits can be obtained if it is used to facilitate lengthier discussion among members of the organization. The outcome of such discussions should be a report which provides a general overview of progress to date, identifies specific successes achieved, or problems experienced along the way, and should include an action plan for the future. The extent to which customer (external and internal) requirements are being satisfied, or have been improved upon, should form a central feature of the report.

The feedback thus provided to the quality programme steering committee or management board will enable top management to decide if strategy needs to be redirected in any way, perhaps to concentrate on particular customer requirements, or whether the programme needs to be developed or extended in any way. The quality programme must be constantly managed in this fashion and not simply allowed to run itself, once up and running, without regular careful scrutiny of its achievements. A total quality programme designed to enhance the service an organization provides to its customers, needs to be regularly evaluated in order to create an environment for continuous improvement.

7   The role of audits in organizations

INTRODUCTION

This final chapter will focus on the four corporate audits (culture, climate, communication and customers) in respect of specific organizational practices like training, management development, corporate strategy and organizational communications systems. It looks specifically at how audits can be used as an integral part of corporate management. Human resources audits can, and should, be well-used instruments in the hands of personnel managers and planners because of the information they supply.

Corporate human resources audits have many side benefits. They can inform recruitment and strategic planning. They can help to analyse organizational competencies and might help determine the efficacy of performance appraisal. They have the advantage of making the implicit explicit – bringing out into the open and systematically assessing the views of employees. This book has considered four major human resources audits: culture, climate, communication, and customer audits, though there are others – occasionally specialist, detailed audits are required by organizations to assess particular problem areas. This final chapter, will examine applications of these audit processes and will then explore further supplementary audits.

AUDITING FOR DEVELOPMENT, STRATEGY, AND TRAINING

What part can corporate audits play in organizational strategy? As mentioned at the beginning of Chapter 1, all strategic planning, if it is to be effective, should be informed by careful, meticulous, and empirical audit of various features of the organization. Audits provide for the planner a snapshot of the state of the organization before, during or after major change events. They can therefore be used for a number of purposes.

Development

Organizational development (OD) is concerned with the diagnosis and improvement of organizational health and performance, and the ability of the organization to adapt to (predict and exploit) change. French and Bell (1984) offer the following definition:

> A top-management-supported, long-range effort to improve an organiz-ation's problem-solving and renewal process, particularly through a more effective and collaborative diagnosis and management of organiza-tion culture with – special emphasis on formal work team, temporary team, and intergroup culture – with the assistance of a consultant-facilitator and the use of theory and technology of applied behavioural science, including action research.
>
> (p. 2)

The implementation of OD strategy and the monitoring of its effective-ness often concerns the use of audits. Climate surveys help to determine the attitudes, beliefs, perceptions, and behaviours of all or some specific members/groups in the organization. Results are then fed up to senior management (and, hopefully, to work groups for interpretation and analysis. Various group members participate in discussions on the impli-cations of the audit, the diagnosis of problems and the development of action plans to help overcome the problems identified.

'Organization development' has become a catch-all phrase meaning very different things to different people. In the beginning, it tended to focus mostly on improving human relations, but the best practitioners have long since broadened it to encompass all aspects of managing an organization. The key aims of OD are to raise an organization's capacity to learn about and manage itself autonomously – particularly where major change is involved. OD specialists try to improve *processes* (how things are done), rather than *content* (what is done).

The general methods of OD have spread into many related fields – for example, organization design; strategic management; quality and service development; and the 'culture of excellence'. Indeed, the term 'OD' is sometimes no longer used, even though the approach is currently more common than ever before. These days, OD practitioners cannot concen-trate purely on interpersonal (or *individual*) processes, but also need to be conversant with *task* processes (e.g. as used in strategic management) and even with technical content (e.g. in organization design, or mergers). Subject specialists may also choose to work in a developmental way: it's more a style than a function. Audits can, and should, be used to diagnose not only the necessity for OD but the efficacy of OD interventions. Indeed specific OD audits could be devised.

Strategic planning

How can audits help in organizational development or strategic planning? The following model, albeit a simple one, gives some idea of this process. Once mission, strategy, structure, and processes have either been decided upon or have historically evolved, a corporate audit can help management to establish benchmarks for company performance, to assess whether performance criteria are being met, and to identify where problems and barriers to effective performance exist.

Figure 7.1 illustrates the process.

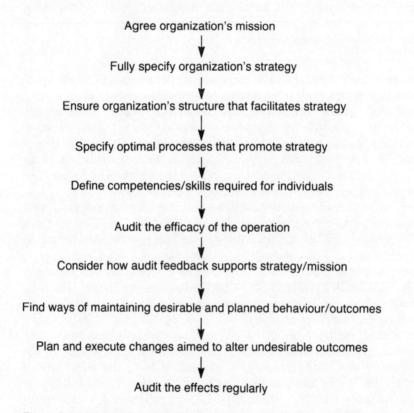

Agree organization's mission

↓

Fully specify organization's strategy

↓

Ensure organization's structure that facilitates strategy

↓

Specify optimal processes that promote strategy

↓

Define competencies/skills required for individuals

↓

Audit the efficacy of the operation

↓

Consider how audit feedback supports strategy/mission

↓

Find ways of maintaining desirable and planned behaviour/outcomes

↓

Plan and execute changes aimed to alter undesirable outcomes

↓

Audit the effects regularly

Figure 7.1 Linking HR auditing processes to organization strategy

Again, audits are an integral part of strategic planning. Data for audits tell the strategic planner whether employees understand, believe or adhere to the company's mission; whether the organizational structure contributes to different subcultures in the organization and whether strategy is working. Strategic planning, particularly with respect to human resources, can benefit greatly from the data that emerge from regular and appropriate audits.

Training

Audits can be used to define training needs and then to monitor the performance or success of a training programme. Audits are also needed to measure the effectiveness of training. For instance, consider the design from Smith (1976) shown in Figure 7.2.

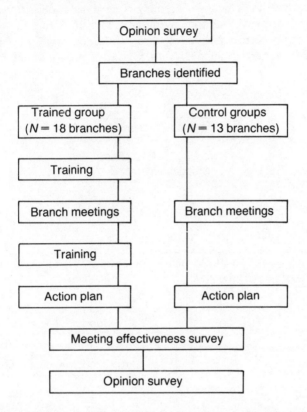

Figure 7.2 Management modelling training to improve morale and customer satisfaction
Source: Smith (1976). Reproduced by permission of the publisher.

Audits can be used to demonstrate the efficacy (or not) of training. In one study, thirty-one branches completed an opinion survey about a variety of topics. Then, comparable groups were arranged those trained and those not trained. The training programme was guided by the results of a survey conducted at the outset, and a second audit was used to assess the efficacy of action plans drawn up either with, or without, prior training.

This is a traditional 'before-and-after' use of corporate audits. They are used to assess, and hence justify, the efficacy of training programmes. Note that it may not be the employees (trainees) who complete the opinion survey at the beginning and end of the course: it may be customers and clients. Indeed, given the post-course evaluation bias that may occur (such as pleasing the trainer or believing one has improved dramatically), with some research it is indeed better if non-participants do the evaluation. Even more importantly, those doing the evaluation of staff are not aware of which groups have been subjected to training. This 'double-blind' procedure ensures that the efficacy of training is most accurately assessed.

Smith (1976) provides another similar model. In Figure 7.3 a customer survey is done before and after three different types of training are conducted in various branches (with a control group where no training takes place).

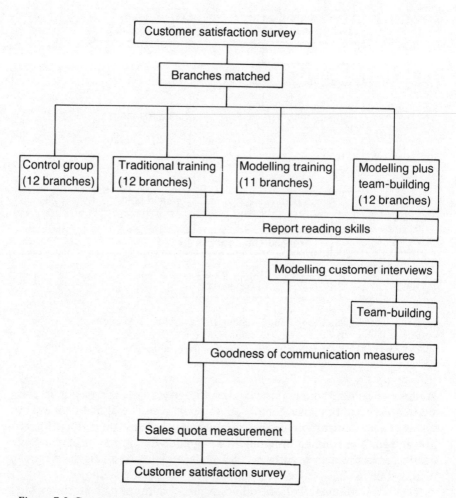

Figure 7.3 Customer survey to assess efficacy of training
Source: Smith (1976). Reproduced by permission of the publisher.

Note that the customer survey is not the only way of measuring the efficacy of training: a sales quota measure is also put in place. Here, following a customer audit, branches are divided into four groups: one group experiences no training (control), another traditional training, a third modelling training, and the fourth the most complex training (modelling plus team-building). All are measured after the appropriate training on both actual sales quota, as well as another customer satisfaction survey. What the researchers are looking for is the degree of difference between the four groups to ascertain the level and kind of effect (or non-effect) of type of training on revenue generated and customer satisfaction (for they may not be the same).

THE ROLE OF AUDITS IN ORGANIZATIONAL DEVELOPMENT

Audits can help to inform a number of OD issues specifically.

Organizational commitment

This includes a sense of belonging in the organization, a sense of excitement in the job and confidence in management. A prevalent approach to organizational commitment is one in which it is considered an affective or emotional attachment to the organization. Thus, a strongly committed individual identifies with, is involved in, and enjoys membership in the organization (Kanter, 1968). Commitment has been associated with quite specific feelings and behaviours of all employees in an organization: belief in, and complete acceptance of, the organization's goals, values, products and services; a general willingness to exert effort on behalf of the organization beyond the requirements of their employment contract, and a desire to remain in the organization (Buchanan, 1974; Mowday, Steers and Porter, 1979; Porter, Crampon and Smith, 1976). Organizational commitment is voluntary and very personal, and cannot be imposed by others. Usually there is a clear reciprocal relationship between employee commitment to the organization and the organization's commitment to its members.

There have been a limited number of attempts to devise an audit instrument to measure organizational commitment. The organizational commitment questionnaire (OCQ) was developed to measure the commitment construct (Mowday, Steers and Porter, 1979). This fifteen-item scale has been demonstrated to have acceptable psychometric properties. A British equivalent to the American OCQ has been tested on blue-collar workers and shown to be psychometrically adequate and stable (Cook and Wall, 1980).

Meyer and Allen (1987) developed a three-component conceptualization of organizational commitment, and identified three forms of commitment which they called 'affective', 'continuance', and 'normative'. They reported that while all three represented a link between the employee and organization that decreased the likelihood of turnover, the nature of that link in each case varied: 'Employees with strong affective commitment remain because they *want* to, those with strong continuance commitment because they *need* to, and those with strong normative commitment because they feel they *ought* to' (Allen and Meyer, 1990, p. 3).

In the latter paper, these two authors describe a study designed to establish independent measures of these distinct psychological states. They found that three components could be empirically as well as conceptually differentiated (see Table 7.1), and that each one had different implications for employee performance.

Organizational conflict

Conflict, which may have many causes (poor communications, psycho-pathic personalities), frequently occurs between competing subgroups, and is often an inherent feature of all organizations because of their structure. Conflict which arises because of goal incompatibility can be understood at the individual, group or organizational level. Of course, there are subtle and important differences between arguments and competition which may be beneficial, and conflict which is not. Contrasting views may have positive outcomes such as an increase in qualitatively and quantitatively different and improved ideas/practices, a clarification of individual views, and a chance for people to test their abilities. On the other hand, negative outcomes include an increase in mistrust, suspicion, turnover, and individuals/groups concentrating on their own narrow interests. As climate audits have shown, conflict can result from differences in perception, competition over limited resources, departmentalization and specialization, the nature of the work activities themselves, and violation of territory. Human resources audits may help to identify the causes of and solutions to organizational conflict.

Organizational change

Whether they like it or not, organizations are subjected to various sources of change: changing technology, product/service obsolescence, changing nature of the work-force, and differences in the quality of working life. Change can be planned or unplanned, resisted or accepted, externally (market-place) initiated or internally initiated. Both individuals and organizations resist change, and audits can pinpoint precisely where the major pockets (and causes) of resistance are. For instance a culture audit can be undertaken before a merge or acquisition, and then one after the event to note change.

Management development

Managers have various demands, constraints and choices placed upon them, and many thus tend to develop specific behavioural roles and styles in responding to work pressures. Organizations attempt to instil both management efficiency (which is concerned with doing things right, and relates to inputs and what a management does) and effectiveness (which is concerned with doing the right things and relates to outputs of the job and what the manager actually achieves). The process of management development should be related to the nature, objectives, and requirements of the organization as a whole. A prerequisite of management development is effective manpower planning, coupled with procedures for recruitment and selection. Performance review audits attempt to identify training, development, personal career, and organizational succession planning.

Mumford (1989) believes the fundamental questions to ask about the effectiveness of management development schemes are:

- Does the scheme achieve what it sets out to achieve? (Answering this question, particularly in relation to courses, has often been described as a validation.)
- Has the process produced results in terms of the demonstrated effectiveness of managers?

In addition, he believes there are certain very useful questions which may be asked to evaluate any management development system:

1 Do you have a policy or statement about developing managers?
2 Have these policies or systems changed significantly over the last fifteen years? If so, how?
3 What stimulated any changes?
4 Have there been partial or smaller-scale initiatives within the total system which have been important (e.g. a particular process or activity)?
5 Is there anything else about the history of management development in your organization which will help us understand the comments we will receive?
6 How significant have formal processes been in developing managers as compared with informal processes?
7 Do you have any prospective changes in your management development processes in mind?
8 How do you evaluate your investment in management development?

(p. 95)

Furthermore he is equally aware of measuring whether the management development system operates in the way intended. Mumford lists the following eight questions that may be answered in an audit:

- improved competence in the existing job

Table 7.1 Varimax rotated factor matrix based on correlations among the items on the effective, continuance and normative commitment scales

	Factor 1	Factor 2	Factor 3
Affective commitment scale items			
1 I would be very happy to spend the rest of my career with this organization.	55	47	−07
2 I enjoy discussing my organization with people outside it.	56	10	−07
3 I really feel as if this organization's problems are my own.	52	39	−06
4 I think that I could easily become as attached to another organization as I am to this one (R).	45	21	18
5 I do not feel like a 'part of the family' at my organization (R).	63	15	−04
6 I do not feel 'emotionally attached' to this organization (R).	81	23	03
7 This organization has a great deal of personal meaning for me.	79	19	02
8 I do not feel a strong sense of belonging to my organization (R).	82	18	−05
Continuous commitment scale items			
1 I am not afraid of what might happen if I quit my job without having another one lined up (R).	−10	02	39
2 It would be very hard for me to leave my organization right now, even if I wanted to.	22	14	58
3 Too much of my life would be disrupted if I decided I wanted to leave my organization now.	33	27	44
4 It wouldn't be too costly for me to leave my organization now (R).	18	12	46
5 Right now, staying with my organization is a matter of necessity as much as desire.	−24	−01	59
6 I feel that I have too few options open to consider leaving this organization.	−14	00	67
7 One of the few serious consequences of leaving this organization would be the scarcity of available alternatives.	−17	−07	60
8 One of the major reasons I continue to work for this organization is that leaving would require a considerable personal sacrifice – another organization may not match the overall benefits I have here.	15	−01	50

Normative commitment scale items

1	I think that people these days move from company to company too often.	14	67	−06
2	I do not believe that a person must always be loyal to his or her organization (*R*).	29	43	00
3	Jumping from organization to organization does not seem at all unethical to me (*R*).	07	63	01
4	One of the major reasons I continue to work for this organization is that I believe that loyalty is important and therefore feel a sense of moral obligation to remain.	17	59	07
5	If I got another offer for a better job elsewhere I would not feel it was right to leave my organization.	17	49	09
6	I was taught to believe in the value of remaining loyal to one organization.	15	49	10
7	Things were better in the days when people stayed with one organization for most of their careers.	05	56	11
8	I do not think that wanting to be a 'company man' or 'company woman' is sensible any more (*R*).	17	47	−03
	% of variance accounted for	58.8	25.8	15.4

Source: Allen and Meyer (1980). Reproduced by permission of the publisher.
Note: The following items were adapted from items used in previous research: ACS items 1 and 3 from Buchanan (1974), and CCS items 1 and 2 from Quinn and Staines (1979). Factor loadings greater than 0.40 are underlined; decimal points have been omitted. *R* = reversed keyed items.

- competence developed in advance of a future job
- more effective career decisions
- turnover of managers at the level desired by the organization (which might be nil or 50 per cent)
- enhanced commitment to the purpose of the organization
- reduction of frustration within individual jobs
- increased satisfaction within individual jobs.

(1989, p. 96)

Organizational effectiveness

Various writers (e.g. Furnham, 1992) have attempted to pinpoint the criteria for effectiveness: action-orientation and a tendency to get things done; listening to and learning from customers; innovation and risk-taking as an expected way of doing things; treating members of staff as a source of quality and productivity; having well-defined basic philosophies with top management keeping in touch with the 'front line'; continuing to do what they know well and can do well; simple structural forms and systems, and few top-level staff and operational decentralization, but strong centralization with a few, core issues. Mullins (1989) maintains that other important factors include having clear, specific, explicit key areas of performance and results, and doing regular audits to determine disparities between strategy formulation and policy decisions, and actions necessary for their successful implementation.

THE ROLE OF AUDITS AS A FEEDBACK COMMUNICATION PROCESS

It is a major role of a corporate human resources audit to provide an organization with clear, objective, explicit information on the beliefs, values, behaviours, and practices of its employees. Most commonly, audits provide management with feedback about the culture and climate that they create or maintain. This upward feedback, if measured properly, can provide management with powerful and useful information. Ilgen, Fisher and Taylor (1979) have conceived of feedback as a special case of the general communications process in which a *message* (feedback) is conveyed to a *recipient* (work performer) from some *source* (e.g., a supervisor or co-worker). They have developed a process model that attempts to integrate human performance and information-processing research findings from laboratory studies with the social context in which feedback occurs in organizational settings. Although this model is developed to conceptualize individual feedback, it is equally appropriate for modelling corporate feedback, and provides a helpful framework for the designs of a corporate audit with a focus on internal communications processes.

There are three general categories of feedback sources: *others*, the *task*, and *self*. 'Others' are those individuals who have observed the recipient's behaviour or output and have some type of information about its effectiveness. In organizations, this category consists most frequently of supervisory personnel, with co-workers, subordinates, and non-organizational members with whom the recipient has contact as part of the work role (such as customers/clients).

The task itself can provide feedback to a work performer. In many jobs, feedback is an inherent part of the task activities, particularly where the task predominantly involves some quantifiable output. Employees may be able to evaluate their own job performance and provide themselves with feedback. It is likely that several factors, such as the measurability of task output, the level of the individual's experience on the task, and the individual's self-esteem, affect the extent to which individuals make such evaluations, and the extent to which they utilize them.

As Figure 7.4 reveals, Ilgen *et al.* hypothesize that the recipient's reaction to feedback involves a four-part process leading to the actual behavioural response. Source, message, and recipient characteristics may affect each of these four parts of the process. The four parts or stages of the recipient's processing of and reaction to performance feedback are:

1   perception of feedback;
2   acceptance of feedback;
3   desire to respond to feedback;
4   the intended response.

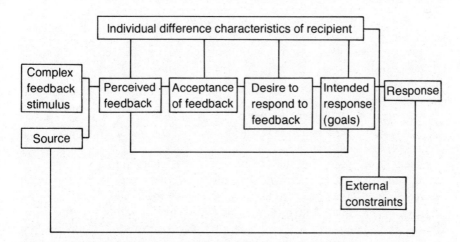

Figure 7.4 A process model of the effects of feedback on recipients
Source: Ilgen, Fisher and Taylor (1979). Reproduced by permission of the publisher.

Perceived feedback

The accuracy with which the recipient perceives the feedback from any given source is labelled as *perceived feedback* in the Ilgen, Fisher and Taylor (1979) model. Various factors may differentially affect the degree of attention paid to the source by the recipient and, thus, influence the accuracy of the perception. Ilgen *et al.* also identified three message factors that appear to affect perceptions of accuracy. These message factors are the temporal interval between the individual's behaviour and the feedback about the behaviour (timing), the positive or negative tone of the information about behaviour (sign), and how often feedback is given to the recipient (frequency). Characteristics of the recipient also are suggested by Ilgen *et al.* as influences on the accuracy of perceived feedback. They stress the importance of self-perceptual sets or frames of reference as influences on the selective sensing and interpreting of feedback from various sources. This is equally true of how, why, and when corporations accept audit feedback.

Acceptance of feedback

Ilgen, Fisher and Taylor (1979) use *acceptance* to refer to the recipient's belief that the feedback is an accurate portrayal of his or her performance. 'Source credibility', the degree of credibility attributed to a source by the recipient, is seen as the principal source characteristic affecting the acceptance of feedback. Ilgen *et al.* suggest that credibility, in turn, is influenced by the recipient's perception of the source's *expertise*, the recipient's trust in the source's motives, the *congruence* of the feedback with the source's role, and the *reliability* of the source. Hence the fact that many audits are done by outside consultants.

The most important message characteristic in terms of its impact on the acceptance of feedback is the *sign* of the feedback. Generally, positive or favourable feedback is more readily accepted by the recipient than is negative or unfavourable feedback. This can lead to very serious problems: For instance some human resources auditors disguise, censor or ignore negative feedback, because it 'causes too many problems'. Message *consistency*, or the extent to which the feedback received from a given source is either *all* positive or *all* negative, is also a major influence on the acceptance of feedback.

Ilgen *et al.* suggested that certain recipient characteristics may affect acceptance of feedback. Individuals with an internal rather than an external *locus of control* may be more likely to accept feedback about performance. Age or age-correlated factors, such as experience or seniority, appears to be inversely related to the willingness to accept feedback. It may also be that older (more experienced, more senior) workers may rely more on their own past experience and knowledge as a source of feedback, and less on external sources. Clearly not all individuals or groups are equally happy to accept audit feedback.

Desire to respond

The willingness to respond to feedback in a manner congruent with that feedback (e.g., maintaining behaviour for which positive feedback was received, or improving that performance for which negative feedback was received) is labelled as *desire to respond to feedback* by Ilgen, Fisher and Taylor (1979).

The source characteristic of most importance in influencing the desire to respond to feedback would appear to be *power*: the extent to which the recipient perceives that the source has control over outcomes and rewards valued by the recipient. Increased source power would be expected to enhance recipient compliance even if the feedback were not accepted.

Frequency of feedback is usually associated with improved performance, but must depend on the sign and timing of the feedback. The sign and frequency of feedback are probably confounded in many instances. Sources are more likely to give positive feedback than negative feedback. Also, if feedback is usually associated with performance improvement, then the recipient's performance should improve over time, resulting in a greater and greater proportion of favourable performance and feedback. Timing may also be confounded with sign and frequency. Sources are more likely to give positive feedback more quickly following the appropriate behaviour than they are to give negative feedback following behaviour appropriate for such feedback.

Ilgen *et al.* regard the view that feedback enhances performance, because it serves as a reinforcer of appropriate work behaviours, as not very helpful in understanding of feedback effects. They favour a more cognitive orientation that focuses on the informational value of feedback rather than its possible reinforcement value. Viewing feedback as providing information about the likelihood that various outcomes or rewards may be received given certain types or levels of work performance appears to be fruitful. Since actual rewards cannot generally be administered to an employee at the completion of each work unit, an important function of feedback is to lead the employee to anticipate a reward at some time in the future (to serve as an incentive). Feedback can provide descriptive and evaluative information about past performance that can be used by the employee to establish perceived relationships (or *instrumentality beliefs*) between performance and rewards that are received. The absence of such feedback is likely to result in the individual establishing incorrect perceptions about the relationship between rewards and behaviours. Providing feedback about an individual's success (or partial success) may serve to increase the individual's belief that more effort expenditure will result in more successful performance.

Intended response

In the Ilgen, Fisher and Taylor (1979) model, the desire to respond to feedback is the major input to the establishment of the response that the recipient intends to make. Performance or response intentions may be thought of as the goal or target set by the recipient. This goal may not always be met; hence, the actual response or performance level is likely to differ in some way from the intended response.

Feedback provides, of course, an important resource both for the individual and the organization. Ashford and Cummings (1983) suggest that feedback may satisfy several motives and, thus, that it is reasonable for individuals to seek feedback in the work environment.

How does giving an individual manager, or department, feedback on their performance or views change their behaviour? Feedback is simply information received by an individual that indicates the correctness, accuracy, or adequacy of past behaviour. Feedback directs: when the feedback indicates certain deficiencies in *what* is being done, the message being transmitted is one that indicates to the employee that subsequent behaviour should change in a direction designed to reduce the noted inadequacies.

Feedback can also serve a motivational function. When information about previous performance is used to focus an employee's attention on achieved levels of performance, or *how much* is being done, the message the employee is receiving is one that instructs him or her to orient future efforts toward increasing subsequent performance. The former function of feedback may be viewed as primarily a qualitative orientation, whereas the latter represents a quantitative emphasis. The effectiveness of the motivating function of knowledge of results depends on the goals an individual sets in response to the knowledge contained in the feedback. Corporate audits can be conducted to compare the perceptions of employees at different levels of an organization's hierarchy regarding the flow of various types of information, or to solicit feedback concerning how the organization could be better run.

Identifying discrepant perceptions

The importance of the management feedback which corporate human resources audits can supply is underlined by research indicating that managers and subordinates may hold different views about organizational functions, the treatment of staff by the organization, and the treatment of subordinates by their managers. Corporate audits can help to bring such discrepant perceptions into line, building a quicker degree of consistency in the views held about the organization and the way it is managed throughout all levels of employees. Such a development can, in turn, guarantee quicker understanding of where disagreements or difficulties among particular sections of the work-force may stem from. For example, managers may place

greater importance on one category of information regarding staff performance, while their subordinates may wish or expect to be assessed in different
terms. Discrepant views about priority issues among managers and
subordinates may lead managers to fail effectively to deal with the
problems of change showing concern to their staff.

Staff need to be supplied with information by their managers, as well as
to give out information. Such communication may contain information
which requires subordinates to carry out their tasks or to achieve objectives
or goals set for them. It may also consist of feedback from management
regarding how well they are performing, or in what respect performance
could be improved. Again, differences of opinions can arise with regard to
how well managers communicate these different messages to staff down the
line. Managers may believe (quite genuinely) that many are supplying the
necessary feedback on different matters. Subordinates, in contrast, may not
perceive the communications processes to be working as effectively.
Corporate audits conducted at different levels of the organizational
hierarchy can identify when these differences of opinion occur, and
quantify how significant or serious they are.

Without an audit, difficulties or misunderstandings concerning internal
corporate communications may never be brought out into the open and
discussed. Communications breakdowns may continue to occur indefinitely
unless a dialogue between senders and receivers of important messages is
set up with feedback loops, enabling both parties to check that the
meanings transmitted equal the meanings received, and that the meanings
sent are regarded as relevant by the receivers.

Auditing solicited feedback from employees

An increasingly commonplace feature of organizational life are mechanisms which invite members of staff at all levels to provide input in the form
of written or oral comments and suggestions regarding work systems and
practices. Among these, employee participation programmes (EPPs) such
as quality circles and quality of life programmes have become especially
popular. Despite their growing implementation, there is still dispute about
whether these programmes have positive benefits for employee and
organizational performance.

There is some evidence that EPPs can enhance individuals' effective
response toward work (Locke and Schweiger, 1979; Miller and Monge,
1986). Whether or not they lead to improved performances is less clear.
What is known, however, is that responses to EPPs, at whichever level
they occur, can be moderated by other factors. Important among these
is the propensity for employees to participate actively in organizational policy-related decisions. Some individuals want to have a voice,
and exhibit what has been termed 'organizational citizenship behaviour'

or 'civic virtue'. Another moderating factor is individual discontent with the extent of worker participation in decision-making.

The effectiveness and nature of any impact of EPPs can be established through corporate auditing techniques. An audit can also be used to investigate the significance of moderating influences on employees' responses to such as communications feedback and involvement programmes. Using the instrument shown in Table 7.2, Graham and Verma (1991) found that attitudes of employees towards EPPs are closely associated with how closely involved they are with the programme, and for those who are directly involved, with the duration of their involvement. In particular, employees who would not normally speak up about organizational matters, exhibited especially strong appreciation of EPPs. In addition, employees who were dissatisfied with the opportunities given by the organization to involve the work-force in decision-making processes, were likely to respond favourably to EPPs.

ALTERNATIVE AUDITS

This book has considered in detail four broad categories of corporate human resources audits: those of culture, climate, communications, and customers. Quite apart from the happy coincidence that they all begin with the letter C, they have a great deal in common. These audits all attempt to document varieties of beliefs and behaviours of an organization's employees with respect to corporate values and norms, reactions to organizational procedures, the use of corporate communication channels, and perceptions and reactions to internal and external customers. They share various common features, in that each audit:

* systematically examines the individual employee perceptions of the organization and reported patterns of behaviour;
* attempts to be comprehensive, in the sense that they examine a wide range of employees' (and management) views.

The question remains about alternative audits. Why not have an audit about pay, or about industrial relations? One obvious reason is that nearly all climate surveys are multidimensional (see pp. 138–52) and often include sub-sections on these issues. Despite the fact that there is a growing consensus about what dimensions one should include in a climate survey, there is nothing to prevent a researcher including items about a highly specific issue.

The focus of this book has been on human resource audits, but of course, other audits are possible that look at wider, or more fashionable areas. Thus, for instance, one might conduct a 'green' or environmental audit which focuses on how employees respond to their physical environment, are in favour of recycling, approve of power-saving devices. Strictly

Table 7.2 Attitude towards employee participation programmes

1 I like my job a lot better since EPPs started.
2 EPPs have done a lot to increase co-operation and teamwork at (name of firm).
3 Interest in EPPs is definitely fading around here.[a]
4 As far as I am concerned EPPs are a big waste of time and money.[a]
5 I hear a lot of positive talk about EPPs around this plant.
6 EPPs have made (name of plant) a better place to work.
7 The time's just not right for EPPs at (name of plant).[a]
8 EPP teams have come up with a lot of good ideas for improving things around here.
9 Without EPPs, things would be much worse around here.
10 If this plant survives and prospers as a business, EPPs will be a big reason why.
11 I feel I have a bigger stake in this plant since EPPs were introduced.
12 EPPs have made me appreciate the need to improve productivity if (name of firm) is to survive as a business.
13 I have a better understanding of the need to upgrade our technology since EPPs started.
14 I think more often about the tough competition that our company faces in the market since the EPPs made me more aware of productivity.

Civic virtue–organizational citizenship behaviour (Civic virtue–OCB)
On your job, how likely are you to:
  1 – make suggestions to improve quality/efficiency in the plant?
  2 – keep up on what is happening in the plant by reading announcements on the bulletin boards?
  3 – warn your supervisor in advance of some defect you think may develop in the production process?
  4 – report any wastage of materials, energy, etc. *outside* your work area?
  5 – report any wastage of materials, energy, etc. *inside* your work area?
  6 – help out a fellow worker on the job?
  7 – read the (name of the company newspaper) regularly?
  8 – attend most plant meetings?
  9 – volunteer for serving on committees of any kind?
  10 – raise an issue of some organizational policy or practice with the supervisor?

Participation-gap: participation-gap is calculated by taking the difference between Q1 and Q2:
Q1. How much say do you think workers *should* have in the following areas of the job?
Q2. How much say do you *actually* have in the following areas of the job?
  1 The way the work is done.
  2 In keeping track of quality.
  3 How fast the work is done.
  4 How much work people should do in a day.
  5 Who should do what in your group or section.
  6 When the work day begins and ends.
  7 Who should be fired if they do a bad job or don't come to work.
  8 Who should be hired into your group.
  9 Handling complaints or grievances.
  10 Who gets promoted.
  11 The use of new technology.
  12 The selection of your supervisor.

Source: Graham and Verma (1991). Reproduced by permission of publisher.
Note: [a]Reverse scored item.

these are only peripherally human resource issues and beyond the scope of
this book, though quite worthwhile in their own right. Three such relatively
neglected topics will be briefly mentioned: computing audits, safety, and
health audits.

However, it should be pointed out that all these audits are different
from, though clearly related to, more 'objective' audits such as job analysis
audits and more fashionably, competency audits. These audits attempt not
so much an audit of the beliefs and behaviours of individuals throughout an
organization, as the specification of the skills, abilities, and capacities of
individual employees and the extent to which jobs in the organization
demand those skills to be increased. However, because of the topicality of
competence, the idea of a competence audit will be briefly reviewed.

Competency audits

There are a number of reasons why the term 'competency' has come into
fashion, and hence, the call for competency audits. Essentially the problem
began with the man who first made the term popular. Boyatzis (1982)
defined competency as 'an underlying characteristic of a person' which
could be a 'motive, trait, skill, aspect of one's self-image or social role, or a
body of knowledge which he or she uses.' The word is used to refer to the
overall ability to perform a job, and the set of behaviours that the person
must display in order to perform the task and functions of a job with
competence.

Woodruffe (1991) has noted how organizations derive their highly
specific competency lists. Often people come to a specific workshop to
analyse, agree, and aggregate the types of behaviour that are desirable to
carry out their jobs to a high standard, and they then practise that
behaviour in the context of the jobs.

At other times, managers at all levels are encouraged to list the
corporate/organization competencies that any successful employee in the
company needs to operate successfully. These competencies are then used
in selection, promotion, appraisal, counselling and vocational guidance.
These lists, which managers are encouraged to believe are quite specific to
their organization (or part of it) are derived in a variety of ways. Sometimes
an autocratic CEO simply sketches these on the back of a share certificate;
at other times all the directors undergo a 'focused' interview and the results
are collated. Still other methods include group discussions, the use of
repertory grids, biodata analysis, or more simply 'tweaking' others' lists to
adapt them to one's own circumstances.

Having got their unique and comprehensive list of competencies,
organizations set out to devise ways of measuring them so that applicants
and employees can be compared and contrasted. How well and accurately
this is done is another question. But before that is considered, it is
important to ask, what are competencies? Are they just a new name for

traits and abilities? Or are they like skills? The former imply cross-situational stability and cross-temporal reliability; that is they are relatively permanent.

Furthermore, there is a wealth of theories and studies attempting to specify the basic traits and abilities that are common across all people, irrespective of the organization or where they work. On the other hand, if competencies are not stable how, when and why do they change? Do they decay if not used, and likewise, do they necessarily improve with practice? A number of crucially important questions need to be considered before any list is drawn up or any audit undertaken.

How are the competencies related to one another?   A list of competencies is nearly always just that – a list, but human abilities are clearly interrelated. Depending on intelligence, thinking styles (i.e., convergent vs. divergent), temperament, certain human factors are clearly related (Furnham, 1992). For instance, extroverts tend to be more socially skilled, more likely to be 'evening people'; more likely to excel in brief 'timed' tests; more likely to be involved in accidents etc. than introverts. Inevitably some competencies will be related (orthogonal) and some unrelated (oblique) to each other, but which? What, in short, is the structure of competencies?

Are competencies learnt or inherited (or both)?   Clearly, there are important implications of the question – if they are primarily learnt, they can be taught; if inherited, they have to be selected. This leads one on to the important but thorny ground of the heredity environment debate, and despite caution, the question remains both important and valid. For instance, if they are learnt, are they best learnt at a particular age (say adolescence or younger) and in a particular way? Do some people learn the competencies more effectively than others?

Are they likely to be found in some groups more than others?   It is quite possible that competencies are found among certain demographic, racial, linguistic, religious, etc. groups more than others. Certainly some groups excel at sport; others at science; so it might not be unreasonable to assume that organizational competencies are found more in some groups than others. And how does one square the selection of these people with equal opportunity and other non-discriminatory legislation?

Are competencies dimensional or categorical?   Is it the case that competencies have an all-or-nothing quality about them (e.g. blue and brown eyes) and that people can and should be categorized into *types*, or is it the case that competencies are dimensional and people fall along a continuum from being highly, through fairly, moderately, or average, poor and low competence? If the former (i.e., dimensional), what are the anchors of that dimension and what the intervening markers?

What is the universe of competencies from which specific organizational lists are derived?   Is there a finite, exhaustive, comprehensive, universal list of competencies from which to devise a subset? Indeed where does one find this list? Or are competencies so numerous, so subtle, so variable that no such list could ever be derived? What strikes a reviewer of numerous organization-specific competencies is how similar they are. If competencies are organization specific, by definition organizations cannot be compared – yet this is highly unlikely.

Are they all equally reliably and validly measurable?   The whole point of getting competencies can be assessed on them; compared; tracked over time; rated before and after training courses, etc. But how are they measured? What sort of test should people undergo: behavioural observation; questionnaire; rating (or subordinates; or both?), etc? Each assessment method has problems associated with it leading to systematic bias and error. Furthermore, not all competencies are likely to be equally validly measured. It is easier to measure certain traits (linguistic skills) than others (intelligence). Many proven, psychometrically valid tests exist to measure various abilities, traits, and beliefs, but others ('forward planning', 'coping with change') are very difficult to measure. Comparing people on unreliable measures is of course highly problematic. Indeed how does one measure common sense, or ability to motivate others, etc?

Are the competencies the sole or even the major 'determinants' of behaviour in the organization?   This is similar to the old question of whether personality traits determine social behaviour. Presumably the competencies are chosen because they represent the fundamental abilities/ capacities needed to do the job well. But does having a competency mean that it will be used? And what other factors *prevent* competent people from performing?

For instance, people might not have the most desirable personality traits, thus preventing them from doing the job well, irrespective of their competency. Anxiety, obsessiveness, phobias, poor coping strategies with everyday stress, etc. may mean that competencies are never allowed to manifest themselves in competent behaviour. On the other hand, various organizational procedures and rules may prevent competent behaviour.

Can one 'compensate' for not having a particular competency?   Is it possible that people can function quite well in an organization by not having a particular competency, or indeed, set of competencies? They might do this through hard work, delegation, and redefinition of their job, etc. People with specific handicaps have been shown to triumph over considerable difficulties, so is it not possible that being without some competencies is not necessarily handicapping.

What does it mean not to have a particular competency?   Is the opposite of competency, incompetency or no competency? What task cannot be done effectively if that competency does not exist, or exists in an insufficient amount? There is quite a difference between knowing how to do a job but doing it badly (incompetence), and not knowing how to do it (no competence). Indeed, what is the cause of incompetency?

Are 'people-related' competencies different from 'thing-related' competencies?   Some people are attracted to computers, accounting systems, etc. because they are logical, predictable, rational, while others shun these, preferring to deal with people, so their 'intuition', sensitivity, etc. can be used. Managerial jobs usually demand both competencies but is it possible to find each equally? Is it not acceptable that human resources managers might have more of the former, and engineering managers more of the latter?

Do organizational competencies change over time?   All organizations live in a volatile environment that demands adaptation and innovation. Does selecting a clearly homogeneous work-force (in terms of salient and non-salient competencies) render one more able to deal with change, as there are bound to be some people in the organization who have the requisite competencies to deal with the new, changed environment? From this point of view, perhaps the most salient, overriding competency to seek out is the ability to deal with change (or indeed to seek out change) and the one most important to detect for rejection is rigidity, conservatism and resistance to change.

Psychologists interested in personality and individual differences, organizational behaviour, and in psychometric tests and scales have long debated these questions with regard to personality traits, intelligence and various other human abilities. The questions are neither trivial nor simple, nor should they be dismissed as being of academic interest only. Indeed, the answer to them is of crucial importance for any organization in search of the competencies of their executives and employees. Yet they have to be answered before any sensible audit is undertaken. The idea is an attractive one. An organizational competency audit could specify the skills, abilities, preferences, and predispositions of employees that may be under- or over-used. It also may provide a very helpful list for senior managers coping with change. A skills audit may well do this. But until the concept of competency is clearly defined and the salient competencies for an organization specified, it really is a waste of time bothering with competency audits.

A safety audit

Many manufacturing and transport organizations have safety programmes, and there is often a strong – or even excessive – management commitment to safety. Studies have shown, for instance, that in low-accident organizations safety matters tend to be given high priority in company meetings and production scheduling, based on the conviction that safety is an integral part of production systems, and accidents are actually symptoms of design faults in that system.

There seem to be other distinguishing characteristics that separate organizations with good versus poor safety records. These include: the rank and status of safety officers; the extent to which safety training was an integral part of the initial training; the frequency of safety inspections by appropriate personnel; orderly 'plant' operators, controlled environmental conditions and the use of safety devices; a stable work-force of older workers; and guidance counselling vs. enforcement and admonition ways of promoting safety (Zohar, 1980).

Zohar believed it is possible to form a picture of a highly safe company:

> Management is actively involved in safety management and creates a general administrative control climate in which work is to be performed. This climate results in increased performance reliability of workers, good house-keeping, and high design and maintenance standards for work environments. There are well-developed personnel-selection training and development programs in which safe conduct is an integral part. Communication links between workers and management are kept open, enabling a flow of information regarding production as well as safety matters. Finally, general management philosophy is not strictly production oriented but also people oriented, as evidenced by various supportive policies described above.
>
> (1980, pp. 97–8)

Hence, Zohar has argued that a safety audit needs to include the following facets:

- perceived management attitudes towards safety;
- perceived effects of safe conduct on promotion;
- perceived effects of safe conduct on social status;
- perceived organizational status of safety officer;
- perceived importance and effectiveness of safety training;
- perceived risk level at work-place;
- perceived effectiveness of enforcement versus guidance in promoting safety.

Health audits

Many organizations feel it is both a moral responsibility and their self-interest to promote the mental and physical health of their employees. Hence a health audit may be concerned with specific lifestyle factors that are known to affect health, such as smoking, alcohol consumption, nutrition, weight control and diet, as well as exercise. As well as focusing on these issues, health audits may examine employees' most common stress-coping strategies, no doubt with an eye to giving them advice.

A problem with looking at health-related behaviours on and off the job, is that employees may feel that their employer has no right to delve into their private lifestyles, even if this affects their behaviour at work. However, it is quite possible also to look at employee health beliefs which, through health attitudes and intentions, can be shown to relate to health behaviour *per se*. A number of studies have been done which specifically look at health behaviour.

Stainton Rogers (1991) made a thorough investigation of lay beliefs and explanations about health and illness, and attempted to use social constructionist research methods. Through extensive in-depth interviews, she derived a number of attitude statements which were later reduced to a more manageable non-overlapping set, which seventy subjects were required to Q-sort. For instance, she noted that explanations for good health divided nicely into two categories (those which arise inside and those outside the individual), which were further subdivided. Four types of explanations related to internal explanations:

- **Behaviour** (looking after yourself; adopting a healthy lifestyle; using preventive services like inoculations).
- **Mind** (positive attitudes; not worrying; taking responsibility for yourself).
- **Heredity** (health constitution).
- **The body's defences** (fighting off disease).

External explanations divided into three categories:

- **Chance**.
- **Social policy** (public health measures; good living standards).
- **Medical advice** (inoculations, contraception).

Asked the similar question, 'What makes people ill?' a similar categorization occurred, at least for internal factors (unhealthy behaviour, mind, and heredity), but with rather more external factors: chance, other people (upsetting one or exposing one to germs), disease organisms (infection), products of social forces (inequality, pollution, advertising), and medical intervention.

She was also able to identify six quite different 'theories' or 'accounts' which represented the way different subjects thought about medical and health-related matters:

The 'cultural critique', 'inequality of access', 'willpower' and 'robust individualism' accounts, all assumed that lifestyle and social circumstances are crucial determinants of health status, and hence, all couched their explanations within the interplay between the individual and society. They were, however, informed by opposing models of society. The 'willpower' and 'robust individualism' accounts took a 'structural functionalist' or 'pluralistic' view of society. They assumed that various social or cultural groups (i.e. different social classes, different genders, different ethnic groups) co-exist in a functional manner, and that individuals have a choice about their lifestyles and living conditions. Consequently, health status in this view, is a product of individual decision-making and circumstances. By contrast, the 'cultural critique' and 'inequality of access' accounts, operated with a 'dominance' or 'conflict' world view, in which individuals' choices and life chances – and consequently health status – are largely constrained and defined by their social position. Indeed, individual freedom to choose was at the very heart of 'robust individualism' account's view of the world, whereas the lack of choice for the most vulnerable and oppressed groups was focal for the 'inequality of access' account.

(p. 160)

There is a vast literature that has consistently demonstrated that people with internal as opposed to external expectations (locus of control beliefs) have greater adaptive functioning. Internals, as opposed to externals, tend to assume more responsibility for their health, guard against accidents and disease, seek more information about health maintenance, and learn more about illnesses and diseases that they contract. Externals believe physical disabilities to be more debilitating than internals, who anticipated less handicaps. Internals also appeared to be more sensitive to internal states, alert to biofeedback cures, and motivated to attempt self-control of bodily functions. Naturally, internals prefer treatments that do not inhibit their freedom or control. Thus, congruence in views of patient and health-care professionals appears to enhance behaviour change.

The idea of individualizing patient treatment based on locus of control beliefs has received support. Imagine, for instance, that one can classify dental patients as preventative vs. restorative, and that these types reflect dental locus of control beliefs: preventive patients are internal, believing that as their dental health is in their control, preventive measures are best; while restorative patients are external, believing that their dental health is beyond their control. As these two groups appear to have different beliefs that no doubt affect their dental health and visits to the dentist, it may be that health education and advice should be quite different for each of the two groups.

Some idea of the concept can be got from the following items, which are the first ten items from Lau and Ware's (1981) scale:

- Staying well has little or nothing to do with chance.
- Seeing a doctor for regular check-ups is a key factor in staying healthy.
- Doctors can rarely do very much for people who are sick.
- Anyone can learn a few basic health principles that can go a long way in preventing illness.
- People's health results from their own carelessness.
- Doctors relieve or cure only a few of the medical problems their patients have.
- There is little one can do to prevent illness.
- No matter what anybody does, there are many diseases that can just wipe you out.
- Whether or not people get well is often a matter of chance.
- People who never get sick are just plain lucky.

Wallston and Wallston (1981) have suggested that even more specific health locus of control scales are developed and that they are used in a clinical as well as a health context. It may be that the scales are better at predicting sick-role behaviour than health-related behaviour.

Pill and Stott (1982) have argued and demonstrated that a person's readiness to accept responsibility for his or her health depends partly on views held about the aetiology of illness. In a sample of working-class mothers they found that they attribute illness causation primarily to germs, followed by 'lifestyle', heredity and stress. Nearly half of the sample held fatalistic views on the cause of these and, hence, they believed that they were rarely morally accountable. In this sense they did not act as responsible individuals by availing themselves of appropriate preventive and screening measures and leading healthy lives. By attributing illness to germs, which are external and random in who they affect, the victim becomes blameless. Better-educated women, however, recognized or admitted that individual behaviour had some part to play in illness, and, thus, felt morally accountable if they neglected themselves and thereby reduced the level of resistance to change.

In a later paper Pill and Stott (1985) presented a salience of lifestyle index based on answers to the five questions below:

1   What do you think are the main reasons for people falling ill? Can you tell me a little bit more about how X makes people ill?
2   Do you think some people are more likely to fall ill than others? What sort of people are they?
3   Do you think that people can ever be to blame if they fall ill?
4   Everyone becomes ill in the course of their lives, but some people do seem to get things worse than others: I wonder what you think about that?
5   Do you think some types of illness are more easily prevented than others? What? How?

Once again they confirmed that 'fatalists' accepted less responsibility for their health than 'lifestylists' who are committed to the idea that day-to-day habits of diet and exercise have implications for present and future health.

Just as in many other spheres of behaviour, the locus of control concept seems to be very important in predicting lay people's health beliefs and behaviours. It has been demonstrated, for instance, that internal locus of control beliefs are more adaptive than external beliefs, so the vast bulk of the literature in this area appears to indicate that health educators need to attempt to encourage 'externals' to become more 'internal' and take some responsibility for their health and illness.

Organizations could easily audit the health beliefs of their staff and determine if they were primarily fatalists or instrumentalists. Certainly, given the problems associated with the former, they may choose to attempt some form of training that turns them into the latter.

CONCLUSION

We have attempted in this book to describe and explain the role of human resource audits in an organization. The benefits of collecting audit data and the steps involved in collecting data were described in detail. Indeed, Chapter 2 was dedicated almost exclusively to organometrics, because it was argued that it was imperative to collect reliable and valid data upon which to make important managerial decisions.

Chapters 3 to 6 examined in detail many of the issues concerning four important human resource audits: culture, climate, communication and customer care. Although there was some predictable overlap in these different audits, they did focus on different features of organizational functioning. But, as we have explained in this chapter, these are by no means the only human resources audits that could be done. Highly specific issues like safety or health can be very beneficially audited.

A question addressed in this final chapter concerned what part audits play in organizations. The results of audits provide the sort of data that managers need before often expensive decisions are made. They can provide an accurate picture of the attitudes, beliefs and behavioural norms of the organization as a whole, at a specific point in time. On the basis of this, organization managers can make more judicious and sensitive decisions about training, development needs, the best ways to improve communication, the effects of change, or even the best way to go about change. Audits are neither new nor a panacea for all organizational ills but they are under-used.

Some organizations in fact have annual audits from which they calculate various indexes, like a morale index or a satisfaction index. These figures are taken very seriously by senior management and explanations are sought for unexpected changes. For some organizations they represent an efficient channel whereby information flows upward about all sorts of relevant issues. Although some employees resent the time taken to complete audit questionnaires (or interviews), many are happy to do so if they believe management takes the results seriously, and acts upon them.

For some, audit data are necessary in human resources strategic planning about manpower needs and related matters. For others the data are more often used to evaluate the need for, and effect of, training. For still others, the ever-present problems of change are considered through use of audits.

For years and years accountants and marketeers have done audits to provide the essential data upon which to make management decisions. Given the usefulness, comparative low cost and importance in their area too, it is no surprise that human resources professionals are turning to auditing the organization from their perspective.

References

Abelson, R.F. (1976) 'Script processing in attitude formation and decision making', in J.S. Carroll and J.S. Payne (eds) *Cognition and Sound Behaviour*, Hillside, NJ: Lawrence Erlbaum Associates.

Allen, N.J. and Meyer, J.P. (1990) 'The measurement and antecedents of effective continuance and normative commitment to the organization', *Journal of Occupational Psychology*, 67: 1–18.

Allen, R. and Dyer, F. (1990) 'A tool for tapping the organizational unconscious', *Personnel Journal*, March: 192–9.

Alvesson, M. (1987) 'Organizations, culture and ideology', *International Studies of Management and Organizations*, 17: 4–18.

Arys, C.F. (1917) A preliminary report on 'work with knowledge of results versus work without knowledge of results', *Psychological Review*, 24: 449–55.

Ashford, S. and Cummings, L. (1983) 'Feedback as an individual resource: Personal strategies of creating information', *Organizational Behaviour and Human Performance*, 32.

Ashforth, B. (1985) 'Climate formation: Issues and extensions', *Academy of Management Review*, 4: 837–47.

Atkinson, P. (1990) *Creating culture change: The key to successful total quality management*, London: IFS.

Azumi, K. and McMillan, C. (1978) 'Culture and organization structure: A comparison of Japanese and British organizations', *Studies of Management and Organizations*, 8: 35–47.

Baron, R.A. and Greenberg, J. (1990) *Behaviour in Organizations: Understanding and managing the human side of work*, Boston: Allyn & Bacon (third edition).

Baskin, O.W. and Aronoff, C.E. (1989) *International Communication in Organizations*, Santa Monica, CA.: Goodyear.

Bateson, J.E. (1977) 'Do we need service marketing?', *Marketing Consumer Services: New Insights*, Cambridge, MA: Marketing Service Institute, Report # 77–115.

Beach, D (1970) Personnel: The Management of People at Work, New York: Macmillan.

Beardon, W.O. and Teel, J.E. (1983) 'Selected determinants of consumer satisfaction and complaint reports', *Journal of Marketing Research*, 20: 21–8.

Benson, G. (1983) 'On the campus: How well do business schools prepare graduates for the business world?', *Personnel*, July/August: 63–9.

Berrien, F. (1970) 'A super-ego for cross-cultural research', *Internal Journal of Psychology*, 5: 33–9.

Berry, L.L. (1980) 'Services marketing is different', *Business*, 30, (May–June): 24–8.

Bluen, S. and Donald, C. (1991) 'The nature and measurement of in-company industrial relations climate', *South African Journal of Psychology*, 21: 12.

Bonoma, T. and Zaltman, G. (1981) *Psychology for Management*, Boston: Kent.

Booth, A. (1988) *The Communications Audit: A Guide for Managers*, Aldershot: Gower.

Bowers, D. and Seashore, S. (1966) 'Predicting organizational effectiveness with a four-factor theory of leadership', *Administrative Science Quarterly*, 11: 238–63.

Boyatzis, R. (1982) *The Competent Manager: A model for effective performance*, Chichester: Wiley.

Brooke, M. (1986) *International Management: A review of strategies and operations*, London: Hutchinson.

Buchanan, B. (1974) 'Building organizational commitment: The socialization of managers in work organizations', *Administrative Science Quarterly*, 19: 533–46.

Buono, A., Bowditch, J. and Lewis, J. (1985) 'When cultures collide: The anatomy of a merger', *Human Relations*, 38: 477–500.

Buony, B.A. and Bitner, M.J. (1987) 'Marketing strategies and organization structures for services firms', in J. Donnelly and W. George (eds) *Marketing of Services*, Chicago: American Marketing: 47–51.

Burgess, R.L. (1968) 'Communications networks: An experimental revaluation', *Journal of Experimental Social Psychology*, 4: 324–27.

Campbell, J., Dunnette, M., Lawler, E. and Weick, K. (1970) *Managerial Behaviour, Performance and Effectiveness*, New York: McGraw-Hill.

Carmen, J.M. (1990) 'Consumer perceptions of service quality: An assessment of the SERVQUAL dimensions', *Journal of Retailing*, 66: 33–55.

Carmen, J.M. and Langeard, E. (1980) 'Growth strategies of service firms', *Strategic Management Journal*, 1, (January–March): 7–22.

Cherrington, D. (1989) *Organizational Behaviour*, Massachusetts: Allyn & Bacon.

Child, J. (1981) 'Culture, contingency and capitalism in the cross-national study of organizations', *Research in Organization Behaviour*, 3: 303–56.

Churchill, G.A. Jr and Suprenant, C., (1982) 'An investigation into the determinants of customer satisfaction', *Journal of Marketing Research*, 19: 491–504.

Collard, R. (1990) *Total Quality: Success through People*, London: IPA.

Cook, J. and Wall, T. (1980) 'New work attitude measures of trust, organizational commitment and personal need non-fulfilment', *Journal of Occupational Psychology*, 53, 39–52.

Cook, J., Hepworth, S., Wall, T. and Warr, P. (1981) *The Experience of Work*, London: Academic Press.

Cooke, R. and Lafferty, J. (1989) *Organizational Culture Inventory*, Plymouth, MI: Human Synergistic.

Cooke, R. and Rousseau, D. (1988) 'Behavioural norms and expectations: A quantitative approach to the assessment of organizational culture', *Group and Organizational Studies*, 13: 245–73.

Cronbach, L. (1987) *Essentials of Psychological Testing*, New York: Harper & Row.

Crosby, P.B. (1978) *Quality is Free: The Art of Making Quality Certain*, New York: New American Library.

Daft, R.L., Lengel, R.H. and Trevino, L.U. (1987) 'Message equivocality, media selection and manager performance: Implications for information systems', *MIS Quarterly*, 11, 355–66.

Dastmalchian, A., Blyton, P. and Adamson, R. (1991) *The Climate of Workplace Relations*, London: Routledge.

Dawson, S. (1989) *Analysing Organizations*, Basingstoke: Macmillan.

Deal, T. and Kennedy, A. (1982a) 'Organizational climate: Its homogeneity within organizations', *Journal of Applied Psychology*, 67: 361–2.

Deal, T. and Kennedy, A. (1982b) *Corporate Cultures*, Reading, MA: Addison-Wesley.

Degot, V. (1987) 'Corporate culture and the concept of rationality in corporate models', *International Studies of Management and Organizations*, 17, 19–39.

de Vaus, D. (1986) *Surveys in Social Research*, London: George Allen & Unwin.

Dieterly, D. and Schneider, B. (1974) 'The effect of organizational environment on perceived power and climate', *Organizational Behaviour and Human Performance*, 11: 316–37.

Dodds, W.B. and Monroe, K.J. (1984) 'The effect of brand and price information on subjective product evaluation', *Advances in Consumer Research*, XII.

Downey, N., Hellriegel, D. and Slocum, J. (1975) 'Congruence between individual needs, organizational climate, job satisfaction and performance', *Academy of Management Journal*, 18: 149–55.

Duncan, J.W. (1984) 'Perceived humour and social network patterns in a sample of task-oriented groups: A reexamination of prior research', *Human Relations*, 37: 895–907.

Eldridge, J. and Crombie, A. (1974) *A Sociology of Organizations*, London: George Allen & Unwin.

Emanuel, M. (1985) *Inside Organizational Communication*, New York: Longman.

Enz, C. (1986) *Power and Shared Values in the Corporate Culture*, Ann Arbor, MI: UMI.

Evan, R. (1978) 'Measuring the impact of culture on organizations', *International Studies of Management and Organizations*: 91–113.

Evans, D.W. (1990) *People, Communication and Organizations*,

Evans, W. (1968) 'A systems model of organizational climate', In R. Taguiri and G. Litwin (eds) *Organizational Climate: Explorations of a Concept*, Boston: Harvard University: 107–24.

Feather, N.T. (1968) 'Change in confidence following success or failure as a predictor of subsequent performance', *Journal of Personality and Social Psychology*, 9: 38–45.

Field, R. and Abelson, M. (1982) 'Climate: A reconceptualization and proposed model', *Human Relations*, 35: 181–201.

Fiol, C. (1991) 'Managing culture as a competitive resource', *Journal of Management*, 17.

Fisher, C.D. (1979) 'Transmission of positive and negative feedback to subordinates: A laboratory investigation', *Journal of Applied Psychology*, 64: 533–40.

Fiske, J. (1982) *Introduction to Communication Studies*, London: Methuen.

Forehand, G. and von Gilmer, B. (1964) 'Environmental variations in studies of organizational behaviour', *Psychological Bulletin*, 62: 362–81.

Forsyth, D.R. (1983) *An Introduction to Group Dynamics*, Monterey, CA: Brooks/Cole.

French, W. and Bell, C. (1984) *Organization Development*, New York: Prentice Hall.

French, W., Kent, F., Rosenzweig, J. (1985) *Understanding Human Behaviour in Organizations*, New York: Harper & Row.

Furnham, A. (1992) 'Corporate Assessment: A new multi-dimensional and international instrument to audit employee perception', *International Journal of Commerce and Management*, 1: 39–57.

Furnham, A. and Gunter, B. (1992) *The Corporate Culture Questionnaire*, London: ABRA.

Garvin, D.A. (1983) 'Quality on the line', *Harvard Business Review*, 61: 65–73.

Gavin, J. (1975) 'Organizational climate as a function of personal and organizational variables', *Journal of Applied Psychology*, 60: 135–9.

Gayle, A. (1988) *Management Audits: The Assessment of Quality Management Systems*, London: McGraw-Hill.

Geertz, C. (1973) *The Interpretation of Culture*, New York: Basic Books.

Gellerman, S. (1960) 'The company personality', *Management Review*, 48: 69–76.

Gerwin, D. (1979) 'Relationships between structive and technology at the organisational and job level', *Journal of Management Studies*, 16: 70–9.

Gilmer, B. (1966) *Industrial Psychology*, New York: McGraw-Hill.

Ginsberg, L. (1978) 'Strategic planning for work climate modification', *Amacon*, 10: 2.

Glaser, R. (1983) *The Corporate Culture Survey*, Bryn Mawr, PA: Organizational Design and Development.

Glauser, M.J. (1984) 'Upward information flow in organisations: Review and conceptual analysis', *Human Relations*, 37: 613–43.

Glick, W. (1985) 'Conceptualizing and measuring organizational and psychological climate: Pitfalls in multilevel research', *Academy of Management Review*, 10: 601–16.

Goffman, E. (1961) *Encounters: Two Studies in the Sociology of Interaction*, Indianapolis: The Bizzs-Merrill Company.

Goldhaber, G.M. and Rogers, O.P. (1979) *Auditing Organizational Communications Systems: the ICA Communications Audit*, Dubuque: Kendall/Hunt.

Gonzalez, R. (1987) *Corporate Cultures Modification: A Guide for Managers*, Manila: National Books Co.

Gordon, G. (1991) 'Industry determinants of organizational culture', *Academy of Management Review*, 16: 396–415.

Gordon, G. and Cummins, W. (1979) *Managing Management Climate*, New York: D.C. Heath.

Graham, J.W. and Verma, A. (1991) 'Predictors and moderators of employee responses to employee participation programme', *Human Relations*, 44: 551–8.

Graves, D. (1972) 'The impact of culture upon managerial attitudes, beliefs and behaviour in England and France', *Journal of Management Studies*, 1: 40–56.

Graves, D. (1986) *Corporate Culture – Diagnosis and Change: Auditing and Changing the Culture of Organizations*, London: Frances Pinter.

Green, S. (1988) 'Understanding corporate culture and its relation to strategy', *International Studies of Management and Organizations*, 18: 6–28.

Gregory, K. (1983) 'Native-view paradigms: Multiple cultures and culture conflicts in organizations', Administrative Science Quarterly, 28: 359–76.

Greller, M.M. and Harold, D.M. (1975) 'Sources of feedback: A preliminary investigation', *Organizational Behaviour and Human Performance*, 13: 244–56.

Gronroos, C. (1982) 'A service quality model and its marketing implications', *European Journal of Marketing*, 18: 36–44.

Guion, R. (1973) 'A note on organizational climate', *Organizational Behaviour and Human Performance*, 9: 120–5.

Hall, J. (1971) 'A comparison of Halpin and Croft's Organizational Climate and Likert's Organizations System', *Administrative Science Quarterly*, 16: 586–96.

Hall, O. and Mansfield, R. (1975) 'Relationship of age and seniority with career variables of engineers and scientists', *Journal of Applied Psychology*, 60: 201–10.

Halpin, A. and Croft, D. (1963) *The Organizational Climate of Schools*, Chicago: University of Chicago Press.

Hampden-Turner, C. (1990) *Corporate Culture: From Vicious to Virtuous Circles*, London: Hutchinson.

Hamser, L.M. and Muchinsky, P.M. (1978) 'Work as on information environment', *Organizational Behaviour and Human Performance*, 21: 47–60.

Handy, C. (1980) *Understanding Organizations*, Harmondsworth: Penguin.

Harrison, R. (1972) 'Understanding your organization's character', *Harvard Business Review*, 5: 119–28.

Hawkins, B.L. and Preston, P. (1981) *Managerial Communication*, Santa Monica, CA: Goodyear.

Herman, J. and Hulin, C. (1972) 'Studying organizational frames of references', *Organizational Behaviour and Human Performance*, 8: 84–108.

Herold, D.M. and Greller, M.M. (1977) 'Feedback: The definition of a construct', *Academy of Management Journal*, 20: 142–7.

Herold, D.M. and Parsons, C.K. (1985) 'Assessing the feedback environment in work organisations: Development of the Job Feedback Survey', *Journal of Applied Psychology*, 70(2): 290–305.

Hersey, P. and Blanchard, K.A. (1982) *Management of Organizational Behaviour: Utilizing Human Resources*, Englewood Cliffs, NJ: Prentice Hall.

Hjorth-Anderson, C. (1984) 'The concept of quality and the efficiency of markets for consumer products', *Journal of Consumer Research*, 11: 708–18.

Hofstede, G. (1980) *Culture's Consequences*, California: Sage.

Hofstede, G. (1981) 'Culture and organizations', *International Studies of Management and Organizations*, 4: 15–41.

Holberton, S. (1991) 'An idea whose time has not only come but will prevail', *Financial Times*, 30 March: 10.

Holbrook, M.B. and Corfman, K.P. (1985) 'Quality and value in the consumption experience: Phaldrus rides again', in J. Jacoby and J. Olson (eds) *Perceived Quality*, Lexington, Mass.: Lexington Books: 31–97.

House, R. and Rizzo, J. (1972) 'Toward the measure of organizational practices: Scale development and validation', *Journal of Applied Psychology*, 56: 388–96.

Howard, J. and Sheth, J. (1969) *The Theory of Buyer Behaviour*, New York: John Wiley & Sons Inc.

Hunt, K. (1979) *Conceptualization and Measurement of Consumer Satisfaction and Dissatisfaction*, Cambridge, MA: Marketing Science Institute.

Ilgen, D.R. and Hamstra, B.W. (1972) 'Performance satisfaction and a function of the difference between expected and reported performance at five levels of reported performance', *Behaviour and Human Performance*, 7: 359–70.

Ilgen, D., Fisher, C. and Taylor, M. (1979) 'Consequences of feedback on behaviour in organizations', *Journal of Applied Psychology*, 64: 349–71.

Indik, B. (1965) 'Organization size and member participation', *Human Relations*, 18: 339–50.

Jackofsky, E. and Slocum, J. (1988) 'A longitudinal study of climates', *Journal of Organizational Behaviour*, 9: 319–34.

Jacoby, J. and Olsen, J. (1985) *Perceived Quality*, Lexington, MA: Lexington Books.

James, L. and Jones, A. (1974) 'Organizational Climate: A review of theory and research', *Psychological Bulletin*, 12: 1096–112.

James, L., Joyce, W. and Slocum, J. (1988) 'Organizations do not cognize', *Academy of Management Review*, 13: 129–32.

Jamieson, I. (1981) 'The concept of culture and its relevance for an analysis of business enterprise in different societies', *International Studies of Management and Organization*, 17: 19–39.

Janis, I.L. (1972) *Victims of Group think*, Boston: Houghton Mifflin.

Johannesson, R. (1973) 'Some problems in the measurement of organizational climate', *Organizational Behaviour and Human Performance*, 10: 118–44.

Jones, A. and James, L. (1979) 'Psychological climate: Dimensions and relationships of individual and aggregated work environment perception', *Organizational Behaviour and Human Performance*, 23: 201–50.

Joyce, W. and Slocum, J. (1987) 'Collective climate: Agreement as a basis for defining aggregate climates in organizations', *Academy of Management Journal*, 27: 721–42.

Kahn, R., Wolfe, D., Quinn, R., Snoek, J. and Rosenthal, R. (1964) *Organizational Stress: Studies in Role Conflict and Ambiguity*, New York: Wiley.

Kanter, R.M. (1968) 'Commitment and social organization: A study of commitment mechanisms in utopian communities', *American Sociological Review*, 33: 499–517.

Kar, L. (1972) *Business Communication: Theory and Practice*, Homewood, IL: Irwin.

Katz, D. and Kahn, R. (1966) *The Social Psychology of Organization*, New York: Wiley.

Kets de Vries, M. and Miller, D. (1984) 'The Neurotic Organization', *Psychology Today*. November: 27–34.

Kilmann, R. and Saxton, M. (1983) *The Kilmann-Saxton Culture-Gap Survey*, Pittsburgh, PA: Organizational Design Consultants.

Kirmeyer, S.L. and Lin, T. (1987) 'Social support: Its relationship to observed communication with peers and superiors', *Academy of Management Journal*, 30: 138–151.

Klauss, R. and Bass, M.M. (1982) *International Communications in Organizations*, New York: Academic Press.

Koys, D. and De Cotiis, T. (1991) 'Inductive measures of psychological climate', *Human Relations*, 44: 265–85.

Kozlowski, S. and Doherty, M. (1989) 'Integration of climate and leadership: Examination of a neglected issue', *Journal of Applied Psychology*, 74: 546–53.

Kozlowski, S. and Farr, J. (1988) 'An integrative model of updating and performance', *Human Performance*, 1: 5–29.

Krackhardt, D. and Porter, L.W. (1986) 'The snowball effect: Turnover embedded in communication networks', *Journal of Applied Psychology*, 71: 50–5.

Kroeber, A.L. and Kluckholm, C. (1952) 'Culture: a critical review of concepts and definitions', *Peabody Museum of American Archaeology and Ethnicology*, 47, 1.

La Follette, W. (1975) 'How is the climate in your organization?', *Personnel Journal*, 6: 376–9.

Landy, F. and Farr, J. (1978) *The Measurement of Work Performance: Methods, Theory and Applications*, London: Academic Press.

Lau, R. and Ware, J. (1981) 'Refinements in the measurement of health-specific locus-of-control beliefs', *Medical Care*, 19: 1147–53.

Laurent, A. (1983) 'The culture diversity of western conceptions of management', *International Studies of Management and Organization*, 8: 75–96.

Laurent, A. (1986a) *A cultural view of organizational change*, Insead.

Laurent, A. (1986b) 'The cross-cultural puzzle of international human resource management', *Human Resource Management*, 125: 91–102.

Lawler, E., Hall, D. and Oldham, G. (1974) 'Organizational climate: Relationship to organizational structure, process and performance', *Organizational Behaviour and Human Performance*, 11: 139–55.

Lehtinen, U. and Lehtinen, J.R. (1982) 'Service quality: A study of quality dimensions', unpublished working paper, Helsinki: Service Management Institute.

Level, D. (1972) 'Communication effectiveness: Methods and situations'., *Journal of Business Communication*, 10: 19–25.

Lewin, K. (1951) *Field theory in the social sciences*, New York: Harper.

Litwin, G. (1968) 'Climate and behaviour theory', in R. Tagiuri and G. Litwin (eds) *Organizational Climate: Explanations of a Concept*, Boston: Harvard University Press: 35–61.

Litwin, G. and Stringer, R. (1968) *Motivation and Organizational Climate*, Boston: Harvard University.

Locke, E.A. and Schweiger, B.M. (1979) 'Participation in decision-making: One more look', in B.M. Shaw (ed.) *Research in Organizational Behaviour* (vol.1), Greenwich, CT: Jai Press: 205–339.

Lovelock, C.H. (1981) 'Towards a classification of services', in L. Berry, G.L. Shostak and G. Upah (eds) *Emerging Perspectives on Services Marketing*, Chicago: American Marketing Association: 72–6.

Luthans, F. and Larsen, J.K. (1986) 'How managers really communicate', *Human Relations*, 39: 161–78.

Lutz, R.J. and Kakkar, P. (1976) 'Situational influence in interpersonal persuasions', in B.B. Anderson (ed.) *Advances in Consumer Research*, vol. 3, Cincinnati: Association for Consumer Research.

Meek, V. (1988) 'Organizational culture: Origins and weaknesses', *Organization Studies*, 9: 453–73.

Merton, R. (1957) 'The role set', *British Journal of Sociology*, 8: 106–20.

Meyer, J. and Allen, N. (1987) *Organizational Commitment: Toward a Three-component Model*, University of Western Ontario: Research Bulletin No. 660.

Miceli, M. and Near, J. (1985) 'Characteristics of organizational climate and perceived wrongdoing associated with whistle-blowing decisions', *Personnel Psychology*, 38: 525–44.

Miller, K.I. and Monge, P.R. (1986) 'Participation, satisfaction and productivity: A meta-analytic review', *Academy of Management Journal*, 24: 727–53.

Moser, C. and Kalton, G. (1971) *Survey Methods in Social Investigation*, Aldershot: Gower.

Mowday, R., Steers, E. and Porter, L. (1979) 'The interaction of personality and job scope in predicting turnover', *Journal of Vocational Behaviour*, 15: 780–9.

Moxnes, P. and Eilertsen, D.E. (1991) 'The influence of management training upon organizational climate: An exploratory study', *Journal of Organizational Behaviour*, 12: 399–411.

Muchinsky, P. (1977) 'Organizational communication: Relationship to organizational climate and job satisfaction', *Academy of Management Journal*, 20: 592–607.

Mullins, L. (1989) *Management and Organizational Behaviour*, London: Pitman.

Mumford, A. (1989) *Management Development: Strategies for Change*, London: Institute of Personnel Management.

Nickolson, N. (1990) 'Organizational innovation in context: culture, interpretation and application', in M. West and J. Farr (eds) *Innovation and Creativity at Work*, Chichester: Wiley.

ODI, (1987) *Total Quality. The ODI Survey*, Boston: ODI Ltd.

Odiorne, G.S. (1957) 'An application of the communications audit', *Personnel Psychology*, 7: 235–43.

Oliver, R. (1981) 'Measurement and evaluation of satisfaction process in retail settings', *Journal of Retailing*, 57: 25–48.

Olshavsky, R.W. (1985) 'Perceived quality in consumer decision making: An integrated theoretical perspective', in J. Jacoby and J. Olson (eds) *Perceived Quality*, Lexington, MA: Lexington Books.

O'Reilly, S., Chatman, J. and Caldwell, R. (1988) 'People, jobs and organizational culture', Working Paper, Berkeley: University of California.

Osterhoff, R., Locander, W. and Bounds, G. (1991) *Competing Globally Through Customer Values*, London: Quorum Books.

Pace, C. and Stern, G. (1958) 'An approach to the measurement of the psychological characteristics of college environment', *Journal of Educational Psychology*, 49: 269–77.

Parasuraman, A., Zeithaml, V. and Berry, L. (1985) 'A conceptual model of service quality and its implications for future research', *Journal of Marketing*, Fall: 41–50.

Parasuraman, A., Zeithaml, V. and Berry, L. (1988) 'SERVQUAL: A multiple-item scale for measuring consumer perceptions of service quality', *Journal of Retailing*, 44: 12–40.

Payne, R. (1990) 'Madness in our method: A comment on Jackofsky and Slocum's paper "A longitudinal study of climate",' *Journal of Organizational Behaviour*, 11: 77–80.

Payne, R. and Mansfield, B. (1973) 'Relationship of perceptions of organizational climate to organizational structure, context and hierarchical radical positions', *Administrative Science Quarterly*, 18: 515–26.

Payne, R. and Pheysey, D. (1971) 'C.G. Stern's Organizational Climate Index', *Organizational Behaviour and Human Performance*, 18: 45–62.

Payne, R. and Pugh, D. (1976) 'Organization structure and climate', in M. Dunnette, (ed.) *Handbook of Industrial and Organizational Psychology*, Chicago: Rand McNally: 1125–73.

Peel, M. (1987) *Customer Service: How to Achieve Total Customer Service Satisfaction*, London: Kogan Page.

Pendleton, D. and Furnham, A. (1992) 'The Human Resource Specialist', *The Financial Times*, September.

Peters, T. and Waterman, R. (1982) *In Search of Excellence*, New York: Harper, Row.

Pill, R. and Stott, N. (1982) 'Concepts of illness causation and responsibility', *Social Science and Medicine*, 16: 43–52.

Pill, R. and Stott, N. (1985) 'Choice or chance: Further evidence on ideas of illness and responsibility for health', *Social Science and Medicine*, 20: 981–96.

Porter, L., Crampon, W. and Smith, F. (1976) 'Organizational commitment and managerial turnover', *Organizational Behaviour and Human Performance*, 15: 87–99.

Pritchard, R. and Karasick, B. (1973) 'The effects of organizational climate on managerial job performance and job satisfaction', *Organizational Behaviour and Human Performance* 9: 126–46.

Qualls, W. and Puto, C. (1989) 'Organizational climate and decision framing', *Journal of Marketing Research*, 26: 179–92.

Quinn, R.P. and Staines, G.L. (1979) *The 1977 Quality of Employment Survey*, Ann Arbor, MI: Institute for Social Research.

Raelin, J. (1986) *Clash of Cultures*, Boston MA: Harvard Business School Press.

Randall, A. (1992) 'Hospitals get the quality treatment', *Financial Times*, March 6: 12.

Read, W. (1962) 'Upward communication in individual hierarchies', *Human Relations*, 15: 3–16.

Regan, W.J. (1963) 'The service revolution', *Journal of Marketing*, 27 (July): 57–62.

Rentsch, J. (1990) 'Climate and culture: Interaction and qualitative differences in organizational meanings', *Journal of Applied Psychology*, 75: 668–81.

Rhinesmith, S. (1989) *Cultural-Organizational Analysis*, Cambridge, MA: McBer and Co.

Rogers, E.M. and Rogers, A. (1976) *Communication in organizations*, New York: Free Press.

Rousseau, D. (1988) 'The construction of climate in organizational research', in L.C. Cooper and I. Robertson (eds) *International Review of Industrial and Organizational Psychology*, Chichester: Wiley: 139–58.

Rousseau, D. (1989) 'The price of success? Security-oriented cultures and high reliability of organizations', *Industrial Crisis Quarterly*, 3: 285–302.

Rousseau, D. (1990) 'Normative beliefs in fund-raising organisations: Links to organisational performance and individual responses', *Group and Organizational Studies*, 4: 123–41.

Rousseau, D. (1992) 'Quantitative assessment of organizational culture: The case for multiple measures', in B. Schneider (ed.) *Frontiers in Industrial and Organizational Psychology*, vol.3.

Sackmann, S. (1989) 'The framers of culture: The conceptual views of anthropology, organization theory and management', paper presented at the Academy of Management Annual Meeting, Washington, August.

Sackmann, S. (1990) 'Managing Organizational Culture: The juggle between possibilities and dreams', in A. Anderson (ed.) *Communication Yearbook*, 13. Los Angeles: Sage.

Sarbin, T. and Allen, V. (1968) 'Role theory', in G. Lindzey and E. Aronson (eds) *The Handbook of Social Psychology*, 2nd edn, vol.1, Reading, MA: Addison-Wesley Publishing Company.

Sashkin, M. (1987) *Pillars of Excellence: The Organizational Beliefs Questionnaire*, Bryn Mawr PA: Organization Design & Development.

Sasser, W.E., Olsen, R.P. and Wyckoff, D.D. (1978) *Management of Service Operations: Text, Cases and Readings*, Boston: Allyn & Bacon Inc.

Sayle, A. (1988) *Management Audits: The Assessment of Quality Management Systems*, London: McGraw-Hill.

Schank, R.C. (1980) 'Language and memory', *Cognitive Science*, 4: 243–84.

Schein, E. (1985) *Organizational Culture and Leadership*, San Francisco: Jossey-Bass.

Schein, E. (1990) 'Organizational culture', *American Psychologist*, 45: 109–19.

Schneider, B. (1983a) 'Interactional psychology and organizational behaviour', in L. Cummings and B. Staw (eds) *Research in Organizational Behaviour*, Greenwich, CT: A1 Press.

Schneider, B. (1983b) 'Work climates: An interactionist perspective', in N. Feimer and E. Geller (eds) *Environmental Psychology Directions and Perspective*, New York: Praeger.

Schneider, B. and Bartlett, C. (1968) 'Individual differences and organizational climate', *Personnel Psychology*, 21: 323–33.

Schneider, B. and Reichers, A. (1983) 'On the etiology of climate', *Personnel Psychology*, 60: 459–65.

Schneider, B., Parkington, J. and Buxton, V. (1980) 'Employee and customer perceptions of service in banks', *Administrative Science Quarterly*, 25: 252–67.

Schneider, S. (1987) 'National vs. Corporate Culture: Implication for Human Resource Management', paper given at the International Personnel and Human Resource Management Conference, Singapore.

Sells, S. (1968) 'An approach to the nature of organizational climate', in R. Taguiri and G. Litwin (eds) *Organizational Climate: Explorations of a Concept*, Boston MA: Harvard University Press: 85–103.

Shaw, M.E. (1978) 'Communication networks fourteen years later', in L. Birkowitz (ed.) *Group processes* (pp. 351–61), New York: Academic Press.

Sheth, J.N. (1975) 'Buyer-seller interaction: A conceptual framework', in *Proceedings*, Sixth Annual Conference, Association for Consumer Research, 382–6.

Shostak, G.L. (1977) 'Service positioning through structural change', *Journal of Marketing*, 51: 34–43.

Shrivastava, P. (1985) 'Integrating strategy formulation with organizational culture', *Journal of Business Strategy*, 7: 103–11.

Singh, J. (1990) 'Managerial culture and work-related values in India', *Organizational Studies*, 11: 75–101.

Smircich, L. (1983) 'Concepts of culture and organizational analysis', *Administrative Science Quarterly*, 28: 339–50.

Smircich, L. and Calas, M. (1987) 'Organizational Culture: A critical assessment', in F. Jablin, L. Putnam, K. Roberts and L. Porter (eds) *Handbook of Organizational Communications*, Los Angeles: Sage.

Smith, P. (1976) 'Management modelling training to improve morale and customer satisfaction', *Personnel Psychology*, 29: 351–9.

Smith, R.A. and Houston, M.J. (1983) 'Script-based education of satisfaction with services', in L. Berry *et al.* (eds) *Emerging Perspectives on Services Marketing*, Chicago: American Marketing Association.

Solomon, M.R., Suprenant, C., Czepiel, J.A. and Gutman, E.G. (1985) 'A role theory perspective on dyadic interactions: The service encounter', *Journal of Marketing*, 49: 99–111.

Stainton Rogers, W. (1991) *Explaining Health and Illness*, Brighton: Wheatsheaf.

Steers, R.M. (1977) *Organizational Effectiveness: A Behavioural View*, Santa Monica, CA: Goodyear.

Stern, E. (1967) 'People in Context', Unpublished report: University of Syracuse.

Szilagy, A. (1981) *Management and Performance*, Glenview, IL: Scott, Foresman.

Taguiri, R. (1968) 'The concept of organizational climate', in R. Taguiri and G. Litwin (eds) *Organizational Climate: Explorations of a Concept*, Boston MA: Harvard University Press: 11–32.

Taylor, J. and Bowers, D. (1972) *Survey of Organizations: A Machine Scored Standardized Questionnaire Instrument*, University of Michigan.

Thibaut, A.M., Calder, B.J. and Sternthal, B. (1981) 'Using information processing theory to design marketing strategies', *Journal of Marketing Research*, 18: 73–9.

Trompenaars, F. (1985) 'The organization of meaning and the meaning of organization', unpublished PhD, Leiden University.

Upah, G.D. (1980) 'Mass marketing in service retailing: A review and synthesis of major networks', *Journal of Retailing*, 56 (Fall): 59–76.

Vernyi, B. (1987) 'Institute aims to boost quality of company suggestion boxes', *Toledo Blade*, Section B.: 2.

Von Haller, H., Gilmer, B. and Deci, E. (1977) *Industrial and Organizational Psychology*, New York: McGraw-Hill.

Walker, D. (1990) *Customer First: A Strategy for Quality Service*, Aldershot: Gower.

Walker, C.A. and Guest, R.H. (1952) *The men on the assembly line*, Cambridge, MA: Harvard University Press.

Walley, D. (1974) *Efficient Auditing*, London: Macmillan.

Wallston, K. and Wallston, B. (1981) 'Health Locus of Control Scales', in H. Lefcourt, (ed.) *Research with the Locus of Control Construct*, New York: Academic Press, 189–221.

Walters, M. (1990) *What about the workers? Making employee surveys work*, London: IPM.

Walton, E. (1961) 'How efficient is the grapevine?', *Personnel*, 28: 45–9.

Webster, F.E. (1968) 'Interpersonal communication and selling effectiveness', *Journal of Marketing*, 32: 7–13.

Weitz, B. (1981) 'Effectiveness in sale interactions: A contingency framework', *Journal of Marketing*, 45: 85–103.

Wiener, Y. and Yoav, V. (1990) 'Relationships between organizational culture and individual motivation – a conceptual integration', *Psychological Reports*, 67: 295–306.

Wilkof, M. (1989) 'Organizational culture and decision making: A case of consensus management', *R and D Management*, 19: 143–99.

Williams, A., Dobson, P. and Walters, M. (1989) *Changing Culture: New Organizational Approaches*, London: IPA.

Woodruffe, C. (1990) *Assessment Centres: Identifying and developing competence*, London: IPM.

Woodruffe, C. (1991) 'Competent by any other name', *Personnel Management*, September, 30–3.

Woodside, A.G., Frey, L.L. and Daly, R.T. (1989) 'Linking service quality, customer satisfaction and behavioural intention', *Journal of Health Care Marketing*, 9: 5–17.

Zeithaml, V. (1987) *Defining and Relating Price, Perceived Quality and Perceived Value*, Report No. 87–101, Cambridge, MA: Marketing Science Institute.

Zohar, D. (1980) 'Safety climate in industrial organizations: Theoretical and applied implications', *Journal of Applied Psychology*, 65: 96–102.

Index